# EDWARD SAID AND THE RELIGIOUS EFFECTS OF CULTURE

This book provides a distinctive account of Edward Said's critique of modern culture by highlighting the religion–secularism distinction on which it is predicated. This distinction is both literal and figurative. It refers, on the one hand, to religious traditions and to secular traditions and, on the other hand, to tropes that extend the meaning and reference of religion and secularism in indeterminate ways. The author takes these tropes as the best way of organizing Said's heterogeneous corpus – from *Joseph Conrad and the Fiction of Autobiography*, his first book, to *Orientalism*, his most influential book, to his recent writings on the Palestinian question. The religion–secularism distinction, as an act of imagination and narrative continuity, lies behind Said's cultural criticism, his notion of intellectual responsibility, and his public controversy with Michael Walzer about the meaning and the uses of the Exodus story and about the question of Palestine.

WILLIAM D. HART is Assistant Professor of Religion at Duke University. He has written for *The American Journal of Philosophy and Theology* and is a member of the American Academy of Religion and the Southeastern Commission on the Study of Religion. His interests lie in the intersection of religion and critical thought, and in naturalistic and postcontemporary accounts of religion.

CAMBRIDGE STUDIES IN
RELIGION AND CRITICAL THOUGHT 8

Edited by
WAYNE PROUDFOOT, *Columbia University*
JEFFREY L. STOUT, *Princeton University*
NICHOLAS WOLTERSTORFF, *Yale University*

Current events confirm the need to understand religious ideas and institutions critically, yet radical doubts have been raised about how to proceed and about the ideal of critical thought itself. Meanwhile, some prominent scholars have urged that we turn the tables, and view modern society as the object of criticism and a religious tradition as the basis for critique. Cambridge Studies in Religion and Critical Thought is a series of books intended to address that interaction of critical thinking and religious traditions in this context of certainty and conflicting claims. It will take up questions such as the following, either by reflecting on them philosophically or by pursuing their ramifications in studies of specific figures and movements: is a coherent critical perspective on religion desirable or even possible? What sort of relationship to religious tradition ought a critic to have? What, if anything, is worth saving from the Enlightenment legacy or from critics of religion like Hume and Feuerbach? The answers offered, while varied, will uniformly consitute distinguished, philosophically informed, and critical analyses of particular religious topics.

Other titles published in the series

# EDWARD SAID AND THE RELIGIOUS EFFECTS OF CULTURE

WILLIAM D. HART

*Duke University*

CAMBRIDGE
UNIVERSITY PRESS

PUBLISHED BY THE PRESS SYNDICATE OF THE UNIVERSITY OF CAMBRIDGE
The Pitt Building, Trumpington Street, Cambridge, United Kingdom

CAMBRIDGE UNIVERSITY PRESS
The Edinburgh Building, Cambridge CB2 2RU, UK www.cup.cam.ac.uk
40 West 20th Street, New York, NY 10011-4211, USA www.cup.org
10 Stamford Road, Oakleigh, Melbourne 3166, Australia
Ruiz de Alarcón 13, 28014 Madrid, Spain

First published 2000

Printed in the United Kingdom at the University Press, Cambridge

*Typeface* Monotype Baskerville 11/12½ pt.   *System* QuarkXPress™ [SE]

*A catalogue record for this book is available from the British Library*

*Library of Congress Cataloguing in Publication data*

Hart, William D., 1957–
Edward Said and the religious effects of culture / by William D.
Hart.
p.   cm. – (Cambridge studies in religion and critical thought; 8)
Includes bibliographical references.
ISBN 0 521 77052 1 (hardback). – ISBN 0 521 77810 7 (paperback)
1. Said, Edward W. – Contributions in philosophy of religion.
2. Said, Edward W. – Contributions in the concept of secularism.
3. Religion–Philosophy.   4. Secularism.   I. Title.   II. Series.
BL51.H336   2000
306.6′092–dc21   99-36183   CIP

ISBN 0 521 77052 1 hardback
ISBN 0 521 77810 7 paperback

# Contents

# *Preface*

Edward W. Said is a celebrated cultural critic and Palestinian activist. He is arguably the most influential American critic of the last quarter century. This book arose from my surprise and bafflement at Said's cryptic, fugitive, but persistent reference to the sacred, religious, theological, and Manichaean. Why these religious references by a self-described secular critic, a thinker whose work, on first glance, seems indifferent if not irrelevant to religious matters? I contend that the presence of these references and others signals the persistence of religion as a Western conceptual category. As with Marx, Nietzsche, and Heidegger before him, religion is the great conceptual dragon that Said must slay. I explore the degree to which religion is as important to Said's critique of culture and imperialism as it is to Marx's critique of capital, Nietzsche's critique of decadence, and Heidegger's critique of metaphysics.

Said is a man of many parts. I highlight some of those parts and leave others in the dark. I give much attention to his Marxism and comparatively little attention to his role as a literary critic. He does not describe himself as a Marxist, but Marxist ideas deeply influence his thinking. As I interpret him, Said reinstates Marx's claim that "the premise of all criticism is the criticism of religion."[1] Radical criticism, therefore, has a necessary relation to religion, not an accidental one. I know of no other contemporary social critic who is more insistent on this point. True, Heidegger makes the criticism of theology and being (ontotheology) the premise of his critique, Derrida, "presence" (another term for ontotheology), and Deleuze, "transcendence." But each, in his own fashion, genuflects before Marx. Where Marx speaks with confidence when he says that "the *criticism of religion* has largely been completed,"[2] Said is not so sure. He makes religion an issue precisely to remind critics of what criticism is not, lest criticism, despite Marx's confidence, once again becomes theology. He voluntarily assumes a burden that most radical

critics do not feel or acknowledge: religion being a burden that they take
Marx or Nietzsche or someone else to have dealt with definitively. I take
Said as qualifying Marx's claim that the criticism of religion is now complete. For him, there are signs everywhere of a "return of the repressed"
– an irruption, in ostensibly critical circles, of repressed religiosity. Too
many critics are "theologizing" and "demonizing" rather than criticizing. It is against this cultural and critical drift (where the critique of religion as the premise of criticism has been forgotten) that Said conceives
his own project as secular criticism.

Except where necessary, I ignore Said's critics. But a brief consideration of how others have read him might help the reader put my interpretation in context. This is important, given what some will see as
eccentric if not counterintuitive – namely, the accent that I put on the
religious–secular thematic in Said's work. Before I take up these other
readings, a quick note. The ideal reader of this book has more than a
passing knowledge of Said and at least a passing knowledge of the issues
at stake between religion and secularism. But such knowledge is not necessary. The moderately determined reader can educate herself along the
way. She will likely come to understand why it might occur to me to think
about Said and religion together. For this reader, Preliminary Remarks
and chapter 6 will be especially important to understanding why Said
feels so passionately about religion and secularism.

*My interpretation of Said is an "excessive" act; it exceeds what is explicitly evident
in his corpus. It runs, as William James would say, ahead of the evidence, but only
slightly ahead, in the manner of a hypothesis. Thus I read Said against the grain,
idiosyncratically, by accenting the religious–secular problematic underlying his work,
by pushing, stretching, and, perhaps, overinterpreting in that direction. I find
significance where others might not. I discern, loosely speaking, a "grammar of
motives" underneath his use of religious and secular language. Thus I do not regard
his language as merely a curiosity or a rhetorical flourish. Such an approach cannot
help but have a certain quality of exaggeration: where the "right" to ambiguity and to
"innocent" tropes is now permitted, now prohibited. I think that this approach illuminates Said's work. The ultimate judgment – whether my excesses illuminate or
darken a picture that would otherwise be clear – is for the reader to make. This is how
I read Said.*

But how do others read him? Broadly speaking, there are poststructuralist, Marxist, and area studies (Middle Eastern and Asian) readings
of Said. All revolve, to a significant degree, around *Orientalism*, where
Said's major claim is this: *Western thought is in the grips of a metaphysics which
makes an array of invidious distinctions between a decadent East and enlightened*

*West, and underwrites ideological and military domination of the East by the West.*
Poststructuralist readings[3] of this book are often ambivalently critical:
Said is thought to be one of them, but not quite. These readings are primarily aimed at vindicating poststructuralism in the face of Said's
"heretical" appropriation of Foucault and Derrida. Either he is not
Foucauldian enough or he is not Derridian enough.[4] In either case, he is
too much a humanist. Marxist readings of Said criticize his populist liberalism or his construction of Marx as an Orientalist.[5] But, where the
former criticism (which is largely sympathetic) is concerned, there is not
the Stalinist-inflected ranting against Said that one finds in Aijaz Ahmad
and his followers. Ahmad belongs to that school of Marxist thinkers that
despises Marxist heretics more than capitalist infidels. This inability to
tell friends from enemies (friends are always under suspicion as possible
enemies) says much about Ahmad's judgment. I am at a loss as to what
Ahmad enthusiasts think they see in his account. What is clear to me is
that his account is little more than a footnote, a rather odd footnote, to
Said. Middle Eastern Area Studies (Arab and Islamic) and Asian Area
Studies are a third site from which Said is read. Like poststructuralist and
Marxist readers, they do not take seriously the religious–secular thematic in Said's work.[6] They give it passing attention, a fleeting reference
here or there, if it receives attention at all. The predominant response to
*Orientalism* by scholars in Middle Eastern Area Studies reflects the apologetic interests of professional Orientalists who are anxious to defend
their disciplines from the charge of Orientalism – that is, the notion that
such disciplines encode a rank-ordering and invidious distinction
between Oriental and Occidental peoples. What is most remarkable,
however, is the dearth of engagements by scholars in area studies. Some
affirm the importance of Said's work, only to dismiss it as
"Occidentalism." Others question his qualifications. Said, appropriately, ignores this type of criticism, which is little more than an attempt
to police disciplinary boundaries as a substitute for grappling critically
with his arguments. But this attempt to "trump" Said's argument by
pulling scholarly rank has proven ineffective. The claim by Orientalist
scholars to expertise and the corollary that Said lacks expertise fails
because expertise is a presumption. "The proof of the scholarly pudding
(whether we should take their presumptive expertise seriously or not) is
in the eating." Seldom does one encounter a substantial and sustained
analysis. What one gets instead is an uncritical celebration of Said's critique of Orientalist knowledge and power or, more often, an equally
uncritical trashing.

I strive to avoid both temptations – and many others. Accordingly, I use gender-inclusive language where appropriate. But I do not make a fetish of it, which means that I do not put gender-sensitive language into the mouths of those who, for whatever reasons, are gender-insensitive. I hope that I am sensitive. But I hope even more that I am provocative.

The support of many people has left me a debt that I can only pay with gratitude. Without the tireless work of Jeffrey Stout, whose intellectual comradeship I deeply appreciate, this book would have never been published. I was first introduced to the work of Edward Said in a graduate seminar taught by Cornel West, who encouraged my idiosyncratic interest in Said's cryptic references to religion and secularism. My interest was further stimulated by the mutual interest of Tommy Williams, a fellow graduate student. Together, we read Said's work during the summer of 1991. I cannot imagine how things might have been without the support and good humor of my best friend, Victor Anderson, or without the encouragement of my best colleague, Melvin Peters. Each, in his own inimitable way, has kept me sane. To the editors of the series Cambridge Studies in Religion and Critical Thought – Jeffrey Stout, Wayne Proudfoot, and Nicholas Wolterstorff – and to my Cambridge editor Kevin Taylor, many thanks.

An early version of chapter 1 was presented to the faculty-graduate colloquium of Princeton University's Center for Human Values. The sharp and pointed criticism of my fellow participants challenged me to think more critically. I thank the Center for its intellectual and financial support. Part of Concluding Remarks was previously published as "Cornel West: Between Rorty's Rock and Hauerwas' Hard Place" in *American Journal of Theology and Philosophy* 19:2 (1998), 151–172. I thank Tyron Inbody, editor of *AJTP*, for permission to use this material in an altered form and in a very different context. Also, I thank Edward Said for permission to reproduce an exchange of letters between Michael Walzer and him.

Finally, and most important, I offer special thanks to Carrol, Adrienne, and Kwame, my wife, daughter, and son. Without them, I am greatly diminished.

# Abbreviations

| | |
|---|---|
| ALS | *After the Last Sky* |
| B | *Beginnings: Intention and Method* |
| CAI | *Culture and Imperialism* |
| CI | *Covering Islam* |
| ME | *Musical Elaborations* |
| O | *Orientalism* |
| PD | *Peace and Its Discontents* |
| POD | *The Politics of Dispossession* |
| QP | *The Question of Palestine* |
| RI | *Representations of Intellectuals* |
| WTC | *The World, the Text, and the Critic* |

# Preliminary remarks

## EXODUS AND THE QUESTION OF PALESTINE

> There is no Israel without the conquest of Canaan and the expulsion or infe-
> rior status of Canaanites – then as now. (Edward Said, "An exchange: Michael
> Walzer and Edward Said")

The publication of Michael Walzer's *Exodus and Revolution* ignited a controversy of extraordinary bitterness between Walzer and Said. At issue
is the question of representation. What is the most appropriate way of
representing the Exodus narrative and its contemporary political implications? With clarity, subtlety, and simplicity, which are the signature of
his neo-Orwellian style, Walzer presents an argument for the Exodus
narrative as a paradigm for revolutionary politics. This book might have
received little notice (even as I write it has been underanalyzed and
perhaps underappreciated) had it not been for a stinging review of the
book by Said. Walzer's book, he argues, is a sophisticated legitimation of
contemporary Israeli–Palestinian relations, a historical repetition of the
conquest of the land of Canaan. This review led to an exchange of
letters between the two men (one a Palestinian American, the other a
Jewish American) that is nothing if not vitriolic. The ascending spiral of
the vitriol – the review, rebuttal, and surrebuttal – suggests that something very important is at stake in this disagreement. What are at stake,
I argue, are not only competing views of how a religious narrative should
be represented, but differing views on the nature of secularism and the
responsibility of the intellectual.

These views beg to be further sifted, as there is more here than one
might imagine. This sifting is made easier by four compound–complex
questions that I pose below; they help to clarify just what the stakes are
in the Said–Walzer dispute:

(1) Why is religion a good description of ethnic, racial, and national sol-
    idarities? Or, to put this question differently, why do discussions of

ethnicity, race, and nationalism slide easily into discussions of religion? Do these forms of solidarity enable or disable radical critique? Or is the relation between solidarity and radical critique more complicated?

(2) Are religious consciousness and critical consciousness incompatible? Do religious commitments compromise radical critique in nontrivial ways?

(3) In "Contribution to the Critique of Hegel's *Philosophy of Right*: Introduction," Marx says that the criticism of religion is nearly complete. Said has doubts. Let me add to those doubts by asking: will the criticism of religion ever be completed? How would we know?

(4) What kinds of relationship with religion are appropriate for secular critics? Must they renounce their religious affiliations, scrupulously avoid religious language, regard their religious upbringing with embarrassment or contempt, construe religious affiliations as private matters that are appropriate in their proper sphere, or can they cultivate a playful, skeptical, appreciative but ironic disposition toward them? Which is more radical – that is, more likely to produce the results that we want? Which approach is more likely to undermine the nasty aspects of religious affiliation while cultivating what is benign and even useful?

With these questions in mind, let us begin again. Said's review essay, "Michael Walzer's *Exodus and Revolution*: A Canaanite Reading," reveals a man who is deeply invested, politically and existentially, in his analysis. The exchange of open letters shows two men who are equally invested in their responses to each other. In *Exodus and Revolution*, Walzer makes a historical claim about how the Exodus narrative has been understood and about its observable consequences for radical politics. People as historically and geographically different as the English Puritans, American colonists, South African Boer nationalists, members of the African National Congress, and the religious leadership of the American civil rights movement, found revolutionary inspiration in the Exodus story. For them, it was a this-worldly account of liberation from oppression. As Walzer says in the final paragraph of the book, the message that these diverse people got from the story was this:

– first, that wherever you live, it is probably Egypt;
– second, that there is a better place, a world more attractive, a promised land;
– and third, that "the way to the land is through the wilderness."

There is no way to get from here to there except by joining together and marching.[1]

Walzer construes Egypt as a "house of bondage" and is quite effective in providing a word-picture of its oppressiveness. Egypt, he writes, "is oppressive like a hot and humid summer day," except that it is "infinitely worse, of course." The Hebrews were afflicted, burdened, and caused sorrow; they were tyrannized. Walzer quickly takes back or modifies this claim, in as much as "Pharaoh is never explicitly called a tyrant in the Book of Exodus." But, these legalities aside, Walzer knows that we will get the point. Besides, he tells us, Pharaoh, in later Jewish literature, is known as the first of the tyrants. Pharaoh is cruel. So is life in the house of bondage. Repression, alienating and alienated work, humiliation, and infanticide are some of many cruelties that the Hebrews experienced. Walzer focuses in particular on the last of this litany, which he construes "as the first of a series of attempts on Jewish peoplehood that culminated in the Nazi death camps."[2] While understandable, I find this sort of anachronistic reading of the past, from the perspective of the Nazi holocaust, morally pernicious. It robs history of the innocence to which it is entitled by confounding the singularity of history as this particular "slaughter-bench"[3] with other slaughter benches that are totally unconnected. According to this bizarre form of historiography, what the Egyptians did to the ancient Hebrews, the Nazis to twentieth-century Jewry, and what the Arabs are now "doing" to the state of Israel become a single story. Even if Pharaoh was bad, he was not, as Walzer's reading suggests, a proto-Nazi. To say that he was is to inflate that currency beyond moral use, beyond its ability to provoke indignation. When this historical judgment of Pharaoh becomes, in the hands of Walzer, a judgment of contemporary Palestinians, Said's ire becomes ballistic. His anger is well justified.

Thus Said is impressed by Walzer's skills as a writer but not by his skills as a historian and even less as an honest interpreter of the Israeli–Palestinian dispute. The upshot of Said's review is that Walzer's text is a thinly veiled apology for the policies of the state of Israel. Walzer recasts the nature of the contemporary Israeli state by recasting the Exodus story as "the birth of a new polity, one that admits its members to a communal politics of participation in political and religious spheres."[4] Further, he views Walzer's reading of the promised-land episode as symptomatic of the book's apologetic character. I shall have more to say about these matters in a moment. First I note that much in Walzer's book, and from my perspective some of its most interesting parts, does not make it into Said's review or receives little attention. In this respect, his review is not so much unsatisfactory (a review can only do so much) as unsatisfying. But Said is razor sharp when dealing with those parts of the text that he does discuss.

Behind Walzer's deceptive partisanship, Said discerns a complex rhetorical strategy of *découpage* (the selection of evidence and "stage setting"), which Walzer deploys with chatty, disarming style. Through this rhetorical style, Walzer can ignore relevant counterevidence, which exposes the nature of his tactical maneuvers – the tactic of inclusion by deferral and the tactic of avoidance. Thus Walzer, like Foucault whom he criticizes on this very point, can evade by deferral the long arm of "scholarly law enforcement – the presentation of evidence, detailed argument, the consideration of alternative views." Or instead, he can avoid considering the reasons why the Israelites came to Egypt in the first place. What happens to Walzer's account if Egypt was the promised land, an archetype of the promised land? By ignoring this question, he can down play the sense in which Egypt itself was a prototype, an earlier promised land, where the Israelites multiplied and prospered.[5]

Lost in the specificity of Walzer's "stage setting" of the Exodus narrative, which includes Leviticus and Numbers, are many examples of Yahweh's blood lust. Nor is Said just picking on Yahweh when he criticizes the bloodthirsty character of monotheistic politics. Yahweh's blood lust is the Christian God's blood lust and Allah's blood lust too. Said's critique goes to the undesirability of monotheistic politics as such, which he thinks makes the "secular and decent politics" that Walzer wants less likely. Also lost in Walzer's account, less through the strategy of *découpage* than the tactic of avoidance, is how to separate the conquest of the land of Canaan, an essential part of the story, from "the attitudes of the murderous Puritans or of the founders of *apartheid.*" This is certainly a hard blow, but not a low blow. I think that Said is right in posing this question, which is not made less right by it sharp tone.

Early in his account, Said refers to a problematic feature of Walzer's style, which is "insistent and uncompromising in places, indifferent and curiously forgiving in others." I do not think that this style is a problem *per se*, but Walzer's now serious-minded, now light-minded and easygoing style is a problem in the particular case to which Said refers. Walzer's style is also a problem when he ignores the "effective history" of the texts that describe the conquest of the land of Canaan. On this point, Said takes Walzer to task, suggesting that right-wing Zionists are better and more honest readers of these texts than Walzer is.[6] In determining what the Exodus story means, Walzer gives greater weight to the later rabbinic tradition than to those traditions that were more contemporaneous with the event. In contrast, Said gives greater weight to the views of Indian-killing Puritans who saw themselves as the new Israelites and Indians as new-world Canaanites. Walzer wants to protect contemporary Judaism from too close an association with the worst part of the Exodus narrative, the divinely sanctioned genocide of the Canaanite nations, and from any associations that might be made with contemporary Palestine. Said wants Walzer to take more seriously the ugly but effective history of this narrative for Indian-killing Puritans, apartheid-practicing South African Boer nationalists, and for contemporary right-wing Zionists. For Said, Walzer's easygoing style, where matters so grave are concerned, shows just how captive he is to the religious effects of culture.

Said's critique continues relentlessly along similar lines and at a similar pace. One gets the sense that Said is circling his prey, reconnoitering and reconnoitering again before going in for the kill. He regards as bizarre Walzer's effort to derive "a realistic, secular paradigm for 'radical politics'" from the Exodus story. He sneers when Walzer "combines sacred and profane in equal doses." He can barely contain himself when Walzer maintains that the Exodus story is progressive, its account of "deliverance" unique, Western, and revolutionary. He compares Walzer unfavorably to others who have explored biblical narratives. And he questions Walzer for failing to consider the philo-Semitic context of Puritan ideology, not to mention the anti-Exodus strain in some Puritan writings. If the Exodus story is revolutionary, he asks, then why does it merit at most a passing reference in the writings of revolutionary thinkers such as Vico, Marx, Michelet, Gramsci, and Fanon? Why does Walzer fail to consider the relations, if any, between the Exodus narrative and actual events? Antonio Gramsci's "The Revolution Against 'Das Kapital'" might provide a model for this approach. There Gramsci shows the gap between the idea of *Das Kapital* and its historical instantiation or transubstantiation in the Bolshevik Revolution. Why is there no "Revolution Against Exodus?" Perhaps Walzer has not written such a piece because the logic of the red terror and the golden calf episode of the Exodus narrative (where Moses purged, in the most gruesome way imaginable, those who were responsible for this act of idolatry) is the same. Here Said disagrees with Walzer's attempt to give a social democratic[7] interpretation of the purges where Lincoln Steffens', *Moses in Red*, had given a Bolshevik reading. Said's approach, one might say, is to "search and destroy," which is not to say that intellectual search-and-destroy missions are not appropriate, sometimes.[8]

The "proof text," as it were, for Said's critique of *Exodus and Revolution* refers to "the destruction of the Canaanite nations." According to Walzer, "the movement from Egypt to Canaan is taken as a metaphor for a transforming politics." The focus of the narrative is the internal "purges of the recalcitrant Israelites" and not the conquest of Canaan. The conquest is not an important part of the story; it is not, following biblical precedent, part of the story that Walzer wants to tell. "[F]or the Canaanites are explicitly excluded from the world of moral concern. According to the commandments of Deuteronomy they are to be driven out or killed – all of them, men, women, and children – and their idols destroyed."[9]

Said construes this passage, indeed, Walzer's entire account, as a pseudo-secular reading. Walzer's interpretation, he argues, can only serve to justify contemporary sectarian claims that are expansionist (read imperialist) in nature, much as the text itself justifies the many ramified exclusion of the Canaanites from the world of moral concern.[10] In his exchange of letters with Said (see Appendix B), Walzer rejects this reading as exemplary of Said's method of "perverse attribution." He goes on to say that Said knows full well that he opposes this kind of moral exclusion, as should be obvious, even on a "Canaanite reading."[11] Despite Walzer's objections, Said presses this point in his reply. Indeed, he anticipates Walzer's objection in his review article, where he notes the rhetoric of self-description used by Zionist writers during the period when the state of Israel was established. He claims that this rhetoric was generally religious and imperialist in character and not the rhetoric of national liberation. Zionists did not see themselves, and were not seen by their European sponsors, as a national liberation movement, but as an eccentric, though like-minded, version of European colonial undertakings such as Vietnam.[12] He cites Walzer's 1967 article "Israel Is Not Vietnam" (co-written with Martin Peretz) as a pioneering attempt to minimize the conventional interpretation of the establishment of the Jewish state. He describes Walzer's method of analysis as sophisticated obfuscation. He later calls it sophistry, when Walzer takes Camus as exemplary of intellectual responsibility within the context of colonialism and national liberation.

I am a partisan of Said in this dispute. But here I want to take my distance. The measure of this distance is the difference between Said's understanding of secularism and my own. Here I want to preview some conclusions that I develop more extensively in Concluding Remarks. Said and I disagree about the meaning of secularism and about the sort of relations that a secular critic can properly have with religion. Said thinks of secularism as religion-abolished or as religion-strictly-quarantined. I think of secularism as a complex relationship with religion that entails an equally complex art of separation. I cannot imagine secularism without religion; they are symbiotic. I can imagine a time (with great difficulty) where it would no longer make sense to talk about secularism precisely because religion had lost it sense. So while I agree with Said's claim that the Exodus is not about revolution, I cannot accept the claim that the story has not inspired "revolutionary" forms of politics. But Said rightly questions the moral quality of the Exodus story's political and ethical legacy. On this matter, I take Said as denying Walzer's claim that social democracy is an aspect of that legacy. Said's wholesale rejection of the story, however, need not be accepted. On the retail level, there are resources for a progressive politics in the Exodus story, but these resources are accessible only after a thoroughgoing critique of considerable subtlety and dialectical skill. This critique, Walzer's failure aside, is precisely the job of the critic, even the secular critic. We begin where we are with the resources at hand, including religious narratives! We make connections and render judgments. Sometimes the connections we make are slippery and dangerous. How could they not be potentially dangerous? Some connections that we draw, like the revolutionary appropriation of the Exodus, obscure other connections, like divinely sanctioned genocide. If criticism is inherently slippery and dangerous, then there can be no safe positions. Nontrivial forms of criticism are necessarily troubled and troubling; they dance, so to speak, on the edge of the abyss. Radical criticism *is* a slippery slope. This is reason for caution, but not for dispensing with the critical task of trying to make ethical and political sense of the storied-traditions that history has given us. On my view, we have to make retail sense of these stories because we cannot abandon them wholesale. On occasion, however, we may be required to abandon particular stories, when we are convinced that they are more likely to sanction evil than good. Perhaps the Exodus is that kind of story? On the other hand, perhaps the legacy of this story and Said's exchange with Walzer say something about the limitations of Said's notion of secularism – but more about that later.

For now, the following observations will do. The Said–Walzer exchange is a sad and strange spectacle in which two ostensibly secular intellectuals find themselves locked in a tendentious contest of wits over what is (literally and figuratively) religious ground. As secular intellectuals, how could they not be shaped by cultural practices shot through with religious sentiment? Walzer tries to make a particular kind of sense of his religious heritage, one that is compatible with his secular, social democratic politics. Where Marx (whose family converted from Judaism to Christianity) takes Judaism as a simile for capitalism, Walzer takes it (or at least the Exodus narrative) as the birth of revolutionary politics. Said (who was baptized in Jerusalem, in St. George's Anglican Cathedral) has long since rejected his Christian upbringing – Anglican on one side, Baptist on the other. He makes a different kind of sense of his heritage. The only good option, as he sees it – for a conscientious secular critic whose religious heritage is circumscribed by bloody conflict between Jews, Christians, and Muslims, on the one hand, and, on the other, between Israelis and Palestinians – is strict rejection.

## RELIGIOUS–SECULAR HIEROGLYPHICS AND THE ROSETTA STONE

I regard "Secular Criticism" and "Religious Criticism," the introduction and the conclusion to *The World, the Text, and the Critic,* as a dossier that contains the spirit and broad outline of Said's cultural critique. These documents have a special place, an interpretive preeminence in my account. I return repeatedly to these documents, which I take as synecdoches – parts that represent the whole – of Said's cultural critique. I also regard these documents as a Rosetta stone that helps to decipher the hieroglyphic character of Said's use of terms such as sacred and profane, religious and secular, Manichaean and theological. These documents-as-Rosetta-stone allow us to read and to understand what we may previously have regarded as merely a curiosity of Said's style, a rhetorical flourish. I take them, on the contrary, as keys to what Said desires and to what he fears. To that extent, they are keys to his cultural critique.

In "Secular Criticism," Said tells a complex and arresting story. He speaks of the humanist scholar Erich Auerbach's Nazi-enforced exile in Istanbul, where, without the benefit of a library, he wrote *Mimesis,* one of the most influential books in Western literature. According to Said, Auerbach's exile, his national and cultural homelessness, and the cosmopolitan spirit that it produced, made this great book possible. But the freedom and critical distance that are available in a condition of exile and homelessness are always threatened by the recuperating and dogmatic powers of culture. Culture is fluid-like; it saturates "everything within its purview." But it does so by separating the best from the "not best," the normal from the abnormal, the insider from the outsider. Cultural judgments, the distinction between good and bad, enlist the enforcement power of the state. Culture and the state – as Matthew Arnold argues approvingly in *Culture and Anarchy*, which I discuss in chapter 1 – cover each other with a sacred veneer, with what Said disapprovingly calls a "quasi-theological exterior." Those who are inside are comfortably at home, and those outside are homeless. Culture is a sacred canopy that includes and excludes simultaneously:

in the transmission and persistence of a culture there is a continual process of reinforcement, by which the hegemonic culture will add to itself the prerogatives given it by its sense of national identity, its power as an implement, ally, or branch of the state, its rightness, its exterior forms and assertions of itself: and most important, by its vindicated power as a victor over everything not itself (*WTC* 5–14).

This process inspires resistance, the most important of which (for Said's purpose) is offered by the intellectual, not the party man or woman, but the isolated individual consciousness. Said, as we shall see, is torn between this solitary, romantic–individualist, Julien Benda-like intellectual and Antonio Gramsci's organic intellectual who, as the word organic suggests, is a component of a larger social organism. The task of this intellectual is to resist the "quasi-religious authority" of culture; the "authority of being comfortably at home among one's people, supported by known powers and acceptable values, protected against the outside world" (*WTC* 15–16).

Having described the task of the critical intellectual, Said then provides a detailed account of "filiation" and "affiliation," which he claims are "at the heart of critical consciousness." Filiation refers to those natural or cultural relations (Said is ambiguous on this point) such as biological procreation and kinship that are authoritative and precritical. Affiliation refers to those relations that compensate for and criticize the failure of filial relations. Said takes T. S. Eliot's conversion from "mere" Protestantism to Anglicanism (or Anglo-Catholicism) and the changes that occur in his poetry from *Prufrock, Gerontion*, and *The Waste Land* to *Ash Wednesday* and *The Four Quartets* as exemplary of the shift from filiation to affiliation. Eliot subscribed to the antecedent authority of Anglican divines such as Lancelot Andrewes, who was "able to harness the old paternal authority [of Roman Catholicism] to an insurgent Protestant and national culture, thereby creating a new institution based not on direct genealogical descent but on what we may call, barbarously, *horizontal affiliation*." This shift bears "strange fruit" in Eliot's poetry, which is consummated by the essays in *After Strange Gods*, with its semi-belligerent "credo of royalism, classicism, and catholicism." This poetry and these essays, and his conversion to Anglo-Catholicism, are compensatory affiliations for the failed filial pieties of Eliot's earlier republicanism, romanticism, and Protestantism (*WTC* 17–18). The anguish, alienation, orphanhood, homelessness, and critical distance of the earlier poetry gives way before the restored authority of the later poetry. Affiliation as a critical form loses its fluidity and reimprisons what it had once liberated. This return of repressed filial authority is what Said elsewhere calls the return of repressed religiosity.

It helps if we think of Said's use of religion and associated terms with Emile Durkheim in mind. If for Durkheim religion is the idealism (or moral force) of social life, then for Said it is an immoral and demoniac force. Accordingly, the critic must avoid two formidable temptations, irradiated by religion, that threaten to misdirect their critical attention. "One is the culture to which critics are bound filiatively (by birth, nationality, profession); the other is a method or system acquired affiliatively (by social and political conviction, economic and historical circumstances, voluntary effort and willed deliberation)" (*WTC* 18–19, 24). The failure to resist these temptations is what Said calls religious criticism. Religious discourse is "an agent of closure, which blocks the road of inquiry. Religion and culture are similar in that both provide "systems of authority" and "canons of order" that coerce and seduce a large following. They are charismatic; they produce moments of collective effervescence, divine madness. These "organized collective passions" are sometimes beneficial. They gather and bind people together, and provide them with a sense identity and group solidarity. But these passions often cause deadly harm. They produce large ideas with deadly consequences such as the Manichaean distinctions between East and West, Islam and modernity, the sons of Enlightened reason and the sons of Oriental despotism. The critique of religious discourse, therefore, is not merely a critique of irrationality, against which "a purely secular view of reality" is no guarantee. The object of Said's critique, and what he holds to be distinctive of religious discourse, is the appeal to "the extrahuman, the vague abstraction, the divine, the esoteric and secret."

In contrast, a secular attitude enables one to resist the religious temptation. It encourages a healthy skepticism toward the "official idols" of culture (filiation) and system (affiliation) such as the New Criticism and the new New Criticism – that is, discourse analysis, schizoid analysis, deconstruction, and neopragmatism. But Said fears that the work of the secular critic has only gotten harder. A once repressed religiosity has returned in secular guise. Criticism is no longer the criticism of religion but religious criticism. This is an oxymoron from Said's perspective. For how can religion be critical? Is not religion, by definition pre- or anticritical? On Said's view, the resurgent interest in Walter Benjamin exemplifies the return of religion, since it is Benjamin's mysticism and messianism that are in vogue not his Marxism. Said's conclusion is this: "Once an intellectual, the modern critic has become a cleric in the worst sense of the word. How their discourse can once again collectively become a truly secular enterprise is, it seems to me, the most serious question critics can be asking one another" (*WTC* 290–292).

## HOW I USE THE WORDS RELIGION AND SECULARISM

When I use the words religion, religiosity, religious, and sacred or secularism, secularity, secularization, and secular, I have ordinary dictionary meanings in mind. Besides more familiar meanings, religion refers to "any object of conscientious regard and pursuit," to any form of piety. Sacred, among other things, refers to "respect or reverence accorded holy things" and to things "set apart for, and dedicated to, some person, place, purpose, sentiment," and so on. Secularism, and its various linguistic forms, refers to the separation of church and state, "to release by church authority from religious vows and from connection with a monastery or similar religious institute." Secularism also refers "to change from religious to civil ownership or use," to the act of depriving something of its "religious character, influence, or significance."[13] Manichaean refers to a world-view that is radically dualistic, where moral and cosmological distinctions are made between the "sons of light and the sons of darkness." Theological refers to "God-talk," to anything related to God or godly things. I think that Said has many if not all of these things in mind when he uses these words. He does not define them with the care that I do. But I shall not hold that against him, which means that I shall hold him responsible for the various meanings of these words.

Said is not a religious thinker. But this does not mean that he is indifferent. On the contrary, religion is something that he can neither tolerate easily nor leave alone. Religion is an issue for him, unlike those who are indifferent, whom we mistakenly call secular. Secularism, in this respect, is a particular kind of relationship with religion. It is a skeptical, wary, or hostile interest. Secular thinkers are preoccupied with bound-ary-drawing and boundary-maintenance, with where secularism ends and religion begins. Secularism is the desire to separate and keep apart things that do not go together well such as church and state and the public and the private. It is also the desire to confound what religion holds apart. Thus secularists revel in contaminating what religionists hold as pure; they ridicule the fetish for purity, but often in the name of a different kind of purity.

Said is a secular thinker, which means that religious matters, broadly conceived, are important to his vision of things. Religious matters are important to his conception of cultural critique and to his image of the secular critic. *Secular Criticism*, as he conceives it, is the other of religious criticism. Without the counterpoint of religious criticism, it has no point. Accordingly, Gentile (or secular) history is the other of sacred history, and critical consciousness (or secular consciousness) is the other of theo-logical and Manichaean consciousness. Said describes those things that he does not like as sacred, religious, or theological, and what he does like as secular. Secularism is a term of approbation and religion is a term of disapprobation. Thus dogmatism, obscurantism, and jargon-ridden lan-guage are religious, as are ideas and social relations such as nationalism, Orientalism, and imperialism. To be sure, Said is no fan of René Girard,[14] but Said's notion of culture has affinities to Girard's notion of sacred violence. Culture, according to Said, has violence-producing effects. Where Girard discerns a primordial, sacrificial logic at work, Said sees organized collective passions. Where Girard accents cosmol-ogy, Said accents history. Where Girard recovers Freud's notion where murderous violence equals guilt equals the sacred, Said turns to Marx's analysis of fetishism and capital accumulation and to Foucault's notion of discourse and exclusion. He turns, that is, to the profit motive and to the discursive[15] construction and maintenance of identity to explain the violence-producing effects of culture.

Religion, therefore, refers to many things: from distinct traditions such as Buddhism, Christianity, and Santería to "sacred violence" (war, sacrifice, and the scapegoat syndrome) to disparate rituals and ideas that gather and bind people as a community. While distinctions can be made between religion proper and "improper," literal and figurative, these very distinctions themselves are figurative. So a clearly metaphorical use of the term such as "he acquires material goods religiously" is just as proper as any other. Christianity is not more religious than ethnic, racial, and national pieties; *religio* (piety) toward God is not more religious than *religio* toward ethnos, race, or nation. Said recognizes the differences between these various senses of religion, but the differences are often less important than the similarities.

As a specific kind of relation to religion, secularism is not indifference. On the contrary, the secular thinker is the captive of several moods – anger, fear, gratitude, esthetic appreciation – perhaps serially, perhaps simultaneously. Whatever the mood, or combination thereof, the one thing that the secular thinker cannot be is indifferent. This is what fascinates – in Nietzsche, or in militant atheists, or in Said – and what seems so strange. The Said–Walzer spectacle seems strange because of our mistaken habit of regarding religious and secular spaces as different places. What if they are the same place under different descriptions? Would not this explain why this ground is so fiercely contested? Is not Said and Walzer's dispute precisely a question of the relations of religious and secular descriptions of this common ground? Said views religion as a plague that, like any other, is best dealt with through quarantine. It should be relegated to private places. There it is less likely to cause harm by contaminating public places or what Said calls the secular world. This is a standard, liberal–Enlightenment view; it sounds Jeffersonian with a strong dose of French anticlericalism. In his dominant mood, Said construes secularism as public suspicion, exclusion, and trivialization of religious matters. Walzer has a similar mood, but his dominant mood is one of accomodation and co-optation. He construes secularism as secularization: as the transformation of religious culture, the distillation of a secular kernel from a religious husk. This accounts for his secular reading of the Exodus story, and for his anxiety-ridden attempt to make secular sense of his ethnicity and religious upbringing.

If I understand Said's argument correctly, Walzer's secularism is shaped and circumscribed by his religious and ethnic heritage, which uncritically, if not surreptitiously, skew his reading of the Exodus.[16] I think that Said is right, but not because I assume that things could be otherwise such that Walzer could totally escape the formative influences of his ethnicity and religious upbringing. To be sure, the critical horizon must extend beyond the constraints of ethnic and familial bonds, but the critic can never stand completely outside those constraints or shed those constraints like snakes shed skin. On the other hand, Said is surely right when he questions the ethical character of "connected criticism." While criticism is impossible without solidarity with some community, justice may demand that present solidarities be broken so that they can be remade. Sometimes those loyalties must be abandoned altogether (which is never done lightly and without considerable anguish) so that new solidarities can be forged. The ethical and political ambiguity of the Exodus story demands that we not only question our "connections" but be willing to break them.

ITINERARY

On Said's view, Walzer's efforts are emblematic of what is wrong with contemporary cultural criticism. In Walzer, he finds an eloquent testimony to the religious effects of culture: the allure of Orientalism, nationalism, and imperialism. Walzer exemplifies the religious seduction of the secular critic. Though no practitioner of "high theory," his work epitomizes, in a less abstract form, the *return* of repressed religiosity in contemporary critical theory. It is these interlocking themes – the religious effects of culture (ideas and affiliations for which people live, die, and kill), the religious seduction of the secular critic, and the return of repressed religiosity – that Said vigilantly criticizes.

These themes, which I separate for analytic purposes, are parts of one interlocking ensemble. *The religious seduction of the secular critic*, refers to Said's preoccupation with the truth-telling vocation of the intellectual. He is concerned, as Julien Benda might put it, by the treason of intellectuals, their failure to resist temptation. They succumb to temptation when they put solidarity before truth-telling, when they bow before the patriotic gods of the nation and the ethnocentric gods of culture. This way of constructing cultural critique, as commentary on a conflict now latent now manifest between religion and secularism, is a quintessentially modern idea. Said wrestles with the specter of religion, the ghost of modernity, whose relation to "real emancipation," in typical Marxist fashion, is the very premise of his cultural critique. The motif of religious and secular conflict is integral to his effort to grapple with the claims that culture, through the various solidarities and loyalties that it produces, makes on even the most conscientious of critics. He construes culture as a site of moral and esthetic refinement, a site of political and ideological contestation. Culture is a battlefield on which the responsible intellectual struggles; he struggles, among other things, against the religious–cultural effects of nationalism, Orientalism, and imperialism. In chapter 1, I discuss Matthew Arnold's influential idea of culture, which is the best example of which

I am aware of how culture becomes an object of religious devotion. By exploring Arnoldian culture and its affinities or lack of affinities to Saidian culture, I lay the groundwork for what Said calls religious–cultural effects.

*The religious effects of culture* refer to those social phenomena that block the road of inquiry, enforce conformity, and subjugate whole populations through the violent passions that they produce. *This book, as the title and my use of italics indicates, is as much about the religious effects of culture as about Said's particular construction of the idea. Each chapter is as much about other people – Michael Walzer, Matthew Arnold, Theodor Adorno, Antonio Gramsci, Karl Marx, Friedrich Nietzsche, Michel Foucault, and Noam Chomsky – as about Said. This book shows how Said illuminates their views and how their views illuminate his. These figures help to illustrate his notion of intellectual responsibility and his account of nationalism, Orientalism, and imperialism as religious–cultural effects. Thus Said is as much an occasion for thinking as an object of thought.* That Said has written extensively on these topics is no coincidence. Nor is it a coincidence that he takes religion as the best description of the kinds of identity that they create and the kinds of loyalty that they inspire. These passions are religious precisely because they are life and death passions; they are ideas and forms of solidarity for which people live, die, and kill. I treat nationalism, Orientalism, and imperialism in chapters 2, 3, and 4. These chapters will be of special interest to those who know Said as the author of *Orientalism* and of *Culture and Imperialism*. They intensify the discussion of culture in chapter 1, and foreshadow the discussion of responsibility and the secular critic in chapters 5 and 6.

*The return of repressed religiosity* refers to the abdication of responsibility by intellectuals within the domain of high theory. It refers to a special case of religious seduction, where ostensibly the most radical forms of cultural critique exemplify the secular return of religious ideas such as Original Sin and messianism. Such developments force Said to reconsider Marx's claim that with Feuerbach the criticism of religion is complete. In chapter 5, I trace the genealogy of Said's notion of intellectual responsibility and speculate on its relation to a particular trajectory of religious and antireligious thought. Chapter 6 extends and completes the story that I begin in Preliminary Remarks and further develop in chapter 5, by connecting "Exodus and the Question of Palestine" to "Marx and the Jewish Question." Chapter 6 puts a finer point on the arguments that I make throughout this study about religious–cultural effects and the religious seduction of the secular critic. Before doing that, I thoroughly explore Said's claim that even high theorists such as Michel

Foucault and Jacques Derrida, and their American postmodernist followers, are not immune to the return of repressed religiosity. If this book begins with Said's account of *how not to read a religious text*, then it ends with his account of *how religion has become the text* of contemporary critical theory.

# CHAPTER I

# Culture as the transfiguration of religious thought

Said's work, as exemplified by *Culture and Imperialism*, is affiliated with an English-language tradition of cultural thought that extends backward through Raymond Williams' *Culture and Society* to Matthew Arnold's *Culture and Anarchy*. Matthew Arnold was a man caught between two worlds: the world of traditional Christian belief and the world of modern scientific reason, one dead, the other powerless to be born. In a world where national identity (increasingly racialized) had displaced religion as the center of value and the highest object of loyalty, Arnold was a proponent of cultural criticism as the *Aufhebung* (negation, preservation, and transformation) of religious thought. Through the mediations of T. S. Eliot and the New Critics, in whose work religious themes are prominent, Said appropriates and transfigures aspects of the Arnoldian cultural idea while rejecting others. He joins Arnold in praise of high culture as "the best that has been thought and said," but cannot celebrate culture insofar as it is transfigured religion. Instead, he joins Marx in opposing a wide array of cultural fetishes. If Arnold construes culture as the transfiguration (*Aufhebung*) of religious thought, then Said construes the critique of culture – that is, the critique of transfigured religion – as the premise of all criticism.

Arnold's cultural critique simultaneously negates theological dogma, both popular and philosophical, preserves Christianity's core (its moral truth and existential efficacy), and transforms Christianity from an offense to modernity's scientific spirit to a deferential but skeptical accomplice. The task of religious thought would no longer be that of telling us how the world is, in a cosmological or metaphysical sense, but of how we should live. Culture plays the same role in Arnold's thought that Reason does in Hegel's. Where speculative reason overcomes the divisions of modern society caused by a one-sided rationality, culture overcomes the divisions caused by industrialism. Arnold wants to restore a unified sensibility, one that is mediated, however, by scientific reason. He longs for a postconventional ethical life (*Sittlichkeit*) that provides some level of meaning and consolation in a world shorn of its sacred canopy. This longing bore fruit in Arnold's reconception of religion. On this view, religious appeals to miracles and supernatural verification had lost all legitimacy with the triumph of the scientific world-view. The watchword of science was verification. Arnold argued that religious faith could only be verified[1] experientially by the evidence of the moral law's efficacy in human history. That religion was a "power making for righteousness" was a proposition that Arnold believed was verifiable. Like Spinoza, he believed that religious criticism should be rational, imaginative, and, most important, edifying. In the tradition of Kant, Arnold struggled to reconcile religion and science. This effort was "a daring attempt to steer between the Scylla of logic and Charybdis of semantics." In other words, he sought to satisfy the evidentiary demands of science without reducing religion to a set of meaningless propositions. He sought to specify the proper spheres of religion and science and thus prevent the illicit encroachment of one on the other.[2] Under the regime of modernity, religion could no longer be dogmatic and doctrinaire. It could only survive as a moral sensibility linked to action, that is, as a form of pragmatic moralism.

If Arnold reduces religion to morality, then it is equally true that he amplifies and raises religion to new emotional heights. Religion is "morality touched by emotion," the notion that "Righteousness tendeth to life." Arnold calls this moral notion the natural truth of religion; it is accessible through "natural" reason and is subject, especially in its Christian form, to scientific verification. The natural truth of religion, however, is obscured by extra belief (*Aberglaube*), by beliefs that go beyond strict verification such as popular supernaturalism and theological metaphysics. The object of *Literature and Dogma*, one of Arnold's more self-consciously religious works, is to reassure those who are attached to Christianity and the Bible, but who accept the fact that ideas such as the supernatural and miracles are losing credibility. Reassurance does not mean disguising this fact or engaging in apologetics. On the contrary, miracles and the supernatural have justly and necessarily been discredited and this should be frankly admitted. The loss of the miraculous dimension of human life (understood in Humean terms) is part of the "same natural and salutary process" that destroyed the credibility of witchcraft. Arnold's notion of reassurance concedes all of this, while affirming the natural truth of Christianity, the notion that righteous conduct promotes life.[3]

Arnold attempts to provide this reassurance by drawing a distinction between a literary and a dogmatic use of language. The former recognizes the metaphorical and poetic character of language, as well as its use-determined meaning. The latter mistakes religious claims for "moves within a scientific language-game."[4] Dogmatists, whether scientists or theologians, the latter of which inappropriately pursue a kind of scientific exactitude, confuse poetic expression with scientific intent. Arnold's critique of the scientific pretensions of religious discourse is similar to Rudolf Bultmann's program of demythologizing. To demythologize "is to reinterpret the biblical mythology so that the essential message of the Bible can be understood for what it is." Liberating the Bible's essential message from an "outmoded world-view" means articulating the moral and existential intentions of the biblical myth in non-mythological terms.[5] Extra belief (*Auberglaube*) represents a mythical, prescientific cosmology whose moral and existential meaning is accessible for moderns only when divested of scientific pretense. To divest is not to discard. Though the product of an outmoded cosmology, the mythopoetic quality of extra belief need not be discarded any more than common and equally outmoded expressions such as "the sun rises in the East and sets in the West." Recognizing the nature of the "language-game," we do not confuse this common-sense claim with physics, with a theory of mechanics. We neither take such a statement to mean that the earth does not rotate on its axis nor that, Copernicus notwithstanding, the sun revolves around the earth. Myth is the poetry of truth. Arnold, accordingly, did not oppose the use of cosmological, metaphysical, or anthropomorphic language in communal worship or personal devotion. What he did oppose was their public role, the claim of speculative validity and scientific verifiability made on their behalf. As the transfiguration of religious thought, culture banishes the extramoral truth claims of religion to a purely private realm. On this liberal Protestant view, the public square is the realm of culture, and scientific verification is the gate keeper.[6]

While Said is silent on this aspect of Arnold's work (his cosmological views), I cannot imagine him disagreeing with much of it. Like Arnold, he thinks that religion is fine when relegated to its proper place, as a properly private affair. Said and Arnold's disagreement turns on the proper relationship between religion and cultural critique. Cultural criticism, as Arnold understands it, is a response to the decline of religion as a public authority. It is an attempt to reconstruct a viable canopy on sacred ruins. In culture, the cosmological claims of religion are negated, the moral claims preserved and transformed, but the existential claims exhibit a bit of ambiguity. Will culture perform the existential work in Arnold's new world that religion has historically performed? Or must this work be reserved to religion alone? Arnold is not clear on this point. The preponderance of the evidence within his own texts, such as it is, suggests that only religion can adequately do this work. He does suggest at one point, in some indefinite future, that the arts and sciences might displace religion as an adequate motivation for moral conduct.[7] But, on the question of whether science can provide the existential assurance and consolation that religion does, he is often silent. This I think reflects his uncertainty about just how much cultural work science could do, and whether the anxieties and uncertainties associated with a disenchanted world were irremediable.

Arnoldian culture is the disenchantment and reconstitution of the Christian gospel. Culture is neither vulgar curiosity nor "an engine of social and class distinction, separating its holder, like a badge or title from other people who have not got it." On the contrary, culture is a quest for total perfection through knowledge of those things that concern us most: "the best which has been thought and said in the world." This knowledge is "a stream of fresh and free thought" that flows across our common ideas and habits.[8] As Raymond Williams observes, this concept of culture belongs to a tradition that is distinctly English, which extends from Burke through Coleridge and Carlyle to Arnold.[9] In part a moral concept, culture is a humanitarian impulse, a desire to diminish and overcome human error, confusion, and misery, "the noble aspiration to leave the world better and happier than we found it."[10] Said shares this aspiration. He is part of the tradition of cultural thought that Williams describes. For those associated with this tradition, cultural critique is not a scholastic affair, where several degrees of abstraction separate theory from the transformation of ordinary practices. On the contrary, cultural criticism should make the world a better place.

Among the attributes of the tradition of perfection through culture is its distinctive missionary character. Arnold describes culture as the harmonious development of our many-sided humanity and the general development of every part of society. It is a "disinterested endeavour after man's perfection," which Arnold describes as "making reason and the will of God prevail." Culture is the desire to make manifest the

Socrates in every man's breast. Arnold regards this broad, inclusive, and dynamic view of culture as a craft, as a form of soul-making or soulcraft. The purpose of culture is not the production of esthetic objects, but the cultivation of human spirits as works of art. Culture is neither a market-place nor a museum, neither commodity nor possession, "not a having and a resting but, a growing and becoming." It is a bulwark against the market morality of industrial society, the inexorable leveling down of virtue and intellect. Horrified by the economic liberalism of his day, Arnold looked on in disgust as royal subjects were transformed into mindless consumers, pursuing an endless array of goods. Arnold regarded this kind of behavior as mechanistic: "machinery" being a trope for the modern idols of science, technology, and the market. Religious institutions, especially those that he called "hole-and-corner" churches, and the scientific pretense of theological dogma (as opposed to the natural truth of religion) are also part of the machinery of modern industrial society. According to Arnold, they help make modern society ugly and stupid.[11] Like Coleridge before him, Arnold believed that an acquisitive, rigidly stratified, and technological society could lose its soul within its own machinery, if it did not promote social forms of beauty and value.

But note well, his critique of industrial society has none of Marx's revolutionary desire. Where Marx discerned the "laws" of historical materialism, Arnold saw a dialectic of Hebraism and Hellenism.[12] From this perspective, the ugliness and stupidity of industrial society is the result of an imbalance of morality and intellect in social life. The leading idea of Hebraism is conduct and obedience. Hellenism, in contrast, is the desire "to see things as they really are." Arnold refers to these governing ideas, respectively, as "strictness of conscience" and "spontaneity of consciousness." Hebraism is a single-minded pursuit of perfection through morality that is characterized by the willingness to "sacrifice all other sides of our being to the religious side." It is the enemy of the Arnoldian concept of totality – that is, "the harmonious perfection of our whole being," and the development of our many-sided humanity. Hellenism, in contrast, falls short of totality because of its moral laxity and susceptibility to moral anarchy. Hebraism and Hellenism are broad social tendencies that represent our moral and intellectual impulses respectively. "At the bottom of both the Greek and Hebrew notion is the desire, native in man, for reason and the will of God, the feeling after the universal order, – in a word, the love of God." Although the means are different, the goals of both are the same, which is to promote human perfection.[13] While no age is totally lacking in evidence of Hebraic and Hellenistic tendencies, each age tends to be dominated by one or the other. Arnold discerns this tale of two cities, this dialectic of Athens and Jerusalem, in the relations of ancient Israel and classical Greece, medieval Christianity and Renaissance humanism, the Protestant Reformation and the Enlightenment.

He regards Hellenism as progressive, as having the spirit of modernity on its side. This spirit demands Hebraism's acquiescence, for want of such, modernity has about it "a certain confusion and false movement." In Arnold's scheme of things, Hebraism is little more than a form of resistance, a sometimes atavistic drag on the historical utopianism and anarchy of unfettered liberty.[14] Arnold notes a sense of uneasiness, what we might call the Pauline spirit of gravity, that pervades Hebraism. This inability to be at ease in Zion is produced by an awareness of the power of sin and evil, which insinuate themselves into the highest aspirations, best intentions, and purest will. In contrast, Hellenism has a Socratic spirit that is oblivious to sin as an obstacle to human perfection. Its hallmark is a naïve, free play of intellect. While Hellenism appears to embody all the essentials of the totality or sense of plenitude that Arnold longs for (spontaneity of consciousness, a free play of the mind, and respect for the harmonious development of our many-sidedness) it lacks Hebraism's self-restraint and strictness of consciousness. It is inadequate to the task of repressing multileveled anarchy and so is destined to play the role of cultural superego for an indefinite time. In culture, the utopianism of Hellenism and the all-encompassing moral claims of Hebraism, both of which are conducive to anarchy, are negated, preserved, and transformed, even as their separation in thought and action is overcome.

If Said is troubled by the ideas of Hebraism and Hellenism, it has much to do with the nineteenth-century tradition of racial thinking of which those ideas are part. The idea of Semitism – Semitic people, languages, and cultures, to which Ernest Renan made pioneering contributions – is often compared invidiously to Greek- and Roman-derived culture. This distinction between Indo-European language users and cultures and Semitic language users and cultures is deeply implicated in nineteenth-century racial thinking, the distinction between Aryan and Semite being only one on a long list. This "racial" distinction is integrally connected to invidious distinctions between religious traditions, between Christians and Jews and between Christians and Muslims. Arnold greatly admired Renan and it is hard to imagine him not being influenced by Renan in these matters. Arnold's distinction between Hebraism and Hellenism is an instance of what Said calls Orientalism – the invidious distinction between East and West, which I address in chapter 3. But the important thing to ponder now are the fluid relations between Orientialism, racial thinking, and invidious religious distinctions

Arnold's response to intellectual and moral decline, economic stratification, and the ever present threat of social anarchy, is not the liberal ideal of equalizing acquisitive opportunities while leaving the rest to the market. He seeks instead to educate desire through culture, replacing the pursuit of commodities with the cultivation of character. "Through culture," he argues, "seems to lie our way, not only to perfection, but even to safety." Culture is an ark of safety that is inseparable from the state.

Thus the very framework and exterior order of the State, whoever may administer the State, is sacred; and culture is the most resolute enemy of anarchy, because of the great hopes and designs for the State which culture teaches us to nourish. But as, believing in right reason, and having faith in the progress of humanity toward perfection, and ever labouring for this end, we grow to have clearer sight of the ideas of right reason, and of the elements and helps of perfection, and gradually come to fill the framework of the State with them, to fashion its internal composition and all of its laws and institutions conformably to them, and to make the State more and more the expression, as we say, of our best self, which is not manifold, and vulgar, and unstable, and contentious, and ever-varying, but one, and noble, and secure, and peaceful, and the same for all mankind, – with what aversion shall we not then regard anarchy, with what firmness shall we not check it, when there is so much that is so precious which it will endanger! (Ibid., 204)

This passage is from Arnold's signature work *Culture and Anarchy*, and says much about his anxious desire for a stable social order. *Culture and Anarchy* was written against a background of growing social unrest, including a crisis in England's financial markets, two consecutive years of disastrous agricultural harvests, and an outbreak of the rind pest virus that led to soaring beef and milk prices. Added to this was a severe outbreak of cholera in the slums of the East End of London, which exacerbated what were already depressing conditions. The economic conditions in England were desperate and much of this desperation spilled into the streets in the form of demonstrations and rallies of various kinds, the most important of which was the famous Hyde Park demonstration of 1866. This protest by working-class people and their advocates signified, both literally and figuratively, the transgression of aristocratic and bourgeois social space.[15] This so-called riot seems rather harmless in retrospect, the price that a democratic society must pay. But to Arnold, it revealed the deep-seated anarchy of the working class and the unwillingness of public officials to act swiftly and brutally to repress disorder.

The Hyde Park demonstration contributed to Arnold's theoretical marriage of the moral authority of culture and the police power of the state. In *Culture and Anarchy*, he developed a notion of culture as the antithesis of anarchy, a collective superego, to speak anachronistically, holding a collective id – with its multileveled anarchy of religion (spirit), body (sexuality), and the body-politic (social class) – at bay. Culture is a bulwark against the apotheosis of science, technology, and market forces in modern industrial society. Arnold's cultural thought is a critique of the destabilizing inequalities created by industrialism, which produced a materialistic upper class, vulgar middle class, and brutalized impoverished class.[16] Like Plato, he favored a form of education that discouraged protest and reconciled people, especially the poorer classes, to their stations in a rank-ordered society. Where education failed, and people were moved to protest openly in the streets, as they were at Hyde Park, Arnold had recourse to his father's brutal wisdom:

I remember my father in one of his unpublished letters written more than forty years ago, when the political and social state of the country was gloomy and troubled, and there were riots in many places, goes on, after strongly insisting on the badness and foolishness of the government, and on the harm and dangerousness of our feudal and aristocratic constitution of society, and ends thus: "As for rioting, the old Roman way of dealing with that is always the right one; flog the rank and file, and fling the ring-leaders from the Tarpeian Rock!"[17]

Arnold inherited this notion of the draconian state from his father, Thomas Arnold. From Edmund Burke he inherited a religious reverence for society and the state. On this Burkean view, the perfection of our own natures is impossible without civic piety, without the joint dominion of God and the state. It is hard to distinguish the two, as the state is "the source and original archetype of all perfection."[18] Arnold inherited this Burkean mind-set where the state is the necessary agent of human perfection.[19] On this view, culture is inextricably bound up with multiple forms of repression (or character formation) at the apex of which is the state. If culture is a collective superego, then the state is the embodiment of the national ego. It is our "best self" in "its collective and corporate character." Unlike the self-interested ordinary self, it is the incarnation of right reason. The best self has no class loyalties or other parochial interests that encumber the ordinary self.[20] Arnold's distinction between "the ordinary, empirical self or ego and the true or real spiritual self," has a religious provenance.[21] It is indebted to the New Testament distinction between the carnal and the spiritual man. True religion requires the sacrifice or subordination of carnal desires to spiritual ones. As the collective and, therefore, highest manifestation of our best self, the interests of the state come before those of the ordinary, individual self. The state is a sacred trust, a religious and political entity.

Said is deeply suspicious of this view. He describes *Culture and Anarchy* as "a very rigorous apology for a deeply authoritarian and uncompromising notion of the State." It would be wrong, he argues, to view the Arnoldian state as a precursor of "Orwell's Big Brother state" or as a precursor of actual dystopian states such as Stalin's Russia or Hitler's Germany. There is no cynicism in his notion of the state as a sacred institution, as our best self, "the repository of our best hopes." But, and this is important, Arnoldian culture is invidiously comparative, competitive, and unabashedly nationalistic: "the people, the nation, the culture and the State he speaks about are his own and are meant to be distinct from those of France, India, or America. Arnold's thought and his rhetoric are stamped with the emergence in nineteenth-century Europe of national sentiment." On his view, some nations or races are more civilized and less provincial than others. While a sharp and unrelenting critic of the English, England stands atop the nations of Europe, which stand astride and look down at the rest of the cultures and nations of the world.[22]

The state is the highest expression of Arnoldian ethical life, just as for Hegel it is the highest manifestation of "objective spirit." But Arnold lacks Hegel's subtlety, and is more susceptible to the crude statist arguments that are often made against Hegel. That Arnold has few qualms about the best self and the brutal use of force that it authorizes against the "not best" is clear. And so, he concludes: the best self through the instrumentality of the executive power will act firmly, clearly, and resolutely to crush public disorder. The Arnoldian state can act with brutal decisiveness, because its conscience is free.[23] Arnold has a Hegelian equanimity before the "slaughter bench" of culture and state. But, as Trilling observes, Arnold lacks Hegel's realism and forthrightness. He wants both "force" and "right" – or, in the pernicious language of Joubert,[24] "force till right is ready." So he retreats "before the brutal question of power."[25] Trilling is probably right. But perhaps this question never arises for Arnold, given his idealistic view of the state. One commentator sums up Arnold's view of the state as follows: "power tends to make people better, and absolute power to make them perfect."[26] Arnold's view is not quite that sanguine, but he's clearly smitten. As he notes: "The State is of the religion of all its citizens without the fanaticism of any of them."[27] As culture sublates religion as the object of veneration in the public square, organized religion recedes and is confined to the private realm. If culture is the transfiguration of religious thought, then the state, under cover of sacred authority, is the policing function of religion augmented and transformed by culture.

### A SAIDIAN CRITIQUE

Said is both fascinated and repelled by Arnold's notion of culture. If Arnold sees a stark choice between culture and anarchy (with culture as that ensemble of authoritative habits and customs, hierarchies, and constraints that hold the chaotic forces at bay), then Said is more ambivalent. If Arnoldian culture is Janus-faced, the "best that has been said and thought in the world" on one side, and on the other side the "Tarpeian Rock," then Said is attracted by the first and repelled by the second. He offers qualified approval of Arnoldian high culture, but rejects Arnoldian state-worship. Against Arnold's idea of culture, he advocates a skeptical, if ambivalent attitude. In contrast to Arnold, and in the interest of human freedom and noncoercive knowledge, he advocates a quasi-anarchic attitude toward cultural authority. Said separates Arnold's idea of culture, understood as "the best which has been thought and said in the world," from its explicit affiliation with the repressive police powers and the ideology-spinning institutions (churches, schools, corporate media, and so on) of the state. *Secular Criticism* is a transvaluation of Arnold's culture–anarchy distinction. Anarchy (often personified by Jonathan Swift, with his satirical wit) becomes Said's preferred metaphor for the disruption and transgression of sacred orders of meaning. Culture becomes a trope for atavistic religioud ideas and commitments such as nationalism, Orientalism, and imperialism. *Secular Criticism* breaks with the gods of nationalism and state-worship, by severing the link between critical consciousness and the politics of identity.

Said's appropriation of Arnold's idea of culture is qualified by his unwillingness to wholly embrace the Arnoldian view (even when that view is separated from the enforcement power of the state) because of its residual religiosity. This residue, which takes the form of nationalism and purist notions of cultural identity, creates an excessive veneration of the state, wedded to strong forms of ethnocentrism and xenophobia. On the wrong side of this strong delineation between *us* and *them*, "anarchy, disorder, irrationality, inferiority, bad taste, and immorality are identified, then deposited outside the culture and kept there by the power of the state and its institutions." This is not a theoretical exercise in fear-mongering on Said's part. He has specific historical examples in mind: including "Macaulay's famous Minute of 1835 on Indian education" and the utilitarian philosophy of British colonialists. Said quotes Macaulay as follows: "all the historical information which has been collected in the Sanskrit language is less valuable than what may be found in the paltry abridgements used at preparatory schools in England." According to Said, this cannot be dismissed, as Derrida dismisses Levi-Strauss' recourse to the idea of the noble savage, as a case of textual ethnocentrism. He goes on to make the Foucauldian point that words (discourse) and things (nondiscursive practices) are linked and that discourse has ascertainable results. Here Said refers to the imposition of the English language on the people of the Indian subcontinent. The second example is the relationship between utilitarian philosophy and British colonial policy in India. According to Said, there is a strong "us" and "them" element in the philosophy of John Stuart Mill, which effectively justified the repression of Indian people in as much as they were uncivilized and beyond the pale of representative government and the rights of liberty (*WTC* 11–13). Invidious distinctions between us and them, higher and lower, European and non-European are written across the breadth of nineteenth-century European thought. Even a great liberal thinker such as Mill was unable to escape this kind of ethnic and racially dualistic thinking (*WTC* 13–14). Said's revision of Arnoldian cultural thought is also an effort to make good on the cosmopolitan ideal that Mill and Arnold shared. Although it should be said, parenthetically, that Arnold's cosmopolitanism, his concept of the world for purposes of defining the best, did not extend beyond Europe. Arnold's truncated view had much in common with the views of his peers, especially Ernest Renan:

What gave writers like Renan and Arnold the right to generalities about race[28] was the official character of their formed cultural literacy. "Our" values were (let us say) liberal, humane, correct; they were supported by belles-lettres, informed scholarship, rational inquiry; as Europeans (and white men) "we" shared in them every time their virtues were extolled. Nevertheless, the human partnerships formed by reiterated cultural values excluded as much as they included. For every idea about "our" art spoken by Arnold, Ruskin, Mill, Newman, Carlyle, Renan, Gobineau, or Comte, another link in the chain binding "us" together was formed while another outsider was banished. Even if this is always the result of such rhetoric, wherever and whenever it occurs, we must remember that for nineteenth-century Europe an imposing edifice of learning and culture was built, so to speak, in the face of actual outsiders (the colonies, the poor, the delinquent), whose role in the culture was to give definition to what they were constitutionally unsuited for. (*O* 227–228)

Arnold's idea of culture did not embrace Europe's Asian, African, or West Indian colonies. Nor is it clear that it included the English working class, given his lifelong ambivalence toward the "masses." The "ours and theirs" distinctions that Arnold and his peers drew were bolstered, according to Said, by the human sciences, social-Darwinism, and high cultural humanism. It is hard to know how "ours and theirs" distinctions can be avoided, even under the best of circumstances, and Said is no help in understanding how they might be. The following passage does succeed, however, in putting a finer point on what he thinks is at stake:

Most modern readers of Matthew Arnold's anguished poetry, or of his celebrated theory in praise of culture, do not also know that Arnold connected the "administrative massacre" ordered by Eyre with tough British policies toward colonial *Eire* and strongly approved both; *Culture and Anarchy* is set plumb in the middle of the Hyde Park Riots of 1867, and what Arnold had to say about culture was specifically believed to be a deterrent to rampant disorder – colonial, Irish, domestic. Jamaicans, Irishmen, and women, and some historians bring up these massacres at "inappropriate" moments, but most Anglo-American readers of Arnold remain oblivious, see them – if they look at them at all – as irrelevant to the more important cultural theory that Arnold appears to be promoting for all the ages. (*CAI* 130–131)

Said brings this train of thought to a head with the following:

The idea of culture itself, as Arnold refined it, is designed to elevate practice to the level of theory, to liberate ideological coercion against rebellious elements – at home and abroad – from the mundane and historical to the abstract and general. "The best that is thought and done" is considered an unassailable position, at home and abroad. (*CAI* 131)

Said fears the exclusionary power of culture, especially when wedded to the repressive power of the state. Under this description, culture constitutes a church–state in which the "others of culture" (colonized people, the poor, and delinquent) are grouped under the rubric of anarchy. In contemporary British and American scenarios, this means "blacks" and the underclass, or Palestinian "terrorists" and Islamic fundamentalists. They replace English working-class democrats, middle-class philistines, and aristocratic barbarians as the enemies of culture and vectors of anarchy. But Said's relation to Arnoldian cultural thought is not as simple or unambiguous as this. For all his suspicion of high cultural humanism, Said remains a high cultural humanist. Like Arnold, he fears the vulgarity of popular culture, but there is an important difference. Where Arnold has an aestheticized fear of multileveled anarchy, Said fears the loss of the ideology-critical function of high culture. Arnold fears anarchy; Said fears conformity. Said's view conforms to that of the Frankfurt School theorists, especially Adorno, who regard a thoroughly commodified popular culture as depoliticized, if not in complicity with capital. The colonization of high culture ("the best that has been thought and said") by a market-driven popular culture and, consequently, the production of mass conformity, is what Said resists. If I were to draw a sketch of this resistance, it would have the broad outline of the "Frankfurt School" and its details would bear the stamp of Theodor Adorno.

Said describes his views as follows: "My cultural biases are on the whole tinged with conservatism, as the sheer weight in my text given over to the masterpieces of high modernism amply testifies" (*B* xiii). As outlandish as this claim might seem on first reading, especially given Said's well publicized involvement in leftist politics, he is a cultural conservative of sorts. I say "of sorts," because terms such as conservative tempt us to dredge-up associations and commitments that are wrong where Said is concerned. Anyway, if the left can be characterized in terms of a split between an older left that views politics in terms of the state and its ideology-producing institutions, and a newer left that views politics primarily in cultural and rhetorical terms, then Said sits skillfully if uncomfortably between the two. With respect to this newer left that is preoccupied with culture and the politics of difference, Said is a "conservative." He believes that there are "Arnoldian best-that-is-thought-or-said touchstones," and that we should give an account of how they are constructed, where they came from, and why they are authoritative (*ME* 60). It would be wrong to suggest that Said is uninterested in cultural politics and difference. His interest, however, is of a decidedly high-brow variety. Said wants to displace the Eurocentric canon by introducing non-European classics into the *agon* of humanistic discourse. But he otherwise appears committed to a fairly rigid distinction between high and low culture that is often associated, in a pejorative way, with modernism. Said is part of a long history of leftist intellectuals who wed a political and economic radicalism with a high-brow disdain for popular culture, especially its religious forms. As *Musical Elaborations* shows, Said cannot think critically about popular culture without reaching reflexively for his "Frankfurt School Reader."

## BEYOND ARNOLD, THROUGH ADORNO

There are undoubtedly several ways of getting at Said's Marxist view of cultural critique as the criticism of transfigured religion. Perhaps none is more appropriate than his Gramscian gloss on Adorno's music theory. In "On the Fetish Character in Music and the Regression of Listening," Adorno argues that there has been a decline in musical taste led by a thoroughly commodified popular music. Alluding to Marx's famous description of fetishism in *Capital*, Adorno argues that the exchange-value of music displaces its use-value, the worship of money displaces the appreciation of art. As in all forms of fetishism, the social character of a product is obscured, appearing as an alien, objective entity. Human subjectivity and creativity are externalized and objectified and become other, God. Human powers are misrecognized as divine power, which inhibits ideology-critique. Fetishized music inhibits ideology-critique in the same way that religion does. Thus the rebelliousness and subversiveness of precapitalist forms of music, under the regime of capital, have been domesticated and placed in the service of commercial success. Music is no longer a revolutionary and unruly attack on the cultural privileges of the ruling class, but has degenerated into a depoliticized "handmaiden" of consumerism. Depoliticization results from the vulgarization of art, from mindless repetition and irrelevant consumption.

Because musical works are "played again and again," they "wear out, like the Sistine Madonna in the bedroom." An interminable process of "climax and repetition" undermines our ability to see the whole. We lose, that is, any notion of totality, the ability as listeners to conceive of the whole, to think from part to whole and whole to part. The possibility for critique drops out, creating a critical void. In the place of this absent critique, music becomes a diversion, a consumption opportunity. The fetish character of music, its very *quid pro quo*, lies in the deceptive substitution of the use value of music, or the pleasure it provides, by the exchange value, or the monetary compensation that it brings. Because of this thorough incorporation into a market economy, there has been a decline in musical taste that even "responsible" and "serious" art like European classical music cannot escape. This, in turn, has led to a dangerous erosion of the line between serious and light music, and the loss of the utopian spirit and ideology-critical function of serious music.[29]

In this early elaboration of his "culture industry" thesis, Adorno claims that hand in hand with the fetishized character of music is a kind of commodity listening, in which it becomes difficult to separate listening from consumption. Fetishized listening has displaced serious musical appreciation and led to a "regression of listening," a degradation, to the point of infantilism and stupidity, of musical taste. Fetishized music blatantly decontextualizes and recontextualizes "reified bits and pieces," destroying the multileveled and complex unity of the work. The whole dissolves into "isolated popular passages." Adorno describes this phenomenon as regression or infantilism. These forms of hearing and listening exemplify if not expose the "neurotic stupidity," sickness, and stultification that fetishized music produces. The ultimate consequence of fetishized music is distraction, the inability to concentrate. "Deconcentration is the perceptual activity which prepares the way for the forgetting and sudden recognition of mass music." Adorno claims that standardized musical products, "hopelessly like one another," inhibit concentrated listening, which becomes unbearable to listeners no longer accustomed to such demands. "They cannot stand the strain of concentrated listening and surrender themselves resignedly to what befalls them, with which they can come to terms only if they do not listen to it too closely."[30]

Adorno's notion of "regression" has psychoanalytic overtones, which is not surprising given his attempt to marry Marx and Freud. Freud's notion of regression, especially in *Totem and Taboo*, *Inhibitions, Symptoms and Anxiety*, and *Moses and Monotheism*, centers around the psychosexual development of the individual and the group. On this view, the developmental history of the individual organism (ontogeny), recapitulates the evolution of the species (phylogeny). The neurotic, as Freud observes "regularly presents to us a piece of psychic infantilism; he has either not been able to free himself from the childlike conditions of psycho-sexuality, or else he has returned to them."[31] Children, child races, savages, primitives, and neurotics, including religious people, share a common psychic structure. They are infantile because they have yet to mature or have regressed, religion being the prototypical form of regression. "Most of these infantile neuroses are overcome spontaneously in the course of growing up, and this is especially true of the obsessional neuroses of childhood." For those who do not outgrow such neuroses there is psychoanalytic treatment. Some childhood obsessions, however, persist into adulthood – religion, again, being the prime example. Freud concludes that "Religion would thus be the universal obsessional neurosis of humanity; like the obsessional neuroses of children, it arose out of the Oedipus complex, out of the relation to the father."[32]

This is not a thorough account of Freud's theory of religion, which goes beyond my immediate purposes, but it is an account of infantilism, wish-fulfillment, and regression in the formation of culture. Adorno's "regression of listening" is homologous to Freud's notion of religion as regressive and infantile behavior. Commodity listening, a metonymy for popular culture, and religion are forms of fetishism. Both distract us from reality (the reality principle) through entertaining diversions (commodity fetishism) or wish-fulfillment. Both "get in the way" of the unmasking activities of science (the reality principle) or ideology-critique. In a late essay entitled "Culture Industry Reconsidered," Adorno recapitulates and elaborates this thesis. Operating from above, the "culture industry intentionally integrates its consumers," effaces the distinction between high and low art and makes the pursuit of cultural objects a function of the profit motive. The culture industry progressively erodes the relative autonomy of art and, as a result, its ideology-critical significance. Cultural objects become commodities entirely, as anything that might exceed or transcend the commodity function is eroded. What appears as new and progressive is merely the masquerade of the eternally same, the changing same, the profit motive. The culture industry is anti-enlightenment in its effects, thus, nature is subjected to progressive, technical domination, which produces mass deception, which fetters consciousness. The culture industry makes "autonomous, independent individuals who judge and decide consciously for themselves" much rarer.[33]

Adorno's famous essay, his music and esthetic theory as a whole, have influenced Said deeply. Exploring Said's view of music as an elaboration of civil society gives us a clear sense of just how subtle and sympathetic is his reading of European classical music, which can be transgressive of "domination and sovereignty," as compared to his notion of religion, whose cultural effects are disastrous. I do not want to leave the impression that Said follows Adorno without deviation. On the contrary, he proceeds by summarizing Adorno's position into three points from which he then takes his distance. First, he cites Adorno's claim that after Beethoven "music [by which both he and Adorno mean European classical music] veered off from the social realm into the aesthetic almost completely." Said approves of Adorno's claim for the ideology-critical function of modern music, but disapproves when Adorno locates that critical function in the autonomy of music "from the world of ordinary historical reality." Here he gives a Gramscian reading of Adorno, arguing "that music remains situated within the social context as a special variety of aesthetic and cultural experience that contributes to what, following Gramsci, we might call the elaboration or production of civil society" (*ME* 12–13).

Curiously, on Said's interpretation, "elaboration equals maintenance." Something seems askew here and even mystified, for surely elaboration means more than the maintenance of the status quo. Is elaboration merely the effort by the ruling class to seduce, negotiate, and compel the assent of those whom they rule – is it, that is to say, hegemonic activity? Or are the efforts of the ruling class part of a larger contest between dominant and emergent forms of hegemony,[34] between those forms that one opposes and those that one supports? In this passage, Said appears to elide this important distinction. I cannot imagine that this is what he intends. Fortunately, he gives a fuller description of elaboration in "Reflections on American 'Left' Criticism." There he remarks on the apparently "contradictory but actually complementary" elements of elaboration, which perpetuate an existing world view and transfigure that world view through cultural forms that are themselves a "highly complex and quasi-autonomous extension of political reality" (*WTC* 170–171). I gloss this claim as follows: elaboration is a cultural contest through which society is maintained and transformed by completing social classes. Having said this, and reconnecting with the previous discussion, there is something disturbing about Said's Gramscianism. It should provide, one would think, a finer-tuned ear when it comes to the role of classical music in the contemporary West, especially in comparison to popular forms of music, but these are sounds that Said cannot hear. Thus Said can write the following:

Music therefore quite literally fills a social space, and it does so by elaborating the ideas of authority and social hierarchy directly connected to a dominant establishment imagined as actually presiding over the work. The awe we feel in the Credo, for example, reinforces the separation between ruler and ruled, and this in turn is made to feel "right" in great outbursts of joy ("et resurrexit," and "hosanna"). (*ME* 64)

Here Said refers to the music of Bach. But is this example of elaboration as the maintenance of civil society truer, more effective, or more compelling than the revolutionary ambitions, with respect to civil society, that are clearly audible in Billie Holiday's "Strange Fruit," Nina Simone's "Mississippi Goddam," Bob Marley's "Them Belly Full (But We Hungry)," Stevie Wonder's "You Haven't Done Nothin'," or the mighty anthem of the Civil Rights Movement, "We Shall Overcome"? I think not. Said's preference for elite cultural forms, therefore, does not confirm Aijaz Ahmad's claim that he constructs a bourgeois Gramsci so much as gives license to those already disposed to read him that way.

Said's second point relates to the contrast between critics like Adorno for whom music is an important subject of analysis and the remarkable musical ignorance of contemporary intellectuals. We can attribute this musical ignorance to the fragmenting effects of modernism and the effects of the culture industry. This is closely related to the third point, which Said takes from his reading of Adorno, what he describes as Adorno's "quasi-neurotic insistence" on the "separate, almost mute, and formally nondiscursive character" of musical art. As Said translates this idea, musical performance is "an extreme occasion, something beyond the everyday, something irreducible and temporally not repeatable, something whose core is precisely what can be experienced only under relatively severe and unyielding conditions." Said does not disagree with Adorno's argument; rather, he supplements that argument by claiming that musical performance bridges the gap between its own practiced and cultivated autonomy and the social–cultural sphere (*ME* 15–18). Again, he uses Gramsci to slightly reconfigure Adorno's basic notion. In this way, he can have his Adornian autonomy and his Gramscian elaboration too. Music is simultaneously a product of the culture industry, resistance to the culture industry, and a progressive elaboration of civil society.

Said's subtle reading of classical music is especially evident in chapter 2 of *Musical Elaborations,* entitled "On the Transgressive Elements in Music." He begins this strange chapter with a stimulating discussion of the relations between politics and ethics, on the one hand, and esthetic and intellectual merit, on the other. Paul de Man's wartime activities, which became the subject of controversy in the 1980s, are his point of departure. How, he asks, should de Man's collaboration with the Nazi occupation during World War II affect the interpretation of his later work? Does it invalidate, contaminate, or otherwise make his work suspect? Or, to take an opposing position, are his collaborationist activities and his later work essentially unrelated, the product, ethically speaking, of two different people? How are we to judge in cases such as this? Said's short answer is that we should be suspicious of de Man's later work. His instincts are to argue for the connection between art, theory, and life but not for their identity. From European classical music and its various "complicities" and de Man's wartime activities, Said *segues* to a discussion of Wagner's music. Said follows Adorno in noting how Wagner's indisputable anti-Semitism is constitutive of his music and, yet, he argues, its esthetic merit is unimpeachable. Wagner becomes the touchstone for his reading of European classical music as transgressive of culture and as in complicity with culture, even to the point of such abominations as Nazism. Wagner's music is a *Pharmakon*, both poison and cure. While constituted by its coarser realities, such as anti-Semitism, Wagner's music cannot be reduced to them. So, on this point, Said takes his distance from Adorno:

All retrospective analyses, whether of music or of any other human activity, that judge, theorize, and totalize simultaneously, that say in effect that one thing (like music) = all things, or all musics = one big summarizing result = it couldn't have happened any other way, seem to me to be intellectually and historically flawed, for the same reason that the later work of Foucault, to whom in all sorts of ways I am very indebted, is flawed. (*ME* 49–50)

Besides what I take as an oblique reference to the flaws in *Orientalism*, Said accomplishes several things in this passage. It allows him to put distance between himself and Adorno and Foucault. With Adorno he can affirm the transgressive element in music (what Adorno calls its ideology-critical function) without accepting Adorno's claims for its worldly autonomy. He can explore the effects of the culture industry on European classical music while still arguing for its resistance, as compared to popular music, to the commodifying pressures of market forces. Said rejects Adorno's totalizing account and, with it, Thomas Mann's *Doctor Faustus* and Foucault's account of Western modernity, which are equally cumulative and apocalyptic. This allows him to expose the Eurocentrism and imperialism of "theory," especially its extremely detailed articulation (or scholasticism), self-reflective self-centeredness (or ethnocentrism), fatalism, and esthetic pessimism. Said says that he does not intend to disparage thinkers such as Mann, Foucault, and Adorno

whose pessimistic brilliance and genuine profundity have dignified so much of contemporary intellectual discourse. I am saying, however, that a secular attitude warns us to beware of transforming the complexities of a many-stranded history into one large figure, or of elevating particular moments or monuments into universals. No social system, no historical vision, no theoretical totalization, no matter how powerful, can exhaust all the alternatives or practices that exist within its domain. There is always the possibility to transgress. (*ME* 55)

On this account, Adorno's esthetic theory must be understood in reference to the encounter between the West and its various others. Essentialism, such as the notion of Western music, is a product of that encounter, an artifact of imperialism. Said's Adornian and post-Adornian notion of music is analogous to what he calls secular transgression. Here secular has less to do with "irrevocable action against law or divinity" than with movement "from one domain to another, which tests and challenges limits, mixes the heterogeneous, cuts across expectations, provides unimaginable pleasures, discoveries, and experiences." He cites with approval Pierre Boulez' claim that Wagner's music refuses to carry the ideological message that its author intended. Wagner may be a vicious anti-Semite, but his music is more than that and cannot be reduced to his anti-Semitism (*ME* 55, 61).

Said rejects any "base-superstructure" account of the relation between Western classical music and society. Music, as his nuanced interpretation of Wagner attests, cannot be reduced to "coarse reality" because it not only mirrors but transcends social relations. Music's "transgressive element" is its nomadic quality, its ability to detach from and reattach to various social formations, to alter its rhetoric as the occasion demands. Furthermore, music has flexibility in respect to the gendered-power relations of which it is a part. On this account, Said feels justified in regarding Western classical music as a form of intellectual labor, as an "elaboration" of civil society (*ME* 70). But does not Said bring Adorno and Gramsci together in a peculiar, counterintuitive and, perhaps, impossible way? How is it that Said can rightfully see Western classical music as a form of elaboration, but is incapable of seeing popular cultural forms, especially music in the same light? What do Gramsci's notion of the "national popular," in which popular culture is a site of hegemonic struggle (a complex struggle between the ruling class and subordinate classes for power and influence), and Adorno's "culture industry" thesis have to do with each other? The answer lies in Said's bifocal perspective on culture. He provides a subtle reading of elite culture, which he sees, simultaneously, through Gramsci's populist lens and Adorno's aristocratic lens. In contrast, he loses his Gramscian perspective when viewing popular culture, where he thinks that an Adornian lens is both necessary and sufficient. On this view, popular culture is simply another manifestation of commodity fetishism, an analogue of Marx's "German ideology," whose arch form is religion. It is easy to picture Said writing of popular culture what Adorno did write: "Before the theological caprice of commodities, the consumers become temple slaves. Those who sacrifice themselves nowhere else can do so here, and here they are fully betrayed."[35]

Said's Adornian perspective seems excessively dour and pessimistic where ordinary people are concerned. Said and Adorno construe ordinary people as religious dupes, too easily seduced by the fetishism of commodities, culture, and the state. They are too easily mystified by ideology; accordingly, they know Madonna, the "material girl," but have not a clue about who the Sistine Madonna is. What better evidence is there of their enslavement by the commodity-gods of the culture industry? I am more than a little wary of the celebration of popular culture in cultural studies, where the Gramscian industry has becomes as prominent, though not as lucrative, as the culture industry that Adorno criticized. Sometimes it resembles that industry. But we need not romanticize ordinary people to see critical potential in their everyday practices. Walt Whitman saw the potential and the warts. But Said is nearly blind to the potential that Whitman saw; he can only see the warts. His Adornian lenses are too thick or not thick enough. Thus the deficiencies of his antireligious rhetoric, which follows the deficiency of his sight – or his lack of insight. His ill-informed and banal use of antireligious rhetoric, though endemic to the academy, lacks the knowledge and intellectual seriousness of critics such Hume and Nietzsche. This uncritical and summary dismissal of what he dislikes as religious, reveals Said's hostility toward religious practices as a site of hegemonic struggle by subaltern classes (the ruled) against the ruling class. Religion is an important site of struggle. It is more important, I would say, than Western classical music for the elaboration of civil society and as a form of ideology-critique. Religious practices are popular sites of ideology-critique and for the elaboration of civil society. If we accord the same generosity in reading that cultural location that Said accords to Western classical music then perhaps we can see what Said does not. What I see are ordinary people making choices under circumstances they did not choose. These circumstances include religious practices shot through with ideological traces that both constrain and enable resistance to unjust social relations, which both trouble and comfort those with vested interests in maintaining those relations.

Interestingly, Said characterizes music and its social relations in a way that some characterize religion:

To think of music and cultural exoticism in the mid to late nineteenth century (Verdi, Bizet, Wagner, Saint-Saëns, etc.) or of music and politics during the seventeenth and twentieth centuries (Monteverdi, Schoenberg, jazz, and rock culture) is therefore to map an ensemble of political and social involvements, affiliations, transgressions, none of which is easily reducible either to simple apartness or to a reflection of coarse reality. (*ME 41*)

Why does not Said display the same charity in his characterization of religion that he does in characterizing music, where he skillfully suspends the latter between autonomy from social relations and the simple reflection of them? Is this the only way that he can protect his romantic–individualist interpretation of musical experience as solitude and affirmation from the charge of plagiarism – that is, from the charge that this notion of music borrows freely from common notions of religious experience and that his notion of musical experience is itself religious and theological? What does Said mean when, of Olivier Messiaen's music, he writes: "None of his music that I know fails to produce remarkable pleasures, admittedly local and not theological (for staunch secularists like myself) but always musical and intelligent" (*ME* 99)? Said appropriates religious and theological language of autonomy, privacy, solitude, and affirmation to describe musical experience while using antireligious language to distance what he affirms and baptizes as secular. Do I overinterpret Said here by eliding his distinction between Messiaen's religiousness and the secular pleasures that his music produces? Perhaps. Is this symptomatic of overinterpretations elsewhere? Perhaps. Still, I insist that Said's notion of musical experience sounds much like Friedrich Schleiermacher, William James, and Alfred North Whitehead's views of religious experience. Perhaps it is a displacement of these notions? How ironic if it is.

Culture is a negotiated enterprise a product of consent, accommodation, resistance, and transformation. Primary among these negotiated practices, as even Freud recognized, are religious traditions. Marx also recognized the "oppositional" intent of religious traditions, even if he finally concludes that they are distorted and disenabling. Ultimately, both saw religion as a defect – of psychosexual development or of the prevailing social relations – crying out for psychoanalytic treatment or revolutionary transformation. Neither Freud nor Marx was dialectical enough where religion is concerned. Why should we repeat their errors? Critics should give more attention to what people actually do with their religious traditions, to the diverse relationships that exist between those traditions and political opposition to oppressive social relations. More attention should be given to how religion and politics are articulated, how they actually fit together or do not fit together under specific historical conditions. On this point, Said's analysis seems particularly inadequate. To the extent that Said adds his voice to the reductive and undialectical chorus of antireligious nay-saying exemplified on the secular left by Marx, can he be seen as reiterating the quintessential modern cliché. But let me be clear: this nay-saying is not bad because it is modern but because it is cliché. Clichés put us to sleep and screen out things that we might otherwise see. Let me conclude by saying that it is precisely on the question of religion and popular culture that Said's Adorno gets the best of his Gramsci. Religious life is just as incomprehensible to Said as Jazz is to Adorno. Here we enter Said's blind spot, which is the blind spot of all Foucauldian-derived cultural studies, and encounter the limits of his conceptual imagination. He sees religion through the language of Marx's *camera obscura* rather than, as with Western classical music, through Gramsci's language of hegemony, negotiation, and consent. Said *cannot* see religion in this light because its exclusion is the very premise of his idea of *Secular Criticism*. If Enlightenment modernity is predicated on a prejudice against prejudice as tradition, then religion is the archetypical form of prejudice. In this respect, Said is merely retelling an old tale, in which the criticism of religion is the premise of all criticism.

# CHAPTER 2

# *The religious effects of culture: nationalism*

[T]he role of the modern state . . . is primarily spiritual, even other-worldly, and its driving force is its collective faith, a faith in its mission and destiny, a faith in things unseen, a faith that would move mountains. Nationalism is sentimental, emotional, and inspirational.

(Carlton J. H. Hayes, *Essays on Nationalism*)

If religion has given birth to all that is essential in society, it is because the idea of society is the soul of religion.

(Emile Durkheim, *The Elementary Forms of the Religious Life*)

All religions rise out of the deification of someone's nationalism.

(Molefi Kete Asante, *Afrocentricity*)

The discursive connections between religion and nationalism have long been recognized. Perhaps no one has explored their relationship as persistently as Carlton J. H. Hayes, a prolific historian of nationalism, who did his most important work during the inter-war years of the 1920s and 1930s. While Emile Durkheim is not noted for his reflections on nationalism, his theory of religion sheds light on the question of religion and nationalism. Between Hayes and Durkheim, we can account for most notions of how religion and nationalism are related. The conceptual territory that they have configured and carved-up between themselves has the form of a question: "Is religion the principle – motive, force, and secret-soul – of nationalism or is nationalism the principle of religion?" This question defines the intellectual ground on which Said strategically engages nationalism as a religious–cultural effect. It is the "cultural common sense" that his analysis presupposes. Said's views of nationalism are fragmentary and, perhaps, underdeveloped. I try to develop the implications of his views by placing them within the framework of Hayes' argument. The danger, of course, is that Said's fragments and Hayes' framework will not fit. That is the chance that I take. Thus Said's scattered commentary on nationalism as religious discourse is the subject of this chapter, whose introductory epigrams do the religious work of "gathering and binding" his fragmentary views.

"Nationalism, Human Rights, and Interpretation" is Said's most explicit and substantial essay on nationalism. This essay ends with a consideration of the Palestinian question, which has preoccupied Said since the 1967 Arab–Israeli War. This is the national question that he knows best and about which he is most passionate. Palestine is haunted, according to Said, by its sacred geography, which is, perhaps, "the most drenched in religious, cultural, and political significance of any on earth." So there is not a more compelling justification for a secular interpretation of human rights, which requires a hermeneutic of connection and not a Manichaean hermeneutic of separation, than the inextricable location of human rights within a national context. "For the truth is that Jewish and Palestinian suffering exist in and belong to the same history: the task of interpretation is to acknowledge that link, not to separate them into unconnected spheres." To engage in the later activity – as did President Bush, when he said that Zionism was not racism[1] because of the suffering of the Jewish people – is to engage in religious criticism. It is to sacralize the suffering of one people by demanding that another people suffer; this is sacrificial logic with the enthusiasm of the vengeful. This religious and liberal theodicy – I say religious and liberal because Said, like Marx in the "Jewish Question," establishes an identity between the two – has characterized American and Western thinkers since the Balfour Declaration, which placed the collective weight of several colonial powers behind the Zionist movement.[2]

Said constructs a genealogy of this way of thinking that includes liberals such as John Stuart Mill, civic republicans such as Alexis de Tocqueville, and cultural thinkers such as Matthew Arnold. Arnold's argument for the sacred character of the state, de Tocqueville's support of the brutal suppression of Muslims in Algeria, and Mill's claim that civilized nations had "sacred duties" to each other that they did not owe savage nations such as India, are part of this story. Neither Mill nor de Tocqueville could sustain their principles in the face of nationalist "imperatives" and the siren songs of patriotism. "To identify with one's best self as Arnold would have wished meant, for Europeans in the age of empire, identifying also with one's best *power*, a navy or an army as well as culture and a religion." On this latter point, Said quotes Marwan Buheiry on the way in which de Tocqueville's nationalist and religious sentiments mutually reinforced each other:

Tocqueville judged Islam and found it wanting. He claimed, rather gratuitously, that its principal aim was war. He characterized it as fossilized and especially as decadent without really defining what he meant although he did seem to find the sign in the fact that the Islamic world was unable to resist European domination. The penetrating insights he had [about] . . . European and North American societies were significantly absent in his consideration of Islam. He never asked how Islamic civilization with its literature, law, and social organization, not only survived the relative collapse in politics, but managed somehow to spread into regions far beyond its epicenter. In short, he failed to appreciate its staying power and spiritual content.

This crude and ungenerous hermeneutic, Said adds, is not solely a Western affliction. Young Muslims and Arabs are also taught to venerate the classics of their religion. Skeptics and satirists such as Salman Rushdie are vilified, exiled, or threatened with death. These same tendencies to idealize or deify nation and culture – Durkheim calls these tendencies "collective representations," which are produced during moments of "collective effervescence," and Said calls them "destructive idealizations of what 'we' are about as a nation" – lie behind the Gulf War. But more about that later.[3]

## NATIONALISM AS A RELIGIOUS ARTIFACT

In 1993, Said gave the Reith Lectures on the subject "Representations of the Intellectual." This prestigious lecture series was inaugurated in 1948 by Bertrand Russell. As Said notes, several Americans had preceded him as honored lecturers, including John Searle, John Kenneth Galbraith, and Robert Oppenheimer. Said took these lectures as an occasion to address the relations between the intellectual life as a *vocation* and the *temptations* of money, power, and nationalism. I shall confine my attention to the last.

For Said, nationalism is a god who always fails. Nothing illustrates this better than one scene from the Greek-like tragedy that was the Iranian Revolution. Said tells a story about an Iranian friend whom he first met in 1978. He describes his friend as brilliant, eloquent, and charismatic, an accomplished writer and teacher, an intellectual. This friend, who remains anonymous in Said's account, played an important role in undermining public support for the Shah, and would soon be on intimate terms with the young, emerging, nonclerical leadership that surrounded Imam Khomeini. Like these youthful leaders, who included Abolhassan Bani-Sadr[4] and Sadek Ghotbzadeh, he was Muslim but not militant. Said recounts the initial enthusiasm of his friend for the Imam and his friend's conviction that it was only right that the Imam be the preeminent authority in the revolution. And then a process of radicalization, reminiscent of the Russian Revolution, spiraled out of control. Bani-Sadr was deposed by Imam Khomeini and fled into exile, and Said's friend, not without considerable difficulty, followed suit. For these men, the god of Iranian nationalism had failed. Like all gods, this one had to be fed. Like many gods, it preferred human blood. Said's friend was fortunate to escape. Many others were not so fortunate. He repaid his debt to good fortune by becoming as fierce a critic of the Khomeini regime as he had once been an avid supporter. He even went further in the wake of the Gulf War, his contempt for Muslim and Arab regimes being such as to express his preference for Western imperialism to "Iraqi fascism." Said laments this transformation, but not because of his friend's newfound contempt for Khomeini or his hatred of the Iraqi state. He was saddened, rather, by his friend's susceptibility to "conversion" experiences, his inability to sustain commitment and critical distance at the same time. For Said, this shuttling back and forth, dogmatic conviction followed by equally dogmatic recantation, is symptomatic of a religious disposition, the ecstasy of submission, and the propensity to bow down and worship (*RI* 103–106).

Said's conjuration of the "god of nationalism" indicates strategic movement upon the ground that Hayes and Durkheim divide between themselves. The idea that nationalism and patriotism are like religion has, as I have already suggested, a long pedigree. In 1928, Hayes published his influential book entitled *Essays on Nationalism*, which included a piece called "Nationalism as a Religion." "Why," Hayes asks, "are millions ready and willing to lay down their lives for nationalism?" From where comes its missionary zeal? The all consuming love that it inspires in its disciples? For Hayes the answer lies in emotional intensity and deep feelings of loyalty irradiated by man's basic "religious sense."[5] Why intense emotions are religious is a question that Hayes does not address. Clearly religion is not a problem for him. He can speak confidently even authoritatively about a religious sense, assuming as he does that everyone knows what he is talking about, religion being self-evident, commonplace, and common sense. But maybe religion is not so simple. What happens when we complicate Hayes' account of religion and question the very notion of a "religious sense"?

Hayes' pronouncements on man's religious sense are spoken with the confidence of all unexamined presuppositions. Everyone has presuppositions that they have not examined. But all presuppositions, in principle, can be examined, although it is probably true that many, perhaps most, will never be examined. It is precisely these never examined presuppositions, which make so much sense to us, that so often make little sense to others. These presuppositions are so basic (they make our notion of sense possible) as to be outside questions of sense altogether. And so it is with Hayes' notion of a religious sense. Hayes' notion is analogous to, if not parasitic on, ideas that were readily available at the time, especially Rudolf Otto's notion of the "numinous." Working within the tradition of Friedrich Schleiermacher,[6] Otto argues that religion is a universal feature of human nature that exceeds rational comprehension and that can only be approached or defined by reference to itself. Religion is *sui generis*. And the numinous – which includes profound sentiments of "awe-filled," overpowering urgency, terror, and fascination, the urge to look and to look away[7] – is the essence of religion. Of course, many of us now view with suspicion the idea of an essence that precedes existence, which is something other than a historical artifact, something enclosed in quotation marks to remind us that we are using a term against itself. My purpose here is not to hold Hayes responsible for intellectual developments for which he was clearly innocent, but only to show why what made sense to him makes no sense to me.

Hayes does something that is typical of those who would use religion as an explanatory category when he moves unconsciously and uncritically between the generality of religion and the specificity of Christianity. The religious sense becomes Christian sense, an extension of Christian ideas writ large. (But is this not what it has always been?) Hayes repeats a common practice in theories of religion, *where a Christian-inspired desire to make sense of cultural others is constitutive of what religion is.* Except for a bit of exotic trimming here and there, Hayes focuses his account entirely on developments in Christianity and Europe. I do not want to judge Hayes too harshly. He had to delimit the subject-matter, and there are limits to what any of us can know. But this way of circumscribing the subject confuses the religious, whatever that might be, with what may be distinctively Christian, European, and modern. This ostensibly historical account, abstracts and obscures simultaneously by substituting vague generalities for historical specificity. But then maybe not. Perhaps Hayes is not as confused as he seems. Perhaps the religious is a distinctively Christian way of talking, religion being a Christian category. After all, Hayes' account as a matter of execution is, firstly, an analysis of the similarities between Christianity and nationalism and, secondly, between nationalism and the other "Abrahamic" traditions – that is, Judaism and Islam.

Like Hayes, Said is especially interested in the relation between nationalism and the monotheistic traditions. I shall have more to say about Said along the way. Before saying anything, however, I must catch up with an account that is already running ahead of itself. So, I begin again, with an expanded version of Hayes' central claim:

> From the dawn of his history man has been distinguished by what may be called a "religious sense," that is, a mysterious faith in some power outside of himself, a faith always accompanied by feelings of reverence and usually attended by external acts and ceremonial. Everywhere under the most diverse forms, you find its expression, in the caves of primitive men, in the pyramids of Egypt, in the laws of Moses and the rites of Aaron, in the words of the Delphic oracle, in the tended fire of the Vestal virgins, in the temples of Inca and Aztec, in the tabus of Eskimo and Hottentot. You find it enshrined in the great religious systems, such as Hinduism, Buddhism, Christianity, and Muhammadanism, which through the centuries have counted their devotees by billions. As always, so today, man feels its spell. [8]

Said does not believe in a universal religious sense. As he writes in *Covering Islam*: "I myself am neither religious nor of an Islamic background, although I think I can understand someone who declares himself or herself to be convinced of a particular faith. But insofar as I feel it is possible to discuss faith at all, it is in the form of *interpretations* of faith manifesting themselves in human acts that take place in human history and society." This is Said's considered belief and interpretive intention. His cultural critique, however, presupposes a notion of religion as dogmatic, deferential to authority, otherworldly, subservience-compelling, and violence-producing (*WTC* 290). This polemical and less descriptive notion of religion is construed as transhistorical and transcultural in regard to the effects that I list above. *Now the textual evidence for my claim is scattered, allusive, and often negative. Sometimes my only recourse, if I am to sustain this claim, is to infer Said's notion of what religion is from his claims of what secularism is or is not. This is a possible weakness in my argument that I want to mark clearly for the reader; it is a weakness that I can only acknowledge and, perhaps, remedy by tying together as many of these scattered remarks, inferences, and negative claims as seem necessary to the argument.* My scattered and allusive analysis, which distinguishes this chapter from the rest, mimics Said's scattered and allusive engagement with nationalism. If successful, this effort will show that Said's polemical notion of religion, which cuts against his explicit beliefs, enables him to construct a narrative of religious and secular conflict, a conflict that Enlightenment modernity did not end, which, on the contrary, is an integral feature of postmodern or postcontemporary culture. Thus the notion, alluded to in the previous passage, of an innate, universal religious sense – which Hayes believes but Said does not, yet analytically and polemically presupposes – was "ready-to-hand," part of the intellectual air that Hayes breathed. While it would be unseemly to hold him blameworthy for views that some of us now regard as wrong, we can still take issue with his claims and analyze the consequences of his view for our understanding of nationalism.

Hayes alludes to the Freudian language of "instinct" and "drive," which is appropriate, because the religious sense seems to work as if it were instinctual. Like the psychosexual energy that Freud calls libido, the religious sense can be "repressed" but not destroyed. Invariably, repressed religiosity "returns" – that is, the religious sense will manifest itself in odd ways when normal channels of expression are blocked. The religious sense is indelible. People do not cease being religious so much as find different objects of cathexis[9] or worship, including abstract ideas such as Science or Humanity. The form may be new but the content is always the same – a sense of "awe" that is primordially religious.[10] Hayes is ambiguous about whether the awe-filled response of the religious subject or the object of that awe is more important. I should think that they are inextricable. But, as I read him, Hayes puts greater emphasis on the sameness of the religious sense as opposed to the sameness of the object. The religious sense seems to have a specifiable range (e.g. devotion, sacrifice, violence), while the religious object varies indefinitely. This helps to explain why doubt and skepticism are among the more common vehicles for the return of repressed religiosity. It explains why Hayes regards the following as manifestations of the religious sense: Stoicism and Greco-Roman mystery cults in the world of early Christianity and, during the Enlightenment, Science, Rationalism, Nature, Progress, and Humanity. They are among the countless ways in which the religious sense returns. The most important symptom of the return of repressed religiosity (a Freudian theme that is also important to Said's view) is the deification and worship of the state – and here we return to our subject matter proper.[11]

I have doubts, which I will speak to shortly, about the strong connection that Hayes draws between periods of religious doubt (skepticism toward the gods of traditional religions) and worship of the political state. In the meantime, I note the following examples that Hayes offers in support of his views: the development in tandem of pagan skepticism and the deification of the Roman emperor, the simultaneous emergence of Protestantism and the "theorizing" of the nation-state, and the coterminous development of deism and nationalism in the eighteenth century. For Hayes, religious doubt begins with the intellectual class and gradually filters down to the masses, who find in the political state a new source of certainty and devotion. The nation-state is invested with the sentiments of love and veneration formerly reserved for specific religious traditions. Under the conditions of modernity, the nation is the transfiguration of traditional religious commitments, which calls to mind Said's analysis of Arnoldian culture. Thus Hayes cites the French Revolution as a landmark in the emergence of nationalism as religion. It is easy to see why he would be fascinated by the French Revolution, so obvious are its Christian trappings. Catholicism provided a ready-made language, a rich store of metaphors for the construction and articulation of French nationalism: Reason as God, the Declaration of the Rights of Man as national catechism, and the written Constitution as holy scripture.[12]

## NATIONALISM AS A CHRISTIAN ARTIFACT

My doubts about Hayes' account are twofold. I think that nationalism emerged not because of religious skepticism but religious enthusiasm, the intensification of religious sentiment that followed in the wake of what Protestant Christians call the Reformation. Secondly, Hayes' account shows, unwittingly for sure, why it is Christianity, specifically, and not the vagary called religion (except when understood as a Christian idea) that aids our analysis of nationalism. I shall speak of nationalism, but first I speak of the state.

*The Foundations of Modern Political Thought* is Quentin Skinner's definitive study of political modernity. It traces the birth, or rebirth, of politics as a human-centered activity, the recovery of Aristotle's notion of politics, and the displacing of Augustine's *City of God* model. In brief, Skinner traces political ferment in Renaissance and Reformation-age Europe, culminating in the religious wars and the emergence of the state. On Skinner's view, the state is "what happened" when Europeans found themselves drowning in their own blood for religious reasons. The absolutist claims of the state usurped and displaced the absolutism of

Christian convictions, the *imperium* of the state displacing the *imperium* of the church. The long term denouement of this process was the reinventing of the state as a secular, impersonal, and "nonprincely" public power. From then on, the state would be the supreme object of political allegiance. It would make the law and define the rights and privileges of every association, organization, and corporation, including the church, in its territorial domain. The proximate cause of this development was the Reformation and the ensuing religious warfare, as Catholics and Reformers insisted on their particular versions of what maintaining "'true religion' and the Church of Christ" meant. The Reformation and the religious warfare that accompanied it made certain things clear – namely, the willingness of the protagonists of rival religious creeds "to fight each other to the death." This willingness convinced many *politique* theorists of the necessity of divorcing state power from the duty to support any religion at all. Only then would there be genuine "prospects of achieving civic peace." The religious enthusiasm unleashed by the Reformation made a paradoxical but crucial contribution to the emergence of the modern, secular state.[13]

The emergence of national consciousness, the nation, or nationalism – I use these terms interchangeably – is closely connected to the protracted process of state-formation in Europe. "It is true," as Hagen Schulze says, "that the term 'nation' has existed for a long time, much longer than the 'state', but in *its contemporary sense, embracing an entire population, a nation can hardly be defined without reference to the state* – in this sense nations may still be very young" (emphasis added). Though its history is long and complex, *natio* (nation) originally referred to birth or descent as a distinctive feature of group membership understood in a very narrow sense. Thus *natio* might refer to the aristocracy (Cicero), a school of philosophers (Pliny), or to native, uncivilized tribes as opposed to law-governed, civilized populations. That these meanings of the word nation are now unfamiliar is true. That it took the Germans a long time to "discover" that they were German, far longer than it took the English to discover their Englishness or the French to discover their Frenchness is also true. The motley crew of "nations" that peopled the European continent "even before such expressions as 'nationalism' or 'national consciousness' were thought of," did not emerge by mere chance. Rather, their emergence was governed by assumptions about "their geographical or historical proximity to the ancient civilization of Rome, their share of the Carolingian heritage," and by "the degree to which a state had imposed its judicial and administrative system."[14] These protonational-

ist stirrings were further transformed by Reformation and religious warfare.

If we assume that Hayes is right insofar as he connects the emergence of nationalism to religion, then it is more likely that nationalism is a result of increased enthusiasm than increased skepticism. If this is right, then the national idea emerged as a highly mediated consequence of religious enthusiasm and as a "state-sponsored rationale" for binding the population to an increasingly bureaucratic and impersonal state.[15] Thus it was in the aftermath of empire and in the context of theorizing the secular state that the nation emerged as an object of discourse. Its emergence was not uniform. Here (France and England) it emerged almost simultaneously with the state, there (the Germanic territories) in opposition to the state or multiple states. However it emerged, the nation represented the construction of a *new* form of allegiance and identity, not the consolidation of an older, primordial, prestate-identity.[16] Where the nation was not already a state – as it was in France and England – it usually aspired to be a state, as happened with the Germans. If we set aside Hayes' claim for the religious as opposed to the Christian character of nationalism (I will show why we should set it aside in a moment) and, following Quentin Skinner, view nationalism, the emergence of the European nation-state,[17] as a response to religious enthusiasm, then there is a great deal that we can learn from Hayes' account.

The reader may notice that I slide from talk of nations and states to talk of nation-states. This slippage is important. It represents an influential way of talking about nationalism, which is evident in Hayes' account and my analysis. Thus nationalism refers preeminently, though not exclusively, to those nationalisms that have captured the apparatus of the state or which hope to do so. On my view, the nation, as opposed to the similar but different notion of peoplehood, which presumably one can find always and in all places, is the by-product of empires that have come unraveled. Nationalism is the form that the sense of peoplehood takes under modern conditions. These conditions include the Romantic ideas of common language, culture, soil, and spirit, and nineteenth-century notions, spurred by science and pseudoscience, of common stock, blood, and race. These nationalisms do aspire to statehood, but many, as in The Netherlands and the Balkans, may never attain it. My reference to nation-states circumscribes, though not in an idiosyncratic way, the notion of nationalism. It privileges, as I said before, those nationalisms that have captured the state apparatus or aspire to do so. With this clarification, I return to Hayes' account.

When Hayes asserts that the religion of nationalism "first appeared among people that were traditionally Christian" he affirms what I assume are specifically Christian and European conditions for the emergence of nationalism. Emergent nationalism, according to Hayes, possessed a missionary idealism, civic liturgies, and political theology.[18] This way of characterizing morphological similarities is already explicitly Christian rather than vaguely religious. Missionary idealism is evident in the claims that nationalism makes for itself: that we are a peculiar people, special, and distinctive, and that our peculiarities have universal significance. This, of course, is an "Abrahamic" theme and perhaps affliction. The idea that Abraham's "Jewish seed" were a peculiar people, God's holy nation, is constitutive, in modified form, of Judaism's Christian and Islamic siblings. The nation, state, and nation-state – I use this cumbersome phrase to signify their distinctness but inextricable connection in my account – first emerged in historically Christian territories, in the wake of the Crusades, against the backdrop of religious warfare between Catholics and Protestants and their common war against Jews. We should not be surprised, therefore, that the nation, state, and nation-state would bear the marks of their birth, any more than we are surprised by the fact that the Catholic Church bears the marks of its imperial, Roman birth.

Said is painfully aware of these connections: of the ways in which the monotheistic religions and nationalism interpenetrate and mutually intensify each other. During the 1970s, he watched Beirut, Lebanon, the exile home of his mother (who with the rest of his family was forced to flee Palestine in 1948 before an advancing Zionist insurgency) as it was destroyed by the fatal dance of nationalism and religion. He recollects the following:

I'm ashamed to admit that a great many of my early memories of friends and family expressing religious opinions are harsh and unpleasant. "Moslems," I was told in 1954 by a great friend of my father's, "are dust. They should be blown away." Another good Christian, a prominent philosopher and former Lebanese Foreign Minister, frequently denounced Islam and the Prophet Muhammad to me, using such words as "lechery," "hypocrisy," "corruption," and "degeneration." These, I later discovered, were not isolated opinions. As anyone who has followed the discourse of Christian militancy in Lebanon and elsewhere in the region will know, they have come to constitute the core of minority expression, which in turn furnish the majority Muslim community with a permanent provocation. Such compliments tend to be, and have obviously been, reciprocated. The result is consolidated animosity, what William Hazlitt calls "the pleasure of hating." A feature of this pleasure, Hazlitt said, is that it "eats into the heart of religion, and turns it into rankling spleen and bigotry; it makes patriotism an excuse for carrying fire, pestilence, and famine into other lands: it leaves to virtue nothing but the spirit of censoriousness, and a narrow, jealous, inquisitorial watchfulness over the actions and motives of others." The relevance of these words to that nasty mix of religious zeal and nationalism sweeping through Lebanon, Israel, and Iran – and the United States, which has a history of involvement in all three countries – is perfectly evident. (*ALS* 173–174)

The nation, state, and nation-state, as Said's comments suggest, are the ship of modern identity, all else is the sea. Or as Hayes puts it, the nation is constructed as eternal. She "feeds off the loyalty of her members, whose deaths fuel her fame and glory. She is a protective mother – Plato's Socrates imagines the state as both mother and father – guarding her children from foreign devils, assuring their life, liberty, and happiness. She fosters their arts and sciences and provides them nourishment. The nation-state is a "family" into which "the individual is born" and a "preceptor" who "follows the individual through life, teaching him in patriotic schools the national catechism." Hayes speaks of "pious precept and solemn sacrament" by which the individual comes to know "the beauties of national holiness." Thus he is prepared for a life of service to the state, "the Alpha and Omega of his being, the author and finisher of his blessings." Every significant life-event is bureaucratically recorded, including rites of passage such as birth, marriage, and death. A special place is reserved for the "crusaders" of nationalism, their place of entombment forever bearing the insignia of their loyal service. "And the funerals of national potentates and heroes are celebrated with patriotic pomp and circumstance that make the obsequies of mediaeval bishops seem drab."[19] In summary, the nation (especially the nation-state) constructs its other as the Hobbesian "state of nature," where life is "nasty, brutish and short." It constructs its other, that is, as death. The nation is a soteriology, an embodiment of the doctrine of salvation and immortality. Those who die in the nation, for the nation, never *really* die. In this regard, the nation has filled the existential paradigm of Christianity with a new content.[20] This, in short, is Hayes' account of nationalism, of those claims that the nation makes for itself.

Civic liturgies such as state funerals represent the second way in which nationalism has distinctively Christian markings. Hayes notes the liturgies surrounding the flag: how it should be displayed, raised, lowered, and saluted. We sing hymns, he observes, in honor of the nation and pledge allegiance to it "and to the republic for which it stands." Clearly, Christian liturgies are models for these civic liturgies.[21] National symbols and ideas, therefore, are subject to sacrilege; they can be blasphemed or otherwise desecrated. (Think of the recent outrage caused by flag burning and the effort to pass a constitutional amendment outlawing the practice.) The rituals, ceremonies and pageantry of civic parades, processions, and pilgrimages are all irradiated by Christian language, symbols, and rituals. Through civic iconography and the collection of national relics, we worship. We erect shrines in honor of national heroes (civic saints) and monuments to commemorate those who died for their country. We consecrate battlefields, sites of mass death, as holy places.[22]

Lincoln's "Gettysburg Address" of 1863 and Second Inaugural Address of 1865 are powerful examples of the third Christian-like component of nationalism – its civic theology. And according to Hayes, "[e]very national state has a 'theology.'"[23] He places theology in quotation marks ostensibly to signal his misuse of the word, his metaphorical expansion of what theology means. By theology he means official doctrines, precepts of the founding fathers, and "admonitions of the national scriptures." National scripture refers, presumably, to documents such as the Declaration of Independence and the Constitution. This notion of theology demonstrates well how metaphors help us to see things differently, by playing with differences, blurring distinctions, and encouraging us to see one thing in terms of another. But it also shows how metaphors can prevent us from seeing important differences by undermining our ability to make distinctions that we want to make. And so it is with Hayes' claim that every nation has a theology.

Theology is a distinctively Christian practice, though a case can be made for Jewish and Islamic theology. Beyond the "Abrahamic family," however, it is unclear that there are practices that, with any specificity, can be called theology. Some might regard this point as pedantic or excessively fastidious, but I beg to differ. Here again, Hayes' language obscures the distinctively Christian character of theology. It tempts us to look in the wrong place, after a vague notion called the "religious sense," meanwhile ignoring the specificity of the tradition before us. Just as important, this quest for the religious sense, the idea that theology is constitutive of the religious as such, blinds us to the specificity of other traditions, to those features that make them different. It undermines our ability to even ask certain questions. Do the nationalisms, for example, of non-Christian, non-Abrahamic nations as a matter of fact have a theology? Does theology as something other than a vagary make sense outside "monotheistic" assumptions? If they do, how do we account for it? Can one account for it, as Hayes does, by reference to an essential feature of human nature called the religious sense? Or is the religious sense (and thus theology as a primordial–universal category) an artifact of a thoroughly Western way of thinking called the theory of religion?

Again, my account is running ahead of itself, ahead of fully explicating, that is, Hayes' notion of theology as a constitutive feature of nationalism. Before returning to that account, I should note that Said also speaks of theology. But his comments are vague and widely scattered. These references provide his analysis with a certain mood and tone, but of themselves are not tools of analysis. He does not do with theology what Marx does, even on the level of metaphor. Marx took full advantage of his dialectical connection to Hegel's "System" (which if anything is a theo-logic) and to Feuerbach's anthropological reduction of that philosophy. Thus, when he says that the criticism of religion, after Feuerbach's critique of theology, is nearly complete, his words carry a certain historical weight. Said's invocation of theology does not have this weight, nor does it do the ethical work that Nietzsche's critique of the ascetic priest does, or the ontological work that Heidegger's critique of ontotheology does. But it does do work that is similar to the political work that is done by Hayes' notion of theology. Said, I imagine, would agree with the following: that theology refers to a nation's representation of itself, its highest ideas, its ideal self. It is precisely the issue of self-representation, what Hayes calls national mythology, which he finds so interesting if not vexing. In representing itself, the nation, through nationalist ideology, perpetrates a fraud. Nationalist theology, which is always a product of the intellectual class, "becomes a nationalist mythology for the masses." Here Hayes draws a distinction between what I had previously conflated. Mythology is on a lower cognitive level than theology, more credulous, as the masses are more credulous than intellectuals. Nationalist mythology is more vulgar than nationalist theology, the former a vulgarization of the latter. The arbitrators in this process of vulgarization are various media types such as "sentimental journalists and emotional orators." Present here is the idea that the intellectual class manipulates the masses, presumably to serve their own interests.[24] A few decades later, Frantz Fanon, following Marx and Engels' critique in the *German Ideology*, would make a similar argument, although it is not intellectuals *per se* but the national bourgeoisie in particular that he targets. Nationalism, he argues, is class-based; nationalist ideology, in the long term, serves the interests of the bourgeoisie.[25] Whether Hayes is more concerned about the class implications of nationalist mythology or with the fact that it plays with a truthful account of a nation's history is unclear.

We have now reached that part of Hayes' account that restates the questions with which this inquiry began. "Why are millions ready and willing to lay down their lives for nationalism?" From where comes its missionary zeal? The all-consuming love that it inspires in its disciples? Hayes discounts the economic motive. Most people most of the time are unwilling to give their lives for economic gain, which is not to say that people are unwilling to take enormous risks for money. But that kind of risk-taking is different from sacrifice; it is done with the prospect of reward clearly in view. This is not to say that the idea of reward is absent from a willingness to sacrifice one's life, but clearly the idea of reward is more uncertain here, more highly mediated. It is understandable, then, that Hayes would turn to religion. After all, we are aware of religious traditions that do require or incite a willingness to sacrifice one's life. Christians and Muslims, for hundreds of years and through many Crusades, were willing to die and, perhaps more important, to kill, for their respective religious traditions. Surely, if nowhere else, is not the religious sense evident here? The problem with this claim is apparent in Hayes' account itself. While this claim is true enough of Christianity and Islam (and of Judaism to a lesser degree) it is far from being true of most religious traditions. Most religious traditions did not construct themselves and were not constructed such that the kind of boundary-maintenance and meticulous monitoring of practices and beliefs that are associated to varying degrees with the Abrahamic traditions made sense. In some traditions one can be religiously both x and y. On this point, Wilfred Cantwell Smith makes the following observation:

Western and Muslim students tend to be baffled when they first learn that a single Chinese may be and usually is a "Confucian", a "Buddhist", *and* a "Taoist". They cannot imagine how a person can "belong to three different religions", as they put it, at the same time. The perplexity arises not from something confused or bizarre about China so much as from the conceptualization of religious systems, which is brought to bear but is evidently inappropriate.[26]

In traditions such as those that Smith describes, the intolerance of religious others that is often characteristic of the Abrahamic traditions is rare.[27] This was the case, at any rate, before the raise of relatively new phenomena such as Hindu and Buddhist nationalisms. Before the rise of these new phenomena, the testimony of ethnographers and other students of Hindu and Buddhist traditions among others, invariably, accents their tolerance of other traditions. These traditions were not driven by a missionary zeal, an imperialist imperative, as were those traditions in which the idea of dying or killing for one's beliefs made sense.

### NATIONALIST SENSE AND RELIGIOUS NONSENSE

Part of the problem with Hayes's notion of the religious sense, with the very idea of religion itself, is the sheer elusiveness of the topic. How does one circumscribe, delimit, or pen down the subject? This is another way of asking the question "What is religion anyway?" I cannot address the claims that Hayes makes about nationalism and religion without simultaneously saying something about what I take religion to be. This is difficult for several reasons. Like most people who write about religion and nationalism or religious nationalism, I take for granted something called "religion." But there are different ways of taking religion for granted, and those differences have important consequences for one's analysis. Most accounts that I have read presuppose a primordial, essentialist, universalist notion of religion, as if religion were something that one finds "out there" as opposed to finding it in the workshops of Western scholars. Religion, on this view, is something that explains why people do what they do; why, for example, they are willing to fight, kill, and die. Even critics who otherwise reject essentialist–universalist notions write as if religion (apart from our self-conscious construction of the category) explains something, namely, the willingness to fight, kill, and die. I think that such notions of religion do some interesting and useful work. Although their explanatory ambition may outstrip their explanatory success, they still provide insights that we may otherwise not have had. That people we call Hindu, for example, or those who practice what we call "traditional African religions," have been willing to fight, kill, and die is undeniable. Why this willingness should be called religious, however, is far from clear. If religion means deep motivations, "ultimate concerns," those things for which we are willing to live and die, then religion can explain anything and nothing. It explains nothing in particular and truly is an "empty signifier." On this reading, religion is merely a redundant way of saying "The things for which people are willing to fight, kill, and die." Religion does not explain anything that we did not already know. What religion is, on my view, has everything to do with how the word religion is used; the meaning of religion, therefore, is relative to the purposes of those who use the word. Religion has its meaning in the language (devotional, scientific, declamatory, laudatory, and so on) of which it is part.

Garth Fowden's analysis of monotheism[28] in late antiquity provides an account of why some traditions are more likely to underwrite the will to fight, kill, and die than others. The upshot of Fowden's argument is that features internal to the Abrahamic traditions of Judaism, Christianity, and Islam, but especially the latter two, account for this difference. According to Fowden, "knowledge of the One God both justifies the exercise of imperial power and makes it more effective." He argues that this conviction defined the world of late antiquity, by which he means "the period between the second-century peak of Rome's prosperity and the ninth-century onset of the Islamic Empire's decline." Constantine placed this Christian-derived monologic "at the center of Roman political ideology." His persecution of "polytheistic cults" should not surprise us, given the Constantinian logic of one God, one empire, and one emperor. According to Fowden, this political–religious universalism "provided the nascent Christian empire's motive energy. While monotheism may have been necessary for the rise of religious and political universalism, it was not sufficient. Such universalism is more likely, however, under monotheistic conditions. But universalism may be possible without monotheism and monotheism does not necessarily lead to imperialism. This highlights an important difference within monotheism, between Judaism on one side and Christianity and Islam on the other. Whether Judaism was a missionary religion or not (a question I do not propose to settle or even get into), its consequences in "world-historical" terms are fundamentally different from those of its younger kin. There is no significant Jewish history of world conquest and empire; there has never been a Jewish commonwealth. On the other hand, while noting the Islamic Empire's relative tolerance of internal dissenters, Fowden draws parallels between Muhammad and Constantine, but does not deny important differences between the two. Both see themselves as religious functionaries. Muhammad is Allah's prophet and Constantine is a latter-day apostle. Both construe imperial conquest – one God, one empire, one messenger – as missionary work.[29]

The novelty of Christianity, and I shall add Islam as Fowden does elsewhere in the book, was its missionary aggressiveness and exclusive self-understanding; a fact that was readily apparent to others during late antiquity. Following Fowden, I take Matthew 28: 16 as the "proof-text" of Christian universalism: "All authority in heaven and on earth has

been given to me. Go therefore and make disciples of all nations, bap-
tizing them in the name of the Father and of the Son and of the Holy
Spirit, teaching them to observe all that I have commanded you." These
words (and whether Jesus really said them or not is irrelevant) are the
foundation text of Christianity's missionary zeal. "In the medieval and
modern worlds monotheism continued to fertilize the discourse of cultural and political conquest and colonialism. Those who worshiped the
only God saw themselves as by definition the only people who knew how
to live fully human lives." This assumption, which was second nature to
Muslims and Eastern Christians, also inspired Western Christians, who
"conquered the world, including much of Eastern Christendom and
Islam." Fowden traces this "Western discourse of conquest and colonialism" to the monotheistic-universalism of late antiquity.[30]

Consider, in light of Fowden's analysis, Said's comments on the role
of Palestine in the sacred geography of the three monotheistic religions:

We are drenched in religion, only a tiny corner of which we see, only a small
part of which concerns us. What a fate for Palestine: to have attracted the religious imagination and the dramas of the apocalypse not just once, but three
times: Judaism, Christianity, Islam, the latter the most austere, least known, and
most abominated. Lift off the veneer of religious cant – which speaks of the
"best and noblest in the Judaic, Christian, or Muslim tradition," in perfectly
interchangeable phrases – and a seething cauldron of outrageous fables is
revealed, seething with several bestiaries, streams of blood, and innumerable
corpses.

Said is left aghast by the "utter madness" of what Christian fundamentalists believe will occur in this most contested of holy places:

According to the scenario proposed by these fundamentalist Christians, Russia
and Israel – Gog and Magog – will have an apocalyptic final battle, which
Russia will win, until Jesus intervenes (but not soon enough to prevent the death
of all Jews; Arabs do not seem to figure in it at all). In the meantime, the true
Christians will be suspended over Israel, above the battle, in Raptures, and after
the fighting is over Jesus will restore them to Jerusalem, from which they will
rule the world.

These Christian insanities, he argues, find their complement in the
equally insane views of Jewish fundamentalists of the Third Temple
Movement and the zealots of Gush Emuim:

Not for nothing then has the Islamic chorus risen in response, like a specter in
one of Blake's visions or Shelley's late apocalyptic poems, intended to make you
lose the thread of argument and grasp only the terrifying vague, blood-dripping
imagery. *Jihad* and Islamic law have the reactive forces to stimulate young men

and women for such suicidal struggle as the politics of secular liberation has never dreamed of. (*ALS* 152–153)[31]

It is the specificity of the monotheistic history that Fowden narrates and its contemporary consequences, which Said describes, that account for the "will to fight, kill and die." Only through a vague conceptual abstraction and reification called the "religious" do we get notions such as "religious nationalism." Only by abstracting from the dynamics produced by the missionary incursions of Christianity and Islam upon cultural practices that we construct as religious, such as those of the Indian subcontinent, can we refer to generalities such as religious or Hindu nationalism. I am not saying that there is not Hindu nationalism. Rather, I follow Wilfred Cantwell Smith who argues that a distinct tradition called Hinduism recognized by people who called themselves Hindu was produced by Islamic incursion, pressure, and conflict and later by the Western theory of religion in association with Western colonial administration.[32] So it is the specificity of traditions called Hindu, which is a placeholder for the historical circumstances and events that I just described, that is doing the conceptual and explanatory work and not the idea of the "religious." My speculative thesis is that the imperatives of survival forced many traditions to remake themselves in the image of Christianity and Islam. Hinduism and "Hindu subjects" were produced through Islamic and Christian power/knowledge, that is, through imperial conquest, administration, and the production of Western scholarship. On that point, I return to Hayes' account of religion and nationalism.[33]

In the following passage, Hayes expresses views that are similar to mine. "Vastly more men perished in the recent four-year War of the Nations [World War I] than in the four centuries of mediaeval Christian Crusades." This is certainly true, and I do not believe that technological advances in the arts of war lessen the importance of this claim. For what this claim acknowledges is a gross disproportion between the levels of religiously inspired sacrifice and sacrifice for the nation. In short, Hayes' own account provides an argument for the qualitative difference between the willingness to die for one's religion and the willingness to die for one's nation.[34] Here religious sentiment cannot account for the intensity and scope of national sentiment. This is true even for Christianity and Islam. As we all know, Christians of one nation, state, or nation-state are quite willing to kill Christians of other nations, for *their* nation. The same is true of Muslims. Perhaps Hayes' account can

be rescued by arguing that nationalism broadens and intensifies a fundamentally religious sense. The problem here is providing a notion of the religious sense that is not, for all the reasons I have previously given, vacuous. His notion of religion, furthermore, is as confusing as it is vacuous. Nationalism, as his stirring and concluding rebuke suggests, is religious in that it inspires strong emotions, but antireligious as a moral phenomenon. "Nationalism as a religion inculcates neither charity nor justice; it is proud, not humble; and it signally fails to universalize human aims." And what of its other failures? Nationalists reject Paul's revolutionary message that in Christ "there is neither Jew nor Greek." Instead, they affirm "the primitive doctrine that there shall be Jew and Greek, only that now there shall be Jew and Greek more quintessentially than ever." Hayes concludes this Christian allegory saying: "Nationalism's kingdom is frankly of this world, and its attainment involves tribal selfishness and vainglory, a particularly ignorant and tyrannical intolerance, – and war." Nationalism brings the sword not peace. Its consequences are militarism, international war, and intolerance.[35]

Hayes was a younger contemporary of Durkheim. Durkheim's work preceded Hayes' earliest essays on nationalism by more than a decade. Yet, he offers a remarkably similar assessment of the violence-producing power of nationalist sentiment. He also takes the French Revolution as his example. For Durkheim, the Revolution is the most explicit illustration of the apotheosis of society by society, its "ability to make itself a god or to create gods."[36] Like Hayes, he cites the deification of ideas such as Liberty and Reason and the establishment of civic dogmas, liturgies, and feast days in honor of the Fatherland. The indissoluble connection between religion and national sentiment is captured in the following passage:

Under the influence of some great collective shock in certain historical periods, social interactions become much more frequent and active. Individuals seek one another out and come together more. The result is the general effervescence that is characteristic of revolutionary or creative epochs. The result of that heightened activity is a general stimulation of individual energies. People live differently and more intensely than in normal times. The changes are not simply of nuance and degree; man himself becomes something other than what he was. He is stirred by passions so intense that they can be satisfied only by violence and extreme acts: by acts of superhuman heroism or bloody barbarism. This explains the Crusades, for example, as well as so many sublime or savage moments in the French Revolution. We see the most mediocre or harmless bourgeois transformed by the general exaltation into a hero or an executioner. And the mental processes are so clearly the same as those at the root of religion that the individuals themselves conceived the pressure they yielded to in explicitly religious terms.[37]

This passage recalls Said's description of religious–cultural effects as "organized collective passions whose social and intellectual results are often disastrous" (*WTC* 290). It also recalls Hayes, who regards international war, militarism, and intolerance as the consequences of nationalism. These consequences, both Hayes' accent on militarism and intolerance and Durkheim's notion of the "morbid inflation of the will,"[38] are what Said calls the "religious effects of culture." For Said, nationalism and imperialism, as religious–cultural effects, go hand in hand. The Gulf War is a textbook example. This is an argument that I address in the following chapter. But, in anticipation of that argument, I note Said's disquietude with the dispatch and mindless conformity that characterized America's decision to go to war against Iraq in 1991. This includes the demonizing of Saddam Hussein, which is not to say that he is not an evil man, the vilification of the Iraqi people, the reduction of Islam to fundamentalism and fundamentalism to fanaticism and terror, all of which were attributed to the irrationality of the Arab mind. All of this was confirmed by an endless parade of "experts" solemnly pontificating on the hell-hole that is the Islamic world. Like Hayes, Said sees nationalism as a social acid that destroys more inclusive, universal, and heterogenous forms of social life. But he is more sophisticated than Hayes, recognizing as he does that nationalist solidarity is bought at the expense of intragroup differences. Nationalism is both social glue and social acid, binding the group, the nation, by dissolving and denying internal differences. Unlike Durkheim, he recognizes that nationalism-as-religion does more than bind people together. It simultaneously produces and represses intracultural differences in pernicious ways.

This pernicious and paradoxical production and repression of differences drives Said's account of the Iranian Revolution, the establishment of an Islamic Republic, and the predicament of his Iranian friend to whom I referred at the beginning of the chapter. His friend's failure was an intellectual failure. The proximate cause of failure was the religious character of his commitments. He betrayed the intellectual vocation by becoming a priest in the temple of nationalism; when this god failed him, as indeed gods always fail, he turned to other gods. Now, after nearly ten years in exile and shortly after the end of the Gulf War, he had concluded that Western imperialism was preferable to Iraqi fascism. For a mind clouded by Manichaean visions, no alternatives were imaginable. This "dogmatizing" of the intellect, which elicits the consent of even the best and the brightest, is a consequence of nationalism as religious–cultural effect. Said's friend disappears from the narrative at this point, but Said tries to make sense of his friend's experience by placing it in the larger context of twentieth-century political and ideological conversions (*RI* 105, 110). He writes his friend's experience into Richard Crossman's Cold War book, *The God That Failed*.

Like the Western intellectuals whose enchantment and disenchantment with Soviet Marxism the book chronicles, Said's friend experienced his own conversion to and apostasy from Iranian and Arab nationalism. Only now, to paraphrase Crossman, could he recognize Western angels having met Iranian and Arab devils. Said dismisses Crossman's account as a cheap morality play, the implication being that intellectuals should not be moved by such considerations. When they are moved by these considerations, the reasoned work of the intellectual life is displaced by soul-making and priestcraft, the consequences of which can only be baleful. This desire to make new souls accounts for disasters such as the Soviet show trials, the mass purges, and the Gulag Archipelago. This is what occurs when the intellectual sells his secular birthright for a bowl of religious porridge. This "selling-out," under difficult circumstances to be sure, reproduces the circumstances that produce it. The behavior of Said's friend during the Gulf Crisis mirrored the behavior of Crossman's intellectuals; his anti-Iraqi and anti-Muslim hysteria was their anticommunist hysteria, both contributing to the hysteria that produced them – evangelical in their efforts, self-mutilating in their public performances. In trying to make sense of Crossman's intellectuals and no doubt of his friend, Said asks "Why as an intellectual did you believe in a god anyway?" As he is quick to add, what he is criticizing is not religious belief *per se*, which is "both understandable and deeply personal," but dogmatism. This aside is no doubt sincere, but, as a matter of practice, religion in Said's account is little more than a metaphor for dogmatism and violence. Here the reader should keep in mind that, for Said, the enchantment and disenchantment of the intellectual are but a microcosm of larger religious–cultural effects. Thus the nationalist debacle in the former Yugoslavia with its ethnic cleansing and mass slaughter is terrible but exemplary of nationalism as religious–cultural effect, of politics as missionary zeal and Manichaean vision (*RI* 110–114).

# CHAPTER 3

# The religious effects of culture: Orientalism

It is quite clear which color is a hundred times more important for a genealogist than blue: namely grey, which is to say, that which can be documented, which can actually be confirmed and has actually existed, in short, the whole, long, hard–to–decipher hieroglyphic script of man's moral past!

(Friedrich Nietzsche, *The Genealogy of Morality*, pp. 8–9)

Genealogy does not oppose itself to history as the lofty and profound gaze of the philosopher might compare to the molelike perspective of the scholar; on the contrary, it rejects the metahistorical deployment of ideal significations and indefinite teleologies. It opposes itself to the search for "origins."

(Michel Foucault, *Language, Counter-Memory, Practice*, p. 140)

I have found it useful here to employ Michel Foucault's notion of a discourse, as described by him in The Archaeology of Knowledge and in Discipline and Punish, to identify Orientalism. My contention is that without examining Orientalism as a discourse one cannot possibly understand the enormously systematic discipline by which European culture was able to manage – and even produce – the Orient politically, sociologically, militarily, ideologically, scientifically, and imaginatively during the post-Enlightenment period.

(Edward Said, *Orientalism*, p. 3)

## THE ORIENTALIST AS MISSIONARY AND PILGRIM

By the late eighteenth century, "the classifications of mankind were systematically multiplied as the possibilities of designation and derivation were refined beyond the categories of what Vico called Gentile and sacred nations; race, color, origin, temperament, character, and types overwhelmed the distinction between Christians and everyone else" (*O* 120). I place the following gloss on Said's point: racialized descriptions of national identity, as exemplified by David Hume's essay "Of National Characters" with its infamous footnote on the incapacities of Negroes, displaced religious descriptions. The modern, secularizing categories of race, nation, and culture displaced the medieval category of *religio*, filling the existential paradigms of Christianity with new content.[1] Under the secular rubrics of race and nation, religious emplotments of human history and destiny "were reconstituted, redeployed, redistributed" (*O* 120–121). Among the most important bearers of the old existential paradigm was Orientalism, which Said describes as the dominant ideological frame of Western man. Orientalism, about which I shall say more later, provided a vocabulary and set of techniques that never lost their religious birthmarks, their status as "a reconstructed religious impulse," a naturalized supernaturalism (*O* 121). Said gets his idea of natural supernaturalism from M. H. Abrams who describes it as a romantic reaction to "the rationalism and decorum of the Enlightenment." He also regards it as a reversion:

to the stark drama and suprarational mysteries of the Christian story and doctrines and to the violent conflicts and abrupt reversals of the Christian inner life, turning on the extremes of destruction and creation, hell and heaven, exile and paradise regained . . . But since they lived inescapably after the Enlightenment, Romantic writers revived these ancient matters with a difference: they undertook to save the overview of human history and destiny, the existential paradigms, and the cardinal values of their religious heritage, by reconstituting them in a way that would make them intellectually acceptable, as well as emotionally pertinent, for the time being.[2]

Abrams is part of the discourse of secularization, enunciated by Max Weber's *The Protestant Ethic and the Spirit of Capitalism*, reconfigured by Karl Löwith's *Meaning in History*, refined by Hans Blumenburg's *The Legitimacy of the Modern Age*, and ostensibly deconstructed by John Milbank's *Theology and Social Theory*. Weber's classic account of secularization is part of the often unproblematic background of contemporary thought. On his account, the logic of Protestant Christianity's "inner-worldly asceticism" led to the triumph of industrial capitalism, instrumental–bureaucratic rationality and the disenchantment (what Nietzsche calls nihilism) of the modern world. In even darker language, it produced Weber's iron cage, Adorno's administered society, and Foucault's carceral society. Said has this process of discipline, administration, and incarceration in mind when he construes Orientalism as a discourse of power, knowledge, and redemption. But this is not all that he has in mind. Löwith's reconfiguration of Weber's secularization thesis

(modernity as the secularization of Christian ideas) provides the philosophical rationale, by way of Abrams, for Said's account of Orientalism
as secular Christian theology. Perhaps the most important of these secularized ideas is redemption, which has an ambiguous shape in Said's
account. The Orient is both object and subject of redemption, the
Orientalist both missionary and pilgrim. As missionary, the Orientalist
was a hero who saved the Orient from obscurity, alienation, and strange-
ness, who restored a paradise lost. The Orientalist reconstructed languages, mores, ways of thinking and restored the ancient, classical
Orient through the "specific Orientalist techniques" of lexicography,
grammar, translation, and cultural decoding. By reconstructing the classical Orient through the tools of the human sciences, the Orientalist
transformed the Orient into an object of anthropological and philolog-
ical knowledge. "In short, having transported the Orient into modernity,
the Orientalist could celebrate his method, and his position, as that of a
secular creator, a man who made new worlds as God had once made the
old" (*O* 121). As pilgrim, the Orientalist luxuriated in the ancient wisdom
of the mysterious East and there found restoration.

Here I pause and note a tension in Said's analysis between genealogy
and metahistory. In what by now is a twice-told tale, Hayden White
argues that the historian prefigures the historical field. She never
encounters historical events "in the raw" as "brute facts." There is
always already some notion of the kind of story that should be told. This
prefiguring is metahistorical or tropological, the most important tropes
being metaphor, metonymy, synecdoche, and irony. According to White,
these tropes prefigure four ideal–typical styles of historiography. Each
style is a combination of *modes of emplotment* (or narrative), *modes of argument* and *modes of ideological implication*. A history prefigured by the metaphor trope would have a romantic form of emplotment, be formist
(concerned with morphology) in argument, and anarchist in ideological
implication. In contrast, the metonymy trope has a tragic form of
emplotment, a mechanistic style of argument, and has radical ideological implications. I will come back to these two historiographical styles in
a moment.

As White is quick to point out, these styles are ideal types. One is
unlikely to encounter them in pure form. The more sophisticated the
historian, whether professional or amateur, the less likely they are to
conform to type. Thus Hegel's historiographical style was complex:
tragic on the microcosmic level and comic on the macrocosmic level.
Some combinations, according to White, are counterintuitive if not

impossible. "The very idea of a Romantic Satire represents a contradiction in terms."[3] Let me hasten to add that I am not bound by every detail and assumption of White's account. I do not regard the preconceptual level that White identifies as a "deep-structure" that is outside historical contingencies. So his model is useful to me only as a heuristic device to illuminate Said's critical practice in *Orientalism*.[4] Said, as I interpret him, emplots Orientalism as tragic-romance, an ostensibly redemptive project in which the Orient is restored to its past glory and the Orientalist is spiritually regenerated. But the price of redemption is high and is paid by the brutal and "primitive accumulation" of the territories, cultures, and bodies of the Oriental other. According to Said, these bloody pursuits of identity and capital accumulation represent a secularization of Christian theology, a tragic twist on the romance of redemption. Or to quote him directly:

My thesis is that the essential aspects of modern Orientalist theory and praxis (from which present–day Orientalism derives) can be understood, not as a sudden access of objective knowledge about the Orient, but as a set of structures inherited from the past, secularized, redisposed, and re–formed by such disciplines as philology, which in turn were naturalized, and laicized substitutes for (or versions of) Christian supernaturalism. (*O* 122)

Said traces the theme of the Orientalist as recreator and redeemer in the work of Silvestre de Sacy and Ernest Renan, which he holds as exemplary of the way in which Orientalist disciplines such as philology and anthropology were, as noted above, "naturalized and laicized substitutes for (or versions of) Christian supernaturalism." If Said emplots Orientalism as a romance, there is nothing simple about it, as it clearly has a tragic dimension. This is evident in Said's contention that Orientalism is "a crucial elaboration" of the greatest act of "primitive accumulation" that the world has ever seen. Here Said speaks of the age of empire, of European imperialism and colonialism. He claims that Orientalism tended fatally (I would say tragically) toward "the systematic accumulation of human beings and territories" (*O* 122–123).

To make sense of this logic of accumulation, Said supplements Marx with Foucault. Orientalism, he argues, is a discourse. Here Said refers to Foucault's technical description of that term in *The Archaeology of Knowledge* and *Discipline and Punish*. Under this description, discourse (discursive formations) is not merely language, but a distinctive relation of words and things, a distinctive way of talking and acting. In *Archaeology*, Foucault develops an elaborate description of discourse, which includes a rich but arcane terminology. Though he abandons most of this terminology in subsequent work, traces of it remain evident throughout. I will not reproduce Foucault's description of discourse here. For a detailed description, the reader can refer to the primary texts or to the voluminous secondary literature.[5] I will provide an assessment of Foucault's views where clarity demands or where those views bear in a crucial way on Said's analysis of Orientalism.

Orientalism refers to the East, and the East, according to Said, is a product of the "imaginative geography" of those people who came to know themselves, their culture and territories as European and later as the West. This distinction between East and West is a way of investing space with a many-ramified meaning. Beyond the domain of this imaginative investment of space, but always in concert with it, is the occupation and command of territory by armed force and imperial administration. The Orient is the distorted mirror-image of the Occident – the image, so to speak, which Dorian Gray saw peering back at him from the mirror. In less foundationalist language, it is the quintessential Western representation of otherness, the constitutive other of the West, that without which there would be no West. In summary, Said defines Orientalism as (1) an area of academic study that ranges alphabetically from anthropology to sociology and beyond, (2) a distinctive ontology and epistemology, and (3) a corporate institution that deals with the Orient through the statements, authoritative views, and descriptions that it makes, and through the Orientalist knowledge and the rationale for colonial occupation and administration that it provides. Orientalism is a Western style of domination and authority, through which the Orient is restructured (*O* 2–3).[6]

If Orientalism is a discourse, then one of its constitutive functions is what Foucault calls *enunciative modalities*.[7] These are rules of discursive formation that determine who speaks, the authority with which they speak, and the institutional site from which they speak – all of which are "subject–positions" (speaker, addressee, authorized, nonauthorized) that a person might occupy. Here, Foucault continues his battle against the sovereign, constitutive subject that Kant constructs in *Critique of Pure Reason*. Foucault rejects the notion of a subject who synthesizes or unifies the Kantian manifold of sensibility. On the contrary, enunciative modalities represent the dispersion of the subject, that is, the various subject–positions that she can occupy or be assigned when speaking. Foucault wants to abandon any attempt to describe discourse as expressing subjectivity.[8] Rather than expressing the synthetic activities of a constitutive subject, verbal expressions are ciphers "for a field of regularity for various positions of subjectivity."[9] On this point, Said makes his most important revision of Foucault's analysis and the one that has generated the most critical scrutiny. He argues for the constitutive power of the author in Orientalist discourse. If nowhere else, he argues, the author in Orientalist discourse has a decisive role in what is otherwise a body of anonymous texts (*O* 23).

Said doubts the accuracy of Foucault's claims for the enunciative function of discourse. He doubts its exclusive power to produce and position the subject, at least for Orientalism. He resolutely rejects Foucault's "anti-humanism," but at the cost of what some regard as incoherence.[10] Despite Foucault's strictures against the constitutive power of the author and the transcendental or constitutive subject, Said insists that certain Orientalist authors, such as Silvestre de Sacy and Ernest Renan, are discourse *formative*. This claim is often viewed as a deviation from Foucauldian orthodoxy. It is not clear to me why it should be, in as much as Foucault himself speaks of "founders of discursivity." Said's basic intuition seems correct: a discursive analysis of subjectivity, by itself, is inadequate. Or, to put this another way, what some analysts call a discursive analysis of subjectivity is inadequate when it does not allow for certain kinds of authors. On Foucault's view, or at least on one of them, authors both produce and are produced by discourse, both use and are artifacts of the language that they use. The concept of "founders of discursivity" can only be understood in this sense. According to Foucault, Marx and Freud are such founders. They not only spoke within the archives of their times, but reshaped their respective archives and produced *an endless possibility of discourse*. To put it another way, they made it possible for us to think differently. Thus they are authors of a special sort. Foucault takes psychoanalysis as an example of what this special kind of authorship can produce. He argues that the founding "of a discursive practice is heterogeneous to its subsequent transformations," so one cannot limit the meaning of psychoanalysis to Freud's founding act.[11] On the other hand, this founding act makes psychoanalytic discourse possible. This, it seems to me, provides a partial opening, within Foucault's own framework, for the kind of author that Said wants to posit in his account of Orientalism.[12]

On Said's view, Sacy and Renan are authors of this special sort; they have a privileged place, *as authors*, in Orientalist discourse. He describes Sacy as the father of Orientalism, "a self-aware inaugurator," who created "the fundamental epistemological rules"[13] governing the behavior of subsequent Orientalists. Sacy was the originator, the founder

Orientalism, Renan the architect. Renan played Lenin to Sacy's Marx, routinizing Sacy's charisma. In line with his self-described "hybrid perspective" on discourse and the author, Said argues that Renan was neither totally original nor totally derivative. He was a significant Orientalist whose cultural force is irreducible to his personality or his ideas. He was "a dynamic force" who worked within the lines, paradigm, and vocabulary that trailblazers like Sacy created. Renan must be understood, Said contends, as a model of intellectual and cultural praxis, the model for how Orientalist statements were made within the archive that defined his time (*O* 124,130). In this way, Said registers his reservations about the poststructuralist dissolution of the subject – the Cartesian subject that thinks its existence and the Kantian subject that constructs the objective world – that Foucault enunciates so powerfully in *The Order of Things*.

One of the more important elements of Foucault's discursive theory is the archive, which he describes "as the general system of the formation and transformation of statements."[14] It is not a Kantian transcendental ideal from which discursive orders and regularities can be deduced. The archive, rather, is a lexicon of every statement that has been made in a particular society. It is a *historical a priori* – that is, the accumulation of specific historical events and antecedent circumstances – that constrains what can be said and who can say it. The archive can be described as "the library of libraries," but only if we allow for the loss, theft, alteration, substitution, and the addition of texts. It organizes statements into particular discursive formations, with specific orders and regularities. Foucault speaks "of clinical discourse, economic discourse, the discourse of natural history, psychiatric discourse."[15] Following Foucault, Said speaks of Orientalist discourse. Only in one respect, and even here one has to assume much, does Said's analysis of Orientalism lack the care, rigor, and specificity of Foucault's genealogies. This occurs when he herds multiple discourses together under the rubric of Orientalism, discourses that are discrete both spatially and temporally. When Said does this, assuming a strictly Foucauldian set of premises, his discourse analysis goes awry. It becomes a highly inflated version of Foucault's idea. But this is true only if Foucault's notion of genealogy is beyond criticism and revision. To accord it that kind of status, as James Clifford apparently does, is to construe it as scripture.

According to Clifford, "One cannot combine within the same analytic totality both personal statements and discursive statements, even though they may be lexically identical." This is a curious statement: so let us be

clear about what Clifford is saying, namely, that ideological analysis and discursive analysis are mutually exclusive as are authorial subjects and the subjects of anonymous discourses. To choose one is to foreclose the possibility of choosing the other. He claims, contrary to Said, that this mutual exclusivity is a methodological rather than an empirical point. Thus it does not matter, methodologically speaking, that Orientalists authors such as Sacy and Renan mattered. Clifford's assertions may be true. But how would we know?[16] He gives us no reason to take what he says as true aside from merely asserting that it is. If this assertion relies on claims that Foucault makes, what is the status of those claims? Are we to take them on faith? Only if Foucault is taken as the *inspired author* (how ironic is that?) of sacred texts can assertions such as Clifford's be made so dogmatically. For surely the point of *Orientalism* is to revise Foucault's notion of discourse, methodologically, in light of the empirical evidence. Thus, to say that Said's genealogy "deviates" from Foucault's genealogies is to say that it is more like the genealogies of Nietzsche. Both Nietzsche and Said are more interested in the distinctive signatures of individual authors – which is not a methodological mistake but a difference in methodological accent – than they are in the constitutive powers of anonymous discourses. Neither is afraid to engage in *ad hominem* arguments where such arguments are appropriate, as icing on their argumentative cake.[17] Both paint with a broad brush, and their primary colors are black and white.[18]

Back to Foucault's notion of discourse, especially as developed in *Archaeology*, from which Said draws directly when he refers to Orientalism as "a library or archive of information." He uses Ian Hacking's term, "family of ideas," to account for the unity of the archive (*O* 43). This is an obvious revision of Foucault's description of the archive as a sovereign power, which is constituted by everything that has been said in a given society. In describing how the West, since antiquity, has come to know the Near East as Other, Said names the following markers: the Bible, Christianity, Marco Polo, Mandeville, and Islam. From the literature that belonged to these experiences an archive of Orientalist statements was built. A limited number of statements provided the lenses through which the Orient was experienced, and they shaped the language through which the encounter between East and West took place (*O* 58).

Said appears to conflate the discourse of Orientalism with the "European archive," if one can speak of such; he, apparently, thinks that one can. So he speaks as if they are the same thing. But his position on the archive may not be as important as it would otherwise be, given the greater influence of *Discipline and Punish* on his description of Orientalism. Only traces of the rich conceptual scheme of the *Archaeology* are evident in *Orientalism*. But these traces are very rich indeed. Said refers frequently (though his language is not always explicit) to the Western *archive*, the Oriental as an *object* of discourse, Orientalist scholarship as an *enunciative modality*, Oriental despotism and irrationality as *conceptual formations*. He also refers to the *strategic choices* that produce, on different spatial planes, incompatible objects, authoritative subject positions, and concepts. More important than any discrete element for Said is Foucault's general category of discourse. As he says in the epigram at the beginning of this chapter, Orientalism cannot be understood without the category discourse, without the systematic discipline that it presupposed, and the distinctive relation between the exercise of power and the production of forms of knowledge (power/knowledge) that it represents. But his failure to explain how a discourse produced "during the post-Enlightenment period" could have anything to do with Dante, much less Aeschylus, weakens his argument and underscores the metahistorical character of Orientalism, as Foucault describes the term in the introductory epigram and as Hayden White describes it in *Metahistory*. On this point, it would appear, Said inflates his currency beyond effective use (*O* 3).

To reiterate, Orientalism is several things: a collection of academic disciplines, an ontology, epistemology, and a discourse. In developing his description of discourse, Said appropriates Foucault's ideas of discipline and power/knowledge. By discipline, Foucault means those methods of modern punitive power that establish meticulous control over the body, assuring its constant subjection by imposing a relation "of docility – utility."[19] Discipline, that is, makes human bodies docile and useful, and advertises their availability for political, economic, and cultural uses of many kinds. As an aspect of power/knowledge, discipline is the notion that power and knowledge imply one another. There are no power relations, according to Foucault, without corresponding fields of knowledge, nor is there "knowledge that does not presuppose and constitute at the same time power relations." This political, military, and cultural ensemble, and the field of knowledge that it creates, is what Foucault calls power/knowledge. Subjects are constituted by power/knowledge relations, which represent an inversion of the Kantian notion of the constitutive subject and, therefore, a reconstruction of the relation between subjectivity and discourse – which in Foucault's technical sense is the relation of language and everything else.[20]

The representative figures of Orientalism as power/knowledge are Napoleon and *Description de l'Egypte* – the massive study that he commissioned in preparation for his conquest of Egypt. The conquest and the study established the paradigm for Orientalism as a discourse of power/knowledge. Said accepts Foucault's critique of the "vulgar" Marxist view, where ideology rationalizes domination after the fact. Thus Egypt was an object of Napoleon's imperial desire, which was an imaginative construct derived from experiences "that belong to the realm of ideas and myths culled from texts," before it became an object of conquest. "His plans for Egypt therefore became the first in a long series of European encounters with the Orient in which the Orientalist's special expertise was put directly to functional colonial use." The *Description de l'Egypte* and Napoleon's military engulfment of Egypt were two aspects and instruments of Western power/knowledge (*O* 80, 86).

A speech by Arthur James Balfour before the House of Commons on 13 June 1910 is a restatement of the power/knowledge relation that the Napoleonic expedition had enunciated. Said characterizes that speech as follows:

England knows Egypt; Egypt is what England knows; England knows that Egypt cannot have self-government; England confirms that by occupying Egypt; for the Egyptians, Egypt is what England has occupied and now governs; foreign occupation therefore becomes "the very basis" of contemporary Egyptian civilization; Egypt requires, indeed, insists upon British occupation. (*O* 34)

Orientalism operates with what Said calls a *textual* attitude, which reduces "the swarming, unpredictable, and problematic mess in which human beings live" to textual representations, to what books say (*O* 92–93). What these texts contain, along with the discourse and the archive that regulate them, are a collection of statements that constitute the objects, subject positions, concepts, and themes of Orientalist discourse. A short list of these statements includes descriptions of Orientals as gullible, lethargic, and suspicious, as inveterate liars who lack directness, clarity, initiative, and nobility. The Oriental is constructed as an object of discourse by statements such as: "Orientals are irrational, depraved, and childlike." Orientalist statements refer to things that are Oriental in terms of a constitutive and irremediable lack of peacefulness, liberality, logic, and virtue. Many Orientalist statements begin with the adjective "Oriental." There are Oriental tales, an Oriental personality, despotism, mode of production, and atmosphere. Running through Orientalist discourse as a common thread is a fundamental ontological and epistemological presupposition that is captured well by Rudyard Kipling's famous claim, which I paraphrase: the East is East and West is West and the gulf between the two cannot be bridged. These statements (and the system of knowledge production that they support, along with the power of European and American military domination, bureaucratic administration, and technologies of discipline) constitute Orientalism.

Absent from this list are *positive* statements about the Orient. Said does not deny that such statements are part of Orientalist discourse, but they are at odds with his purpose, which is to expose the *dominant* contours of Orientalist discourse and the way that Orientalist othering structures both positive and negative representations (*O* 31–32, 38–39, 40, 49, 92–93). The charge that Said neglects the sympathetic tradition of Orientalism is a common criticism. In his review of *Orientalism*, Albert Hourani takes Said to task, questioning his fairness and balance, and offers specific criticisms that would be reiterated by subsequent commentators. For example, he asks the following question: "But can it be that he himself has fallen into the trap which he has exposed, and has sunk human differences in an abstract concept called 'Orientalism'?" This is a prototype of the charge of "Occidentalism." Said's writing, according to Hourani, "is forceful and brilliant (sometimes too forceful for comfort; sometimes too brilliant too be clear)." This ironic phrasing cannot conceal a clear rebuke; it is a prototype of the charge that *Orientalism* is a coarse polemic. Hourani defends a certain tradition of Orientalist scholarship on Islam, as exemplified by Louis Massignon, against Said's fierce attack. "Within the limits of this work, those whom the world calls 'Orientalist' were not guilty of what Mr. Said calls 'Orientalism.'" This criticism is a prototype of the charge of reductionism.[21]

## SHADOWS OF GOD: ESSENTIALISM, HUMANISM, PHENOMENOLOGY

Hourani's review is the first in a series of critiques that are, perhaps, the most influential commentaries on *Orientalism*. That list includes the following:

1979   Albert Hourani, "The Road to Morocco"
1981   S. J. al-'Azm, "Orientalism and Orientalism in Reverse"
1983   Dennis Porter, "Orientalism and its Problems"

These texts run the gamut, from the thoughtful to the less than thoughtful, from Hourani to Ahmad, with much ambivalence in between. Ambivalence would seem to be the enabling condition of what Foucault calls "discursivity." Marx and Freud, as I remarked earlier, are founders of discursivity. Their status has as much to do with the disagreements they make possible as with a particular line of thought that they prescribe. They created languages in which agreement, disagreement, and revisions of their views take place. So it is with the critical language that Said has created.[22]

Hourani's critique of *Orientalism* has been refined and pushed in three relatively distinct directions. Most of the criticism can be classified as antiessentialist, antihumanist, or antiphenomenological. Collectively, I call these ideas the shadows of God. Behind them lie notions such as God, Being, image of God, and God's-eye view. Nietzsche characterizes this ensemble as Platonic–Christian, Heidegger calls it ontotheology, Derrida calls it presence. These foundational notions have been the object of much contemporary theory. While relatively distinct, antiessentialist, antihumanist, and antiphenomenological lines of criticism are interdependent. I will address these lines of criticism briefly and in reverse order.

Among the more tempting critiques of *Orientalism* is the charge of essentialism. Said's critics often accuse him of abstraction and reification, of practicing reverse Orientalism, Occidentalism.[23] His rhetoric is said to mimic what he criticizes.[24] There is some truth to this charge, although I think that critics make too much of it. There are good reasons for being suspicious of simpleminded reversals. But we should not lose sight of the rhetorical situation that the critic occupies. To a certain degree the kind of mimicry in which Said engages goes with the critical territory. There is an important ethical–political difference, however, between what Said castigates as Orientalism and the mimetic qualities of his critical rhetoric. There is no good reason to elide the critical difference between the two.[25] For example, Derrida mimes phenomenology, repeating many of its gestures, but his repetitions, purportedly, have different motivations and goals and thus produce a significantly different script.

More serious than the charge of essentialism, within a critical milieu that is often "antihumanist," is the charge that Said is a humanist. This criticism usually holds that Said is not Foucauldian enough, his lack of fidelity to Foucault's austere antihumanism is said to traduce an otherwise admirable critical project. Said's humanism threatens to reproduce the sovereign, constitutive subject in the form of the heroic or representative intellectual. It threatens to undermine one of Foucault's most important critical interventions by replicating a universal and invidious concept of normative humanity. This humanist idea, according to Paul Bové, has underwritten the rigid hierarchies – sexual, racial, and so on – that Foucault's analyses seek to banish.[26] I spend a lot of time addressing this criticism in chapter 5. Here I will only say this: I do not find Bové's argument persuasive. He does not grapple sufficiently with the view that every would-be antihumanism (which purports to be something other than fascist) is a form of humanism.[27] Humanism (like democracy in John Dewey's expansive sense of the term) contains the principle of its own self-criticism and self-overcoming; it is best positioned to correct its own defects to recognize and criticize the inhumane behavior that antihumanists associate with their Heideggerian–derived notion of humanism.

"Madness and the Orient" might be an apt rubric for the third-line criticism directed at *Orientalism*. Here the criticism is directed at Said's phenomenological residues, his ambivalence on the question of whether there is an authentic Orient or not. James Clifford describes Said's Sartrean-derived phenomenology as a "humanist fable of suppressed authenticity,"[28] but he seems unaware of the extent to which his criticism of Said mirrors a criticism that others have made of Foucault. This same "humanist fable" is an important aspect of Derrida's trenchant critique of Foucault in "Cogito and the History of Madness." By now this critique of *Histoire de la folie* (a severely abridged version of which was translated into English as *Madness and Civilization*) is fairly well known in critical circles. In his essay, Derrida discerns an "admirable tension" in Foucault's book. He describes Foucault's undertaking as an impossible but intellectually audacious and seductive attempt to write a history of madness itself. Foucault wants to show what madness is like in its pristine state, before it is captured by reason and imprisoned by knowledge. He would do so by producing an archaeology of a silence, by excavating the lives of those who, buried in silence, do not speak. On Derrida's account, Foucault is attempting to write a history of madness that bypasses reason while simultaneously avoiding any objectivist *naïveté*.

Foucault's undertaking, he suggests, is itself a form of madness. If there is no access to madness outside language, reason, and representation,[29] then to speak as if there were is itself authentic madness.

Said's critics make a similar critique of *Orientalism*. On this view, there is a structural analogy between Foucault's attempt to excavate an authentic pre-discursive madness and Said's claims for the Orient. Catherine G. Martin, for example, criticizes Said's analysis of Orientalism for being too Foucauldian and not Derridian enough.[30] On the one hand, Said rejects the view that there is a pre-discursive, pre-Orientalist Orient, an authentic Orient beneath the ideological distortions of Orientalist discourse. This is the "Nietzschean" Said. On the other hand, he is a Marxist realist who wants to liberate the real Orient from the misrepresentations of Orientalism. In this mode, he speaks of a real Orient, an Orient free of domination, distortion, and coercion, an Orient free from we–they, us–them distinctions (*O* 104). I think that the criticism of Said's phenomenology has considerable technical merit; there is a hint of Sartrean existential–phenomenology, which is a residue from his early work on Joseph Conrad.[31] But this criticism is right only about the marginal case, where Said does use the phenomenologically reductive language of authenticity and purity. I do not want to dismiss the importance of this criticism, but as with Derrida's critique of Foucault in "Cogito and the History of Madness,"[32] the critique of Said's phenomenology does little to dim the luster of his analysis. As Derrida's critique is merely a footnote to Foucault's great achievement, so are similar critiques of Said's achievement. Despite its flaws, and much like *Histoire de la folie*, *Orientalism* remains a powerful analysis of a particular configuration of power/knowledge.

Finally, there is Aijaz Ahmad's critique of *Orientalism*, which is interesting despite its flaws. Ahmad makes the same critical moves that Paul Bové, James Clifford, and Robert Young make. What makes his narrative distinctive, constituting perhaps a fourth line of criticism, is the unabashedly Marxist character of his account. Ahmad is particularly effective in exposing Said's "anti-Marxism" (more on that in a moment), his sometimes magisterial and sometimes muddled eclecticism, and his surprisingly "conservative" high cultural humanism. I place anti-Marxism in quotations because while I think that Ahmad is right (if by anti-Marxist he means anti-Stalinist), he is wrong in a way that is central to my claim that Said's use of the word religion is Marxist. I think that Ahmad is right (in the way that a caricature is right) when he says that Said constructs a bourgeois Marx and a radical Benda. He is right, within that perspective, when he describes the Frankenstein-like construction of Marx as an Orientalist, Said's bizarre attempt, from Ahmad's perspective, to graft Marx into Orientalist discourse. Ahmad shows how Said repeats a gesture that is common on the poststructuralist–postmodernist "left" where Marx is subjected to trenchant, often tendentious criticism, while Nietzsche is largely uninterrogated.[33] Apparently, Nietzsche's work, which is heavily laden with Orientalist statements, does not merit comment. While this shows that Said is no simple Marxist, it does not detract from what remains a Marxist interpretation of religion.

## THE ORIENTALIST CONSTRUCTION OF ISLAM

Said's interpretation of religion or, to be precise, his account of how Orientalists have represented or misrepresented Islam is a prominent thread running through the length of *Orientalism*. This book, as he acknowledges, is "far from a complete history or general account of Orientalism" (*O* 224). To manage the unmanageable wealth of Orientalist material, he uses the narrative device of pairing, comparing, and contrasting two important Orientalists: such as Sacy and Renan, Edward William Lane and François-René Chateaubriand, Alphonse de Lamartine and Gérard de Nerval or Gustave Flaubert, Richard Burton and T. E. Lawrence, Louis Massignon and H. A. R. Gibb, Albert Hourani and Bernard Lewis. Their representations of Islam are very important to Said. His representation of them reveals much about his view of Islam and religion. If the Orientalist representation of Arabs is one pillar of Said's account, then the representation of Islam is the other. Said's hostile critique of religion stands in sharp contrast to his defense of Islam. Why is this? Does it support the contention of some of his critics that he is "soft" on Islam, an apologist, a secret admirer? How does he manage the feat of criticizing religion and defending Islam? Part of the answer is purely pragmatic. For good or for ill, Islam is regarded as a constitutive feature of Arab and Oriental identity. For pragmatic reasons, Said accepts this association. So he feels compelled to defend Islam and thus Arabs and Orientals against the misrepresentations of Orientalists. The reader should note well, in what follows, the specificity and sympathetic character of Said's account of Islam compared to his abstract and hostile depiction of religion. Here, to take up a point that I make in Preliminary Remarks, Said engages in practices, where they suit his own purposes, that he otherwise calls Orientalist –

namely, the use of abstract generalities, reified notions, and Manichaean logic.

Much of the animus that Said discerns in Orientalism is a reaction to Islam. Islamic–Christian conflict and competition is part of the prehistory of modern Orientalism and a central figure in its post-Enlightenment elaboration. Orientalism bears the stamp of European rancor toward and misapprehension of Islam. This attitude is clearly evident, he contends, in European representations of the Prophet Muhammad. "What this discourse considers to be a fact – that Muhammad is an imposter, for example, is a component of the discourse, a statement the discourse compels one to make whenever the name Muhammad occurs" (*O* 71, 74). Within Orientalist discourse, there are no meanings or kinds of significance that exceed, supplement, or challenge what Orientalists claim. Thus Muhammad *is* an impostor – period. This statement requires neither background, evidence, nor qualification. The more one says that Muhammad is an imposter, the greater the weight and authority that pronouncement carries (*O* 72).[34] Said's interest in Islam, as these comments underscore, revolves around the question of representation. He claims that the Western representation of Islam is a misrepresentation and he doubts, in his Nietzschean mood, whether true representations are possible. He supports this claim by noting that representations as such are politically, institutionally, linguistically, and culturally constructed. Representations are necessarily intertwined with and bear the trace of other things. They are, necessarily, true and false or beyond truth and falsehood.

*Orientalism* is Said's guerrilla campaign against Christian, European, and Western (he does not consistently distinguish them) representations of Islam. Much of this campaign deals with the construction of the Prophet as an imposter or with Islam as a threat to the West. He takes Dante to task for his depiction of the Prophet whom he relegates to the ninth circle of Hell. The Prophet is depicted as more sinful than blasphemers, heretics, sensualists, and gluttons, more sinful than suicidal, avaricious, and wrathful people. Said refers to the threat both real and imaginary that Islam posed to Europe from the middle ages to the late seventeenth-century (*O* 59, 68, 272). This is a surprisingly attenuated formulation, given Said's professed distaste for reified notions. What he calls the Islamic threat is more accurately characterized as the threat, real or imaginary, that a specific Muslim civilization, the Ottoman Turks, posed for Christian Europeans.

Be that as it may, Said's most sustained analysis of Islam and the politics of representation is put forth in *Covering Islam*. Islam, he argues, signifies the negative. This is true across the ideological spectrum, from left to right. "For the right, Islam represents barbarism; for the left, medieval theocracy; for the center, a kind of distasteful exoticism." According to Said, Muslims are represented as a problem or threat. Their image is ideologically distorted when they are represented (*covered*) as oil suppliers or potential terrorists (*CI* xv, 26). They are apprehended under the mutually contradictory rubrics of medievalism and funda-mentalism. This raises the question of who governs these representa-tions? Whose interests do they serve? How, Said asks, can one interpret other cultures unless antecedent circumstances have already made those cultures available for representation? Has not European interest in other cultures always been colonial, imperial, and commercial in character? (*CI* 131). If the power/knowledge relations of Orientalist dis-course frame Western interpretations of otherness, then authorita-tive statements about Islam are difficult to challenge, because the "enunciative authority" of Orientalism determines who can speak authoritatively. Most Western interpreters of Islam, he contends, ignore the way that Islam is constructed as a hostile culture, and how such interpretations are tainted by the interests of professional Islamic schol-ars. These scholars work within corporate and governmental spheres of influence, both of which are major players in the field of cultural inter-pretation. Their role in deciding what Islam is and whether it is desir-able and in America's interest should not be underestimated (*CI* 134, 158).

Whatever the accuracy of Said's representation, the consequence, as he sees it, of Western representations of Islam is the unrestrained and immediate image that it produces. As a noteworthy example of such image-making, he cites an essay by Michael Walzer entitled "The Islam Explosion." Walzer's essay, he claims, follows an Orientalist script. Violent political events in Muslim countries are attributed to Islam, which is construed as encroaching on the West with a "frightening moral fervor." Palestinian resistance to Israeli "colonialism" is described as religious, rather than political, civil, or human. Islam is characterized as antithetical to liberalism, secularism, socialism, and democracy, all of which are construed as the fruits of European colonialism. Said quotes Walzer to the effect that "wherever there has been murder, war, pro-tracted conflict involving special horrors, 'Islam has clearly played a part.'" His argument is compelling. Unfortunately, his longstanding dis-agreement with Walzer gets the best of him here. This intense dislike detracts from his argument and underwrites citation practices, where Walzer's argument is concerned, that are tendentious.

Said concludes his point by adding that the interrelated powers of a corporate–government–academic–media complex produce canonical representations of Islam that have less to do with truth or accuracy than they do with the geopolitics of power. Scholars have a choice when it comes to interpreting other cultures or cultural formations such as Islam: they can either place their skills at the service of corporate and government power or at the service of morally informed criticism. "This choice must be the first act of interpretation today, and it must result in a decision, not simply a postponement." If scholars choose the second option, and Said thinks that they should, then the connection between Western knowledge of Islam and "conquest and domination" must be completely severed (*CI* 38, 79, 161, 164).

Said cannot quite decide whether Islam is an object constituted by the power/knowledge relations of Orientalist discourse or an ideological label, a distortion or misrepresentation of Islam *as it really is*. He implies that there is a "real," prediscursive Islam that can be represented more or less accurately. As an object of Orientalist discourse, however, Islam is little more than a set of reckless generalities and clichés (*CI* x–xi). I find this account of the Orientalist discourse on Islam interesting. For what better account could there be of Said's discourse on religion? Interestingly, Said's critique of Orientalist representations of Islam departs from Foucault's description of how objects are constituted. For Foucault, power/knowledge relations produce rather than distort truth. There is no truth or knowledge that is outside power; "power and knowledge directly imply one another."[35] Said's language pries knowledge and power apart. Or, to put a positive spin on it, power is morally plural. Western power, therefore, not only produces Islam as truth, it also distorts, masks, or in the language of the book's title, *covers* Islam. This is the language of ideology not discourse. It is not Foucault's language, which is not to suggest that Said should adopt this language as his own. On the contrary, Said can be fruitfully read as providing a Gramscian (and perhaps an Althusserian) reading of Foucault. For all the insights resident in the idea of discourse as power/knowledge, the idea of ideology is too rich to abandon. It is indispensable to what Said wants to provide: an account of Islam as *both* discursive and ideological. Such an account, of course, cannot be given without challenging Foucault's critique of the very notion of ideology,[36] which Said tries to do. We can argue about how successful he is, whether he uses the idea of ideology with the circumspection that Foucault says is necessary. Or we can challenge the cogency of Foucault's claim that such circumspection is needed. As a skeptical admirer of both Said and Foucault, the question for me is how to make good on Said's analysis of Islam while doing justice to Foucault's insights. Such an account will show that the apparent ambiguity of Said's analysis, which is closely tied to his apparent ambivalence on the question of whether there is a "real" Islam or not, appears less ambiguous and ambivalent in light of what I take his purposes to be.

On Said's account, a responsible representation of Islam would include three levels or concentric circles of importance. Of primary importance is the Qur'an, which is the "bedrock identity of Islamic faith." Second are the various schools of Qur'anic interpretation, including "Islamic sects, jurisprudential schools, hermeneutic styles, linguistic theories, and the like." Third are the various ideological contexts and practices that have influenced or inspired Islam, or to which it has otherwise been linked. Following Maxime Rodinson,[37] he argues that this third level must be carefully distinguished from the first two. With respect to this third level, Said wants to make a basic point: that Islam, like other great religions, is compatible with a wide range of mutually contradictory ideologies. How Islam looks has much to do with the culture of which it is a part. Islam in Iran is different from Islam in Bosnia, which is different from Islam in Singapore. While these cultural variations cannot be distinguished from true Islam, neither can true Islam be reduced to a single version. Islam is too diverse, culturally and geopolitically. Unlike the term religion, Said questions the analytical and epistemological usefulness of "Islam," which he calls an abstraction, and he doubts whether there is a *homo islamicus.* Islam, rather, is a complex object of discourse. It is also an ideology providing cover for the geopolitical interests of Western nations and the national security interests of Saudi Arabia and postrevolutionary Iran (*CI* 53–54, 57–60). Islam as an ideology distorts Islam as a universal community of faith and interpretation. Said is not making any deep metaphysical claim about the way Islam really is. What he is saying is that some representations are better than others, and that knowing whose interests are being served goes a long way in deciding which Islam and whose representations are better.

Consider Said's meditations on Louis Massignon and H. A. R. Gibb, whom he describes as the greatest Islamic Orientalists of the period between World Wars I and II. He describes them as representative types: men whose work exemplified their respective national traditions. Massignon was a Frenchman, Gibb an Englishman. Said speaks elo-

quently and sympathetically about Massignon, and describes his style –
which comes out of "the period of so-called aesthetic decadence" and
also shows the influence of Bergson, Durkheim, Mauss, and others –
with glowing respect. "His essays, to say nothing of the monumental
study of al-Hallaj, draw effortlessly on the entire corpus of Islamic literature; his mystifying erudition and almost familiar personality sometimes make him appear to be a scholar invented by Jorge Luis Borges."
Massignon worked diligently to contextualize the Islamic texts and issues
that he engaged, to bring them to life and to surprise his readers with
cross disciplinary insights. The breadth and depth of his erudition was
unmatched. Said crowns this high praise with the following:

No modern Orientalist – and certainly not Gibb, his closest peer in achievement
and influence – could refer so easily (and accurately) in an essay to a host of
Islamic mystics and to Jung, Heisenberg, Mallarme, and Kierkegaard; and certainly very few Orientalists had that range together with the concrete political
experience of which he was able to speak in his 1952 essay "L'Occident devant
l'Orient: Primaute d'une solution culturelle. (*O* 266–267)

Said characterizes Massignon as an eccentric, whose "unorthodox"
view of Islam begins with a peculiar interpretation of the Abrahamic
religions. In this narrative, Ishmael and his Arab–Islamic descendants
are excluded from the promise that Yahweh made to Isaac and his Jewish
descendants:

Islam is therefore a religion of resistance (to God the Father, to Christ the
Incarnation), which yet keeps within it the language of tears, just as the whole
notion of *jihad* in Islam (which Massignon explicitly says is the epic form in
Islam that Renan could not see or understand) has an important intellectual
dimension whose mission is war against Christianity and Judaism as exterior
enemies, and against heresy as a interior enemy. Yet within Islam, Massignon
believed he was able to discern a type of countercurrent, which it became his
chief intellectual mission to study, embodied in mysticism, a road toward divine
grace. The principal feature of mysticism was of course its subjective character, whose nonrational and even inexplicable tendencies were toward the singu-
lar, the individual, the momentary experience of participation in the Divine. All
of Massignon's extraordinary work on mysticism was thus an attempt to
describe the itinerary of souls out of the limiting consensus imposed on them
by the orthodox Islamic community, or Sunna. (*O* 268)

Only a fool, according to Said, would deny the genius and novelty of
Massignon's interpretation of Islam. Yet, something about Massignon
troubles Said. Despite his great love for Islam, Massignon maps an
asymmetrical distinction between Islam and Western religious traditions

onto the East–West and the modern–premodern distinctions. Despite his undeniable sympathy for Islam, Massignon remains an Orientalist. But, and this merits emphasis, his account of the East–West encounter holds the West responsible for its relentless attacks on Islam, from the Crusades to colonialism to modern stereotypical representations. He fought tirelessly on behalf of Muslim civilization, in support of Palestinian refugees, and for the rights of Arab Muslims and Arab Christians in Palestine. Even Massignon, however, was a product of his national and scholarly tradition. Even someone as sympathetic as he could not wholly resist making invidious distinctions between East and West.

Gibb was Massignon's English peer and alter ego: a defender of "orthodox" Islam against "unorthodox" experimentation and against nationalism, communism, and Westernization. Said criticizes what he regards as Gibb's abstract use of the words "religion" and "Islam." Gibb abstracts "Islam as a religion" from the mundane circumstances of everyday life (*O* 279–280). But how does this differ from Said's usage? And when he criticizes Gibb, in addition, of also doing the opposite of abstracting, of taking everything in the culture into Islam, how does that differ from what Said does throughout *Orientalism*? Said obviously is not as enchanted by Gibb as by Massignon. On the contrary, Gibb exemplifies the superior attitude and impervious disposition that he criticizes as Orientalist:

Between the silent appeal of Islam to a monolithic community of orthodox believers and a whole merely verbal articulation of Islam by misled corps of political activists, desperate clerks, and opportunistic reformers: there Gibb stood, wrote, reformulated. His writing said either what Islam could not say or what its clerics would not say. What Gibb wrote was in one sense temporally ahead of Islam in that he allowed that at some point in the future Islam would be able to say what it could not say now. In another important sense, however, Gibb's writings on Islam predated the religion as a coherent body of "living" beliefs, since his writing was able to get hold of "Islam" as a silent appeal made to Muslims *before* their faith became a matter for worldly argument, practice, or debate.

The Orient and Islam have a kind of extrareal, phenomenologically reduced status that puts them out of reach of everyone except the Western expert. From the beginning of Western speculation about the Orient, the one thing the Orient could not do was to represent itself (*O* 282–283).

What this brief excursus on Massignon and Gibb shows is that better interpretations of Islam than the standard Orientalist fare were possible, even under the constraints of Orientalism. Thus Massignon's interpretation is better than Gibb's. In an effort to provide a better representation of Islam, or to suggest what that would entail, Said offers a crude theory of religion. In addition to being an object of Orientalist discourse, Islam is also an object of religious discourse. Religion is what Foucault calls an *inter-discursive* object, an object at the intersection of several discourses. To get at this issue, we shall look at what Said regards as the *conditions of emergence* for Orientalist discourse. He claims that four elements had to be in place before modern Orientalism could emerge: (1) European exploration and expansion, (2) a sympathetic, pre-Romantic, exotic apprehension of the non-European other, (3) eighteenth-century historicism, and (4) the classification schemes of the new sciences. These elements transformed the narrowly religious context that had previously governed the way that the Christian West examined and judged the Orient and Islam. "In other words, modern Orientalism derives from secularizing elements in eighteenth-century European culture" (*O* 120).

Said, it seems to me, is on the verge of an insight that eludes him nevertheless. Perhaps religion, like Orientalism, is a discourse, a distinctively Western way of thinking, of formulating and organizing concepts, of relating particular words and particular things. Much of what Said attributes to Orientalism, especially during the middle ages, is better understood as religious discourse. Islam is, primarily, an object of Christian discourse and the Western theoretical discourse on religion and only secondarily an object of Orientalist discourse. Long before the emergence of modern Orientalism (the only kind of Orientalism there has ever been!) there was conflict between Christians and Muslims. The geographical imagination of the West (the East–West distinction) was not central to this conflict. The fundamental distinction was between the true God and idols, true and false religion. Said's conflation of Europe and Christianity allows him to elide the historical specificity of his subject matter. He legitimates this move by citing Gibbon's description of Muslim conquest as "coeval with the darkest and most slothful period of European annals" (*O* 59). In effect, Said uses the authority of Gibbon to license his reading of the encounter between Islam and Christendom as East–West conflict. It matters little that Gibbon may have seen it this way. As a self-conscious critic of conventional approaches to the history of ideas, Said owes his readers more. Where Gibbon is insufficiently historical, Said must be more historical. Instead, Said replicates the worst errors of the historian of ideas, projecting as ontology what he is

ostensibly committed to analyzing as contingent historical phenomena.
He does not question Gibbon's anachronistic reading of the encounter
between Islamic societies and Christendom as East–West conflict. Like
Gibbon, he reads back into the encounter the consequences of subsequent historical developments such as the emergence and consolidation
of the "idea of Europe," the ascendancy of European cartography, and
the emergence of the "imaginative geography" of East and West.

To pursue this point a little further, John Hale cites three events that
marked the transition from a geographically amorphous sense of
Christian identity to a specific sense of European identity. The first event
was the ecumenical conference at Florence in 1439 that exposed vast
differences between Greek and Latin forms of Christianity. The second
event was the occupation of southeastern Europe (and in some cases the
conversion of its people to Islam) by the Ottoman Turks. Third, and
most important, were the Reformation and the religious wars that followed. European identity emerged as a safe haven amidst a Latin
Christendom that was "soaked in her own blood." According to Hale,
"The idea of Europe emerged during the latter part of what we have
come to know as the European Renaissance." Only then did the word
"Europe" became a common term. "[T]he continent itself was given a
securely map-based frame of reference, a set of images that established
its identity in pictorial terms, and a triumphal ideology that overrode its
internal contradictions."[38] The process was gradual by which a Greek
myth became a map, became a discursive object, became a specific site
for a geopolitical identity called Europe.

The same anachronism that allows Said to read the encounter
between Islamic civilization and Christendom as East–West conflict is
operative in his reading of Dante, whose complicity with Orientalism,
he claims, is evident. This is true despite his discriminating, refined, and
"poetic grasp of Islam." Said claims that Dante constructs Islam as a
creature of Western power/knowledge, a construction that is simultaneously cosmological, geographical, historical, and moral (*O* 69). To be
sure, by the time that Dante wrote *The Divine Comedy*, the idea of Europe
was in the process of being consolidated. But to place Dante within the
spatializing logic and imaginative geography of Orientalism, as the
Syrian philosopher Sadiq Jalal al-'Azm argued in an early review of
*Orientalism*, is anachronistic and gratuitous. Europe (and later the West)
was constituted, in part, by Christendom and by Islamic civilization.
Islam as an object of discourse, and certainly as a proper name, is a
rather late development. Only recently has Islam displaced terms such

and incorporates a vague knowledge of sixteenth-century European religious warfare, seventeenth-century Puritan America, and seventeenth- and eighteenth-century critiques of religious enthusiasm. His opposition to religious–cultural effects is apparent in the invidious use of terms such as *Manichaean* and *errand into the wilderness*. I will show why these terms have the force that they do by providing a short and episodic outline of the "religious history" of ideology. Said's antireligious language is indebted to that history. And that history helps to underscore his continuing relationship, though highly mediated, to Marx's critique of bourgeois ideology as a religious phenomenon. Here, culture is a battlefield for an elaborate and contradictory outworking of fetishism and mystification.

## THE RELIGIOUS HISTORY OF IDEOLOGY

This is a long history: perhaps I should say prehistory inasmuch as the term ideology was not coined until the late eighteenth century by Destutt de Tracy, for whom the term signified the "science of ideas." But long before this term was coined, and almost completely since, the ideas associated with ideology have had a negative resonance. Jorge Larrain traces the historical emergence of this as yet nameless ensemble of ideas to Niccolò Machiavelli, who was greatly concerned about the role that religion played in supporting or undermining princely authority. Machiavelli came to the conclusion quite early that religion, power, and domination go hand in hand.[1] Accordingly, the prince should do everything he could to cultivate the appearance of religious virtue, while being prepared to act contrary to those virtues behind the scenes. Machiavelli posits a distinction between the appearance of religious virtue and the reality of princely power. Among other things, the prince should cultivate the ability to lie well. It is odd, then, that Larrain does not begin his account with Plato's *Republic*, since Plato enunciates both the political and the epistemological problematics that underlie the notion of ideology. He articulates the political problematic by grappling with the question of how to reconcile men to their various stations in a hierarchically arranged society. To accomplish this end, Plato uses a religious myth where different kinds of metals – gold, silver, iron, and bronze – signify a rank-ordering of birth and social status. According to this "Ur-myth," a god or demiurge created different orders of men by mixing them with a specific metal at birth. Rulers (or philosopher-kings) are of golden-birth, auxiliaries (or the warrior-class) are of silver-birth, and craftsmen and farmers (the artisan class) are of iron- and bronze-birth. Plato knows that this myth is not true, but a necessary form of untruth, what he calls a "noble lie."[2] This initiates the epistemological problematic of "appearance and reality" that underlies the very notion of false consciousness.

Plato aside, the upshot of Larrain's argument is that Machiavelli sees religion in practical terms as a powerful and potentially problematic tool of princely authority.[3] In *The Prince*, Machiavelli makes his famous (or infamous) argument about how virtuous a prince should be. He should not be so virtuous that he cannot act like a beast when necessary and beastly behavior will be necessary, because men are not always good but are often bad. It is important that the prince appears to have certain virtues, but to actually possess such virtues is dangerous. "Thus it is well to seem merciful, faithful, humane, sincere, religious, and also to be so; but you must have the mind so disposed that when it is needful to be otherwise you may be able to change to the opposite qualities." Machiavelli understands the complexities of religion and political power. Religion (and the other virtues) makes people docile and easier to rule, but it threatens to do the same thing to the prince. While it is important above all that he appears religious, the prince can never lose sight of that maxim "from which there is no appeal," namely, that "the end justifies the means." The prince must appropriate divine authority for his own uses and "favor religion (even though it were believed to be false)." The wiser the prince the more he will support "the belief in miracles that are celebrated in religions, however false they may be."[4] In our language, false beliefs are ideological weapons in the service of political interests, especially when those beliefs are religious in character.

From Machiavelli, Larrain moves to Francis Bacon's *New Organon* and his notion of idols. *Bacon's famous discussion of idols of the tribe, cave, marketplace, and theatre, which Said uses in his own analyses, is decisive, according to Larrain, for a number of thinkers who wrestled with the function of religion in social and political life.* Remarkably, Larrain says nothing about the significance of the word "idol" itself. This is odd because the idea of idol worship is an important element in the appearance–reality problematic of ideology. Idolatry could be described as an intrareligious form of false consciousness. This idea is an important aspect of Bacon's use of the term, and is evident throughout his introductory discussion of "idols and false notions" in the *New Organon*. According to Bacon, certain idols (or false notions) "are inherent in human nature." These "idols of the tribe," as he calls them, include the cognitive activity of imposing order and reg-

ularity on natural disorder and irregularity, dogmatic adherence to presuppositions that tailor the "data" and that encourage us to ignore negative evidence, the desire for "final causes, and a tendency toward
abstract thought. (It is this notion of idolatry, I think, that Said has in
mind when he refers to "the various official idols venerated by culture
and by system" (*WTC* ).) "Idols of the den" or of the "cave," as they are
sometimes called, refer to the peculiarities of individuality and the problems that cause the understanding. They pollute the understanding by
promoting partiality (or lack of comprehensiveness), excessive synthesis
or analysis, party zeal (who to favor, the moderns or the ancients?) and
"narrowness of subject." Bacon calls the false notions that derive from
language, from words and names – "idols of the market." Market idols
pertain to the nonreferentiality of some names, to the fact that some
words refer only to imaginary objects, while others refer badly or in a
confused way. Words create objects that do not exist and misperceive
those that do. The fourth set of false notions that deform the understanding are "idols of the theatre." Bacon refers here to three kinds of
theory: to sophistry, empiricism, and superstition. The first refers to the
metaphysics of Aristotelian science, the second to deductive approaches
to knowledge of the natural world, and the third to theology. Theology
(or superstition) is especially pernicious because it corrupts philosophy.[5]

The specificity of the connection between idolatry and ideology has
not escaped notice by other scholars. Moshe Halbertal and Avishai
Margalit construe Bacon as a late figure in a tradition of ideology-critique, whose prototype they suggest is the biblical critique of idolatry.
They argue that biblical Jews and Christians construe idolatry primarily
in moral terms as an interpersonal relationship between an anthropomorphic God and humans. On this view, Israel is God's wife; the church
is the bride and Jesus the bridegroom. As idolatry is the root metaphor
for betrayal or disloyalty within the marital relationship, so it is in the
God–human relationship. For biblical thinkers, idolatry is a moral
offense, a sexual sin, metaphorically speaking, within the God–human
relationship.[6] Postbiblical and modern thinkers, in contrast, construe
idolatry as a cognitive error defined primarily by anthropomorphism.

Halbertal and Margalit claim that Maimonides was the central figure
in the postbiblical shift from idolatry construed as adultery to idolatry as
the great cognitive error of anthropomorphism. This error is present
whenever God is construed as body with emotions and a psychic life, or
when God is conceived as a composite, complex entity. The great metaphysical errors of corporeality and multiplicity that are embodied in

anthropomorphism undermine God's perfection. This shift in the meaning of idolatry, they add, was part of a conceptual chain of intra- and then extra-religious criticism whose ironic consequence is the critique of religion itself as idolatry. They describe this chain as follows: "the criticism of idolatry by the monotheistic religions, the criticism of folk religion by the religious Enlightenment, the criticism of religion in general by the secular Enlightenment, and finally the criticism of ideology."[7] *Said's notion of Secular Criticism belongs to this fourth stage where religion is construed as idolatry and ultimately as ideology.* I will detail Said's view of imperialism and its relation to these themes later, after further detailing the religious history of ideology.

The first link in the conceptual chain of intra- and then extra-religious criticism is characterized by the appropriation of intrapagan criticism of folk religion by the monotheistic religions. This criticism centers around the mythological and imaginative character of folk religion, whose consequence is the distortion of truth. Christians extended this intrapagan criticism to all forms of paganism both folk and elite. They "flip the script," as it were, by applying the same criticism to the pagan "elite" that those critics applied to the pagan "folk." The critique of paganism led to intra-Jewish and intra-Christian critiques of folk religion, whose great error, as Maimonides held, was anthropomorphism. Halbertal and Margalit describe this intra-Jewish and intra-Christian criticism of the crude anthropomorphism of folk religion as the "religious Enlightenment." *Said would likely find this very notion oxymoronic. On his view, religion and enlightenment are antagonists. Religion-soaked tradition is what enlightenment delivers one from.* The authors of this study have a different view. According to them, there was a religious Enlightenment, and it did fall victim to its own logic when enlightened forms of monotheism themselves became the object of secular critique. This "boomerang effect," so to speak, constitutes the third link in the conceptual chain. The secular Enlightenment centers around the epistemic authority of tradition as such, which goes beyond the religious Enlightenment's ambivalent critique of traditional authority. Under the conditions of secular enlightenment, every form of authority becomes suspect and must justify itself before the bar of reason.

Bacon, I should note in returning to Larrain's account, belongs, with some ambiguity, to this third link in the conceptual chain of criticism. As representatives of this Baconian line of thinking, Larrain cites Hobbes, Locke, Helvetius, Holbach, and Diderot – the last three were important figures in the French Enlightenment. Easily the most radical site of Enlightenment, France produced a radical, anticlerical discourse of priestly deceit. The "deceitful priest," it was held, led a conspiracy against the people in the interest of the ecclesiastical aristocracy. In some respects, this perspective was two steps forward. But it also represents one step backward insofar as Bacon's accent on the systematic character of cognitive error or illusion is displaced by the more amorphous notion of conspiracy. This is not to overlook, as Larrain notes, Bacon's ambiguity on whether idolatry is a product of nature or nurture, whether it is immune to human artifice or not.[8] The secular Enlightenment complicates the epistemic picture drawn by the religious Enlightenment by tracing the sources of epistemic error or illusion, not only to imagination and tradition, but to the very structure of the will and cognition as Descartes and Kant argue respectively. By shifting the focus of critique from folk religion to religion in general, the secular Enlightenment paved the way for the explicit idea of religion as ideology. The secular Enlightenment provides a set of images in which religion is construed "as an alien belief in which man subordinates himself to the creatures of his illusional imagination and is thus alienated from his most vital interests."[9]

Marx is the most important figure (after Nietzsche) in the fourth stage of intra- become extra-religious critique. The young Marx[10] is the culmination and termination of the Fichte–Hegel–Feuerbach trajectory in German idealism. Central to German idealism is the notion that the Ego posits its other, the non-Ego, which is a precondition of consciousness.[11] According to Feuerbach, who developed this view most thoroughly, the conscious subject makes himself an object of reflection and becomes acquainted with himself in this way. Only through this process of self-othering (of externalizing consciousness or subjectivity), which then confronts the self as an object, is the self fully realized. We know ourselves or become self-conscious only through the external or objective embodiment of our subjective consciousness. Self-consciousness is nothing less than "being becoming objective to itself." Feuerbach does not hesitate to draw the obvious conclusion that the object of consciousness has no existence apart from self-consciousness. "Consciousness of God is self-consciousness, knowledge of God is self-knowledge. By his God thou knowest the man, and by the man his God; the two are identical."[12] If Feuerbach reduces Hegel's God – who comes to self-knowledge and self-realization in history by going out from himself (self-alienation) and returning to himself (reconciliation) – to the constructive–projective activities of the human mind, then Marx regards the consequences of that activity as idolatry. Religion represents an alienated or unauthentic relationship to the self, where aspects of the self are posited as an alien power to which one docilely submits. According to Marx, "Religion is indeed man's self-consciousness and self-awareness so long as he has not found himself or has lost himself again." Marx, at the height of his rhetorical skill, adds that "Religion is the sigh of the oppressed creature, the sentiment of a heartless world, and the soul of soulless conditions." Far from the manifestation of man's best self, religion is a form of debasement, human suffering, and, simultaneously, a protest against that suffering. For this reason, Marx calls for the "abolition of religion as the illusory happiness of men." Their real happiness demands that they "abandon their illusions" about a condition so bad that it can only be endured through illusions. "The criticism of religion is, therefore, the embryonic criticism of this vale of tears of which religion is the halo."[13] On Marx's view, and in the current jargon, religion is a social construct.

So far, I have provided an upside-down account of Marx's view. When viewed right-side up, his starting-point is labor. Marx criticizes what he regards as Feuerbach's inadequate critique of Hegel's abstract thought. Despite his call for a materialist critique, Feuerbach remains as preoccupied with the mental labor of man as Hegel is with that of Spirit. Both abstract from the materiality of the social relations to which Marx calls attention. As the process by which we reproduce ourselves and the material world, physical labor plays a central role in Marx's concept of alienation. Properly speaking, labor is the self-creation and creative self-expression of human subjectivity. Under this description, labor has a strong normative quality, and is essential to what humans are. Labor is not merely a means to an end – money, but an end in itself. For Marx, a purely instrumental conception of labor is a distortion of its constitutive value. When labor is conceived merely as a means, the worker is alienated from the process and product of her own labor, from her own life-activity and essential nature, or what Marx calls her "species being." The final result of this instrumental conception of labor is the destruction of human community, as humans are alienated from one another. The production of commodities involves the externalization and objectification (alienation) of the self in the product (or object) of production. This process, within a capitalist mode of production, entails the simultaneous impoverishment of the self, both materially and spiritually.[14]

Religion is the spiritual form of this impoverishment. As God is exalted, humans are debased. On this view, religion is a false god, a sham, the quintessential form of "false consciousness."[15] Ideology is idolatry in secular form. Now, admittedly, this is a strong reading; Marx does not explicitly develop the idolatry theme with this degree of self-consciousness. My reading refers more to the logical implications of his argument than to what he literally says. On this view, God is an idol that must be smashed. God has to die because the living God means living death for the worker. God feeds off the estranged, alienated labor, the objectified subjectivity of the worker. The objectification of God, there-fore, is the alienation of man. For Marx, there is no recuperation of alienated subjectivity as there is for Hegel and Feuerbach; alienation is a one-way street and the loss that the worker or the religious subject suffers is irretrievable.[16] Rather than liberating humans, religion debases, deforms, and impoverishes. As the quintessential form of idola-try, religion is an ideological subterfuge for, and a pathetically ineffective weapon against, the rule of private property and monopoly capital. If capitalism is the fetishism of commodities, then religion is the fetishism of the alienated subject. But, where Marx regards this fetishism as pathetically ineffective, Said regards it as socially and politically danger-ous. Imperialism, to strain the analogy just a bit, is the fetishism of the alienated subject *en masse.*

Halbertal and Margalit conclude their account arguing that modern or stage-four idolatry-critique has three strategic forms – replacement, extension, and inversion. Bacon and Marx enact the first strategy, with the former criticizing false ideas and the latter rejecting commodity fet-ishism as false worship.[17] Halbertal and Margalit's account suffers, however, when they fail to attribute a version of the epistemological problematic to Marx. Marx's critique of alienated labor, liberal eman-cipation, and commodity fetishism only makes sense in light of the dem-agogically driven (subjective) and bureaucratically driven (objective) mystification that capitalism produces. They need not accept vulgar notions of false consciousness to acknowledge that some form of misrec-ognition (systematic) or the desire that things be misrecognized (dema-gogic) is going on.[18] What I have been calling the political and the epistemological problematics are inextricable from Marx's scattered and conjunctive account of ideology. *This notion of ideology, which is key to Said's account of Orientalism, is equally germane to his account of imperialism.*

"Extension" is the second form of stage-four idolatry-critique, which is characterized by the extension of criticism to all possible candidates for worship. This could be described as Paul Tillich's "Protestant Principle" or H. Richard Niebuhr's "radical monotheism" gone amuck.

It resembles Nietzsche's analysis of the Christian will to truth, which eventually undermines Christian belief, culminating in the death of the Christian god himself. Halbertal and Margalit cite Wittgenstein as exemplary of this form of idolatry-critique. But I think that it is better described as radical skepticism, and Wittgenstein is no radical skeptic. This form of criticism is driven by a radical fear of being wrong and judging incorrectly (undecidability) and is most apropos of contemporary thinkers influenced by Derrida.

Halbertal and Margalit call the third form of idolatry-critique "inversion." They claim that this is the most radical form of modern iconoclasm, because it inverts the rank-order and normative coding of monotheism and polytheism, Judeo-Christianity and paganism. As they rightly note, Nietzsche celebrates the pagan gods as affirming the healthy, life-enhancing, heroic instincts of the strong, while denigrating the sickliness and degeneracy of the Jewish and the Christian gods.[19] What they do not mention is Nietzsche's enthusiastic celebration of the ancient Israelite god Yahweh and the Islamic god Allah. At the very least, this should qualify their claim that Nietzsche's inversion of traditional idolatry-critique necessarily celebrates pagan deities at the expense of monotheistic ones. Also in need of qualification is their claim that Nietzsche's inverted critique (the death of God) entails self-deification.[20] They arrive at this conclusion undoubtedly from a partial reading of *Thus Spoke Zarathustra*, although they do not cite this book in their notes. *Zarathustra* is often read as advocating the deification of the strong man, superman (*Übermensch*) who overcomes the dwarfish aspects of himself by murdering God. Others read this book as a cautionary tale that shows the impossibility of self-deification,[21] which is most likely to create "superdwarfs" and "superbuffoons." When read this way, Nietzsche's strong man, who realizes that God is the will to nothingness sanctified, knows the same thing as Marx's emancipated worker, who realizes that the deification of God is the alienation of man.

Marx's critique of ideology as fetishism is the intersection of Machiavelli's notion of religion as a ruse of princely power, Bacon's notion of idols as the falsification of consciousness, Hobbes' materialism, and the French Enlightenment's anticlericalism. The fourth link in the conceptual chain of idolatry-critique, as exemplified by Marx, represents a radicalization of the secular Enlightenment. At this point, the struggle against the public authority of religion has largely been won; hence Marx's famous claim: that "For Germany, the *criticism of religion* has largely been completed." But religion takes on new importance as a

metaphor for all forms of mystification – violent and nonviolent, passive and aggressive. If ideology is a form of collective illusion, mass self-alienation, or a make-believe world, then religion is its root metaphor. *Nationalism, class, race, and a host of other reifications – Said's religious–cultural effects – become the new idols of veneration.*

Secularization characterizes the fourth stage, as idolatry-critique becomes ideology-critique. Marx construes the object of critique as class ideology and Nietzsche construes it as slave morality. "Ideologies as interest-dependent social beliefs manipulate the masses by making use of the power of the imagination, as well as illusion-preserving institutions like the educational system and the church."[22] Halbertal and Margalit provide a fairly good description of Marx, but not of Nietzsche, for whom ideology or slave morality is an interest-dependent set of social beliefs that manipulate through *ressentiment* the "higher type" of man. Thus the best in a rank-ordered, aristocratic society is subjected to the worst. In either case, ideology serves one set of social interests at the expense of another. If we focus just on Marx, however, it is precisely in the cultural realm that ideology has it effects. *Culture is the site of Said's critique of imperialism.*

### SONS OF LIGHT AND SONS OF DARKNESS

Culture is a battlefield of competing interests, as both Marx and Arnold understood, but from which they drew different conclusions. Said uses military metaphors such as "theater" (of war) to describe the agonistic character of cultural elaboration. Culture is a site of identity formation, conflict, and contention, "where various political and ideological causes engage one another." Said is a Marxist-oriented thinker with Arnoldian sympathies. He attempts to marry Arnold and Marx: the idea of culture as the transfiguration of religion, and the idea of cultural critique as the criticism of religion. Said buttresses this notion of culture with Freud's theory of repression, according to which the return of repressed infantile sexuality is a form of neurosis, whose quintessential form is religion. Any doubt that this is what Said has in mind is dispelled when he adds: "In the formerly colonized world, these 'returns' have produced varieties of religious and nationalist fundamentalism" (*CAI* xii–xiii). These atavistic returns of religious and nationalist identity mirror the Manichaean propensities of the imperial cultures to which they are reactions. They are part of the same set of dispositions that allowed the imperial cultures of the West to maintain a Manichaean separation between great works of art such as *Mansfield Park* or *The Plague* and the slave and colonial cultures of which they were part.

Said gives two definitions of culture:

First of all it means those practices, like the arts of description, communication, and representation, that have relative autonomy from the economic, social, and political realms and that often exist in aesthetic forms, one of whose principal aims is pleasure.

Second, and almost imperceptibly, culture is a concept that includes a refining and elevating element, each society's reservoir of the best that has been known and thought, as Matthew Arnold put it in the 1860s. (*CAI* xii–xiii)

On Said's view, the Manichaean separation and reification of Marx's metaphorical distinction between "base" and "superstructure" (reality and appearance), between objects that act and agents acted upon, are what imperialism and its culture is all about. Culture is a system of representations that justify before and after the fact the bifurcation of imperialism, which in reality is a single complex ensemble, into a military and administrative "base" and an esthetic "superstructure." Said rejects this notion of culture. He argues, to the contrary, that culture is an ideological site that mystifies social relations, such as slavery and colonialism, by construing esthetic artifacts, like the European realistic novel, as autonomous from the complex ensemble of forces that produce real life. He rejects, to put a finer point on it, the isolated work of art canonized by bourgeois humanism and the vulgar Marxist construction of esthetic artifacts as "reflexes, echoes, phantoms, and sublimates" of real productive forces.[23] This Manichaean perspective is religious because it separates and moralizes, and is ideological because it mystifies and fetishizes. It is these religious–ideological practices that Said criticizes in *Culture and Imperialism*.

Some commentators object to the formulation "culture and imperialism," arguing that the "culture of imperialism" is more appropriate. I think that this argument is persuasive, but what it suggests beyond this barefaced claim is not. Said is hardly ignorant of imperialism as a cultural formation. The very suggestion that he is ignorant is bizarre, since Said is largely responsible for our sensitivity to this issue in the first place. We should not be misled, by an unhappy verbal formulation, to think otherwise. Knowledge of imperialism as culture is the backbone of his critique of imperialism, which is an experience so vast and yet so detailed, whose cultural dimensions are so crucial: "that we must speak of overlapping territories, intertwined histories common to men and women, whites and non-whites, dwellers in the metropolis and on the peripheries, past as well as present and future; these territories and histories can only be seen from the perspective of the whole of secular human history" (*CAI* 61).

Instead of this secular vision, what Said discovers beneath the comparative literary project of Erich Auerbach and other high cultural humanists and beneath contemporary critical theory is a common religious model, a Manichaean model. He traces this model back to the founding religious sources of Western culture: to the Church and to the Holy Roman Empire that guaranteed, in a curious way, "the integrity of the core European literatures," and he traces it, still deeper, to the Christian Incarnation from whose idea "Western realistic literature as we know it emerges." In its idealist, unsystematically Hegelian version, this notion of literary culture obscured the connection between its idealist historicism and the concrete reality of the current imperial world map (*CAI* 44–45, 47–48). Simultaneously, the movement of the Hegelian Spirit (the development of self-conscious reason) was identified with certain geographies, with Western space, European lands. A distinction was made between geographies of light and geographies of darkness, the enlightened nations and the dark continent. The Spirit moved from East to West, while leaving some cultural geographies in utter darkness.

Said draws on Gramsci's *Some Aspects of the Southern Question* to make sense of these geographies of East and West, light and dark. Gramsci, he claims, is a spatial and geographical thinker as is shown by his frequent use of words such "as 'terrain,' 'territory,' 'blocks,' and 'region.'" He finds the political issues that Gramsci grapples with in *The Southern Question* relevant to his critique of the Manichaean disposition in prominent forms of Western thought. Gramsci wants to make sure that important social relations are not obscured; thus he explicitly connects the poverty of southern Italy, with its vast labor pool of unemployed and underemployed workers, to the exploitative economic policies of the north. The histories of the two regions are discrepant, but they overlap in basic ways. Similarly, Said connects "the development of comparative literature and the emergence of imperial geography," and he goes on to connect this imperial geography to progressive movements and to contemporary critical theory. Thus the Manichaeanism of the women's and the working-class movements, which were progressive on their issues but enthusiastic supporters of the American empire. Thus the Manichaean blindness of contemporary theorists. "To read most cultural deconstructionists, or Marxists, or new historicists is to read writers whose political horizon, whose historical location is within a society and culture deeply enmeshed in imperial domination." But few seem to notice or to make critical allowances for it. They see representation as problematic, but rarely "put it in its full political context, a context that is primarily imperial" (*CAI* 49–53, 56–57). Against this Manichaean perspective, Said advocates a *contrapuntal* perspective, which connects what Manichaeanism would put asunder. This effort to connect, over against the religious desire to separate, is what Said calls secular interpretation.

Said begins his secular interpretation with the common-sense notion of culture as something other than the ugly thing that Joseph Conrad said that it was, only to undermine that common sense and underscore Conrad's view. Said focuses less on military conquest, territorial acquisition, and colonial administration than on attitude, disposition, and imagination. Following Raymond Williams' idea of a "structure of feeling,"[24] Said speaks of a "structure of attitude and reference." In this regard, he is most interested in English, French, and American "structures," because of their projective, geographically far-flung, and globalizing imagination. Said describes his method early in the book. He begins with the proposition that Western imperialism created one world, undermining, before the fact, Manichaean conceptions of Western and non-Western cultures. Their histories, he argues, are intertwined and overlapping; so he employs a contrapuntal method that examines these cultures together and not as autonomous subjects that can be understood discretely. This he hopes will make the "politics of blame" and the "politics of confrontation," as exemplified by the Gulf War, less likely (*CAI* xvi–xvii, 18–19).

Said returns to Joseph Conrad, the subject of his dissertation and first book,[25] to illustrate the contrapuntal approach. From Conrad's novella, *Heart of Darkness*, Said derives two visions of the imperial process, two possible arguments about the nature and meaning of the "old imperial enterprise." On one view, imperialism is a thoroughly Western-centered event; this vision is omnifocal, but strictly European and American in perspective. Here Westerners tell a story to themselves about themselves, where their former colonies, now free from official domination, are the objects of Europe's imperial desires. These desires are represented not only in Western constructions of its former colonies as markets, but also "as locales on the ideological map over which they continue to rule morally and intellectually." Such desire is a trace of the imperial past in the postcolonial present. As exemplary of that desire, Said quotes Saul Bellow's aggressive and crude invocation of Western superiority: "Show me the Zulu Tolstoy." This first of "two visions in *Heart of Darkness*," he argues, obscures and conceals the intertwined histories and overlapping territories of the West and its other. The second vision, in contrast, is ambivalent, less certain, more conscious of the contingency of the impe- rial enterprise. Even if the subject of this vision could not imagine an alternative to imperialism, to European domination of the non-Western world, it does allow Conrad's "later readers to imagine something other than an Africa carved up into dozens of European colonies, even if, for his own part, he had little notion of what that Africa might be" (*CAI* 20, 25–26).

Said suggests that there is a connection between "the discourse of resurgent empire," an outgrowth of Conrad's first vision in *Heart of Darkness*, and an ideological shift within the domain of high theory. Hand in hand with a resurgence of imperial desire were Jean-François Lyotard and Michel Foucault's disenchantment with narratives of emancipation. "After years of support for anti-colonial struggles in Algeria, Cuba, Vietnam, Palestine, Iran, which came to represent for many Western intellectuals their deepest engagement in the politics and philosophy of anti-imperialist decolonization, a moment of exhaustion and disap- pointment was reached." Said does not draw a causal connection between the two developments, but he clearly thinks that they are con- nected, part of the same event, the same historical conjuncture (*CAI* 27). On Said's view, the disenchantment of Western intellectuals with narra- tives of emancipation is the other side of the nostalgia for empire.

He enlists Salman Rushdie, who marshals George Orwell and Samuel Beckett, to illustrate the second line of vision in *Heart of Darkness*. This second narrative line suggests a different notion of imperialism as non- Eurocentric, nontotalizing, and profoundly secular. In this vision, Conrad's intellectual honesty outruns his prejudice as he accents, despite himself, realities inaccessible to the imperial gaze. I say despite himself advisedly, because Said also suggests that this honesty is self-conscious and intentional. "Conrad's way of demonstrating this discrepancy between the orthodox and his own views of empire is to keep drawing attention to how ideas and values are constructed (and deconstructed) through dislocations in the narrator's language." Here Said refers to Conrad's narrators as self-conscious, reflective, anxiety-ridden witnesses to European imperialism. Conrad constructs an unstable, discrepant vision of imperialism where things are not always as they appear or as Europeans represent them, where other representations are possible. This vision permits us to see imperialism in all of its benevolent and cruel complexity, as an ensemble of historically intertwined but discrepant experiences (*CAI* 27–31). The first vision in *Heart of Darkness* represents the dominant, asymmetrical view, where the history of colonial territories is merely the history of imperial intervention. On this view, "colonial undertakings were marginal and perhaps even eccentric to the central activities of the great metropolitan cultures." This vision constructs the West, in a Hegelian fashion, as the supersubject of history, shedding light on the dark places of people without history (*CAI* 35). The second vision is a comparative or contrapuntal exploration of imperialism as the overlapping but discrepant experiences of Western and non-Western peoples. Said's analysis builds on this second (secular) vision in *Heart of Darkness*. This vision legitimizes a non-Manichaean interpretation of imperialism, from which the common horizon of ideas such as the canon, *Weltliteratur*, nationality, race, colonialism, and liberation become visible. This contrapuntal vision holds the metropole and its geographically distant colonies in view simultaneously.

Perhaps no example of this contrapuntal, secular mode of interpretation has generated more controversy than Said's reading of Jane Austen's *Mansfield Park*. Austen is pivotal for Said's argument, and in turn, is central to my interpretation of religious discourse as a constitutive feature of Said's intellectual structure of attitude and reference. Religious discourse is to Said's analysis of imperialism as Antigua is to Austen's vision of *Mansfield Park*. On its face, this may sound like a preposterous claim, but I think that it is no more preposterous than, and just as illuminating as, Said's analysis of *Mansfield Park*. Since my analysis is in symbiosis with Said's account, what I think will only emerge as I read Said reading Austen.

Said's basic claim is straightforward. The peace, harmony, and domestic tranquility of the factual and the fictional Mansfield Park depend on the cruelties of slave-based sugar production in Antigua – they depend on each other. The colonial economy mirrors the gender dynamics of the domestic economy.[26] "Austen sees what Fanny does as a domestic or small-scale moment in space that corresponds to the larger, more openly colonial movements of Sir Thomas, her mentor, the man whose estate she inherits." According to Said, Austen was fully aware of the material relationship between the calm splendor of the English place, such as Mansfield Park, and Caribbean sugar plantations, where slavery was not abolished until the 1830s (*CAI* 89). Fanny Price's bourgeois life style and the life of anonymous Antiguan slaves under the cruel whip of the slave-driver are part of a single reality. Said's contrapuntal reading is designed to make explicit what is often implicit in the English realistic novel, that is, a "structure of attitude and reference" that presupposes as ordinary and everyday English overseas colonial possessions. Though aware of this connection, it is not something that Austen need think about too much; again, it is part of her "prejudice," background assumptions, the common sense that makes possible the factual and the fictional Mansfield Park.

On this point, Michael Steffes[27] demurs. He disputes Said's claim that we should read *Mansfield Park* as resisting or avoiding its Antiguan connection, but ultimately failing because of its own "formal inclusiveness, historical honesty, and prophetic suggestiveness" (*CAI* 96). He disputes, in short, the claim that Austen's passing reference to Antigua is a Freudian "slip of the pen." Far from expressing something she wished to repress and conceal, Austen's reference to Antigua is self-conscious, an intentional act that is central to what she wants to say. In this heavily documented essay, Steffes shows how wide-spread antislavery sentiment was in Austen's England, the preponderance of the evidence for her personal opposition to slavery, and the obvious irony in her invocation of slavery. What Austen wants to say by invoking slavery in Antigua, and here Steffes agrees with Peter Smith, is that "*Mansfield Park* rests upon a symbolic equivalence established between the forced labour of African cane-cutters and that invisible figure who stands in the margin of every page Jane Austen wrote, the unmarried gentlewoman who has no money of her own."[28] Austen, then, cannot be read as supporting slavery or of being indifferent.[29] This argument, however, misses the point, which is not that Austen supported slavery, but that she represents through her novel a set of dispositions and attitudes that were constitutive of the latter age of empire.

Referring to what reading Austen entails as attending to the world "outside" the novel, Said remarks: "But all these things having to do with the outside brought in seem unmistakably there in the suggestiveness of her allusive and abstract language" (*CAI* 92). This is precisely the argument that I make for the place of religious discourse in Said's analysis of imperialism – for that matter, in the whole of his critical work. The allusive and suggestive use of "missionary," "evangelical," and "errand into the wilderness" show how religious ideas are constitutive of his analysis of imperialism.

Said's analysis of *Mansfield Park* opens many lines of inquiry, which I cannot pursue. But looking backward and forward, I can say more about the importance of Said's interpretation, which I propose to turn back on him. *Looking backwards*, we see the centrality of *Mansfield Park* to Said's claim that the British realistic novel constructs an imperial "structure of attitude and reference." This structure, as I suggested earlier, is an instance of the "geographical imagination," where "the facts of empire are associated with sustained possession, with far-flung and sometimes unknown spaces, with eccentric or unacceptable human beings, with fortune-enhancing or fantasized activities like emigration, money-making, and sexual adventure" (*CAI* 64). Having discerned this structure, Said describes the first of its fourfold interpretive consequences, namely, "an unusual organic continuity" between earlier British novels such as *Mansfield Park* and later novels such as *Heart of Darkness*. The connective tissue of these earlier and later novels is imperialism. Said denies the claim that this view commits him to the notion that novels have "legislative or direct political authority." They are not, as he puts it, either frigates or bank drafts, but esthetic artifacts, whose political implications are highly mediated and heterogeneous (*CAI* 73). Here and elsewhere, he rejects crudely reductionistic arguments, where esthetic merit is adequately accounted for through the cultural studies language of "production," by situating himself between romantic and antiromantic accounts of esthetics.

Said concludes that, by the mid-nineteenth century, novelists could not "ignore the vast overseas reach of British power." Thus the fourth interpretive consequence of the British "structure" is an anti-idealistic account of how novels relate to the exercise of power and privilege at home and abroad. Said rejects the notion that this connecting structure can be found "outside the novels themselves, which means that one gets the particular, concrete experiences of 'abroad' only in individual novels." This means that critics cannot merely "summarize and judge"; they have to carefully analyze "works whose paraphrasable content they might regard as politically and morally objectionable" (*CAI* 76).

From Said's account, I draw several conclusions. Austen's *Mansfield Park*, with its vague allusions to empire, is part of the same structure of attitude and reference that produced the eerie realism of Conrad's *Heart of Darkness*. Her novel precedes the "scramble for Africa" that defined the classic age of empire, while his novel is contemporaneous with it. Both novels, and all cultural artifacts, must be read with attention to what they include and exclude. These novels did not produce imperialism, but imperialism is unimaginable without them. Imagine no *Kim*, no *Heart of Darkness* and now, after Said, no *Mansfield Park*. Finally, I discern an argument about "a complex ideological configuration underlying" imperialism and the narrative authority of the realistic novel. Said is no advocate of the simpleminded critique of narrative, so fashionable in some circles, as his argument for Enlightenment narratives of emancipation shows. What he criticizes here is a particular construction of narrative: narrative as Christian triumphalism, a quasi-Hegelian narrative with Europe as history's subject and Europe's colonies and former colonies as objects. He argues that this narrative authority helped consolidate, refine, and articulate imperial authority, by constructing and investing social space in particular ways. By imagining geographically distant places as imperial prospects, they facilitated the colonizing, populating, and depopulating of actually existing territories. Again, as Said notes, this structure of attitude and reference (where spatial differentiation is always moralized and the power to narrate is an imperial prerogative) is part of a trajectory, an "imperial imaginary" that precedes the classic age of empire.

*Looking forward*, beyond *Mansfield Park*, which he privileges in describing the imperial structure of attitude and reference, Said explores the presence or absence of a French analogue. He does so while further elaborating his account of culture and imperialism. Said does not find a substantial French analogue to the British structure until after the mid-nineteenth century, which is not to say that there was not an "infrastructure" of attitude and reference. This infrastructure centers on Napoleon's imperial escapades, which fed the French romantic spirit and enabled an emerging "disciplinary order" dominated by "archeology, linguistics, historiography, Orientalism, and experimental biology" (*CAI* 99). The important point here is that French arts and sciences, as Rousseau would put it, were enabled by Napoleon's imperial adventures, especially in Egypt. This helps to illuminate Said's reading of a particular cultural artifact, Verdi's Egyptian opera. According to Said, *Aida* "embodies, as it was intended to do, the authority of Europe's version of Egypt at a moment in nineteenth-century history." It reveals what it tries hard to exclude, namely, the colonial context that is constitutive of "its commission and composition." Read contrapuntally, "*Aida* reveals a structure of reference and attitude, a web of affiliations, connections, decisions, and collaborations, which can be read as leaving a set of ghostly notations in the opera's visual and musical text" (*CAI* 125).

Said follows the same interpretive vein when assessing Albert Camus' novels and Rudyard Kipling's novel, *Kim*. As with Jane Austen, no matter how muted the reference, Camus' novels are clearly constituted by, and constitutive of, a French structure of attitude and reference. They are not merely anguished reflections on the human condition, but cultural interventions in "the contest between Algerian nationalism and French colonialism" (*CAI* 175). Accordingly, the murdered Arab in *The Stranger* and the deaths of countless Arabs in *The Plague* provide an anonymous stage for the dramatic engagements of Meursault, Rieux, and Tarrou. Camus displaces the reality of Arab deaths at the hands of French imperialists on to an anonymous biblical-like plague. Camus has his characters ask existential questions at the point where they should be asking socio-historical ones. He waxes metaphysical precisely at the point where more mundane accounts are available. Said might object to the vigor with which I have developed his views, but they are his views, and I think that he is right. A contrapuntal reading of Camus, therefore, would accent the geographical reality and imagination that circumscribe his novels and the way that they distill "the traditions, idioms, and discursive strategies of France's appropriation of Algeria." With Camus, Said concludes, a massive French "structure of feeling" receives its most exquisite and final articulation (*CAI* 184).

Said's reading of Kipling is interesting, especially when he connects "surveillance and control over India" with British love and fascination and with the esthetic and psychological pleasure that they derived. But this reading otherwise lacks the power of his readings of Austen and Camus. Kipling is so obvious, there is no power of surprise. And Said fails, at least in my view, to defamiliarize Kipling sufficiently so that he can be encountered anew. On my view, this is his least insightful and least persuasive reading. I agree with Said when he says that *Kim* is "a great [imperial] document of its historical moment," but not when he calls it "an aesthetic milestone," though a "milestone along the way to midnight August 14–15, 1947" it certainly was (*CAI* 161–162).

What did those whom Salman Rushdie calls "midnight's children" think of this document? How did they resist, oppose, and contest imperialism, the massive structures (English, French, and American) of attitude and reference that Said describes? In his first novel, *Midnight's Children*, Rushdie represents India on the verge of independence, which became effective at midnight 14 August 1947. By lending an ear to the voices of India's people and to the voices of other colonial peoples aspiring to national liberation, Said departs radically from *Orientalism*. *Culture and Imperialism* explores contrapuntally, as intertwined histories and overlapping events, the Western discourse of cultural imperialism and the "non-Western" resistance and opposition that it inspired. While Said limits his analysis to English, French, and American imperialism as he does in

*Orientalism*, his scope is much broader, including African, Asian, and colonial sites in the Americas. He also gives much-needed attention to Ireland, an important "white colony," and to Ireland's foremost "poet of decolonialization," William Butler Yeats. Poets of decolonialization precede the theorists of liberation in Said's account. Besides the Irish Yeats, Said cites Pablo Neruda (Chile), Amie Cesaire (Martinique), and Mahmoud Darwish (Palestine) as poets of decolonialization. From the very beginning, Said's account is disorienting – Yeats a poet of decolonialization? By beginning with Yeats, Said allows us to see colonialism and decolonialization in a new light. We see the intertextual traces of the Irishman Yeats, a poet of decolonialization, in the work of Chinua Achebe, an African novelist of decolonialization. With the help of Said we can see past Yeats' current canonical status as a great Western poet and see him anew, for the first time, as the critic of English imperialism that he was. And we see just how central Irish nationalism is to his critique.

These poets, Said emphasizes, are nationalists. But he wants to distinguish, though not absolutely, their nationalisms from the imperial nationalisms of the Western powers. If imperialism is the aggressive territorial expansion of nationalism,[30] then decolonialization is the recovery of lost territory. "The slow and often bitterly disputed recovery of geographical territory which is at the heart of decolonialization is preceded – as empire had been – by the charting of cultural territory" (*CAI* 209). This is an important point. What Said suggests is that a "counterstructure of attitude and reference," articulated in many cases by poets of decolonialization, was constitutive of anticolonial efforts. Again, these efforts took a nationalist form, as they had to under the constraints of European modernity, where power is articulated in national terms. These poets avoid nativism, as do most forms of nationalism during the decolonizing phase of anti-imperialism. They rejected absolute distinctions between colonizer and colonized and notions of a pristine precolonial identity. Even as they fight for control of territory, they know that their history and the colonizer's history are intertwined. Yeats, for example, avoids the nativist turn, at least before he became a fascist, when articulating the emancipatory aspirations of the Irish people, who were suffering under English rule. Yeats' contrapuntal construction of nationalist identity, along with those of the other poets of decolonialization, held at arm's length the nativism that would deform many postcolonial nationalisms.

The poets did not recognize and consciously resist nativism so much as they were customarily and habitually indisposed toward it. It fell to a theorist of liberation, Frantz Fanon, to point out the dangers of nativism. And nativism, on Said's view, is the eminent form of nationalism as religious–cultural effect. For the nativist, national identity is defined by the quest for pure essence and lost origins. Nativism is *millenarian* in that it looks backwards by looking forward to the time when a pristine, essential, precolonial, *prelapsarian* sense of peoplehood is restored. Nativism represents the *afterlife* of cultural imperialism in the postcolonial context. Said privileges Fanon's work in his account of theorists of liberation. This account begins with Fanon's rereading of Hegel's master–slave dialectic, proceeds through an account of the *Manichaeanism* of the colonial city, and culminates in a Marxist-derived critique of the national bourgeoisie. Fanon illustrates well the complexities and hybridity of decolonizing and postcolonial critics.

These critics are especially indebted to four decolonializing and post-colonial historians: C. L. R. James (*The Black Jacobins*), George Antonius (*The Arab Awakening*), Ranajit Guha (*A Rule of Property for Bengal*), and S. H. Alatas (*The Myth of the Lazy Native*). These historians provide a bridge, not necessarily chronological, between the poets of decolonialization, such as Yeats, and the theorists of liberation, such as Fanon. Their works, according to Said, represent "the voyage in," colonial intellectuals taking the case for decolonization and liberation from imperial domination into the metropolitan center, Europe's "heart of darkness." This voyage down the Congo River of the European imperial imagination, rewrites and reaccents Conrad's fictional voyage, shedding new light into a different kind of darkness. These works represent a "variety of hybrid cultural work" by intellectuals who recognize the intertwining and overlapping of their history and that of the metropolis. Their work is designed to command both the attentions of the colonial "periphery" and the metropolitan "center." This hybrid, contrapuntal perspective allows them to engage in severe criticism of Western imperialism without denying the commonalities that the imperial experience had wrought. In this way, their work is "fundamental to the cultural coalition now being built between anti-imperial resistance in the peripheries and oppositional culture of Europe and the United States" (*CAI* 261).

Said describes Fanon as the first major anti-imperialist theorist to recognize that orthodox nationalism follows the same path that imperialism created. While the imperialists appeared to cede authority to the nationalist bourgeoisie, in fact they really extended their own hegemony. To tell a simple national story, therefore, is to repeat, extend, and produce "new forms of imperialism." Fanon's great achievement in *The Wretched of the*

*Earth,* according to Said, "is first to represent colonialism and national-ism in their Manichaean contest, then to enact the birth of an indepen-dence movement, finally to transfigure that movement into what is in effect a trans-personal and trans-national force." As the most important theoretical practitioner of this culturally hybrid work, Fanon recognized how the Manichaeanism of colonial social space – the "clean, well-lighted European city and the dark, fetid, ill-lit casbah," can re-emerge and replicate along class, gender, and ethnic lines in the postcolonial city (*CAI* 223, 269–270, 273).

The word *Manichaean* dominates my account of Said's views of cultu-ral imperialism. Not surprisingly, I think that it would be wrong to say that Said uses this word absentmindedly. His use of this term is too self-assured for that, as casual and self-assured as Austen's passing reference to Antigua. My question is what does Manichaean mean and why is Said self-assured in his usage? There is nothing mysterious here: Manichaean refers to the ways of the Manichees, a religious community founded in the third century CE by the Persian-born Mani. But what is Said signify-ing when he uses the word? Why does he find this particular word so useful for describing the culture of imperialism?

Manichaeanism (and a cluster of formative myths and related tradi-tions) has several features that might provide answers to these questions, the most important being its radical dualism. This dualism is simultane-ously cosmological and ethical; it pertains to God and matter, light and dark, good and evil. Manichaeanism is an important example of what, for lack of a better term, we might call ancient Iranian national religios-ity. It was a late, eclectic development of a trajectory that included Zervanism, Zoroastrianism, Mandaism, and Gnosticism. All these tra-ditions presuppose some version of cosmic conflict between radically dualistic principles. The core myth is of Zervanian derivation and con-cerns the birth of cosmic twins called Ohrmazd or Good and Ahriman or Evil. Ahriman was first born and is described as black and evil-smelling, while Ohrmazd is fair and sweet-smelling. Their struggle for supremacy, as predestined, would eventually end with the triumph of Good over Evil. In Zoroastrianism, the cosmic struggle between Ohrmazd and Ahriman is reproduced. In Gnosticism, this cosmological distinction is associated with light and darkness, spirit and matter. These distinctions are constitutive of Manichaeanism and its reconfiguration of the core Zervanian myth.[31] Most of that reconfigured myth is not important for my purposes, but Manichaean eschatology, where the forces of light triumph over the forces of darkness, is important in making sense of Said's critique of imperialism as a religious, metaphysical, moralistic, and geographical act of imagination.

When viewed against the backdrop of this cursory description of Manichaeanism, Said's reference to Fanon's "clean, well-lighted European city and the dark, fetid, ill-lit casbah," takes on added significance. Imperialism creates on the concrete level of lived human experience geographies of light and dark. The symbolic becomes the literal, the virtual becomes actual, as a metaphysically conceived darkness is reproduced on the political level. Fanon, then, is Said's best example of an emancipatory nationalist, someone for whom nationalism is necessary but full of pitfalls. It is a transitory phase between imperial domination and national liberation, with national liberation defined ultimately and paradoxically as a postnationalist form of solidarity. Here at last, the god of nationalism is slain. Nationalism as religious–cultural effect and imperialism as Manichaean vision give way to a truly *secular* vision of human solidarity that binds "the European as well as the native together in a new non-adversarial community of awareness and anti-imperialism" (*CAI* 274).

Both retrospectively and prospectively, Said's entire critique of imperialism can be construed as referring to this underlying Manichaean vision. His call for a contrapuntal approach to the intertwined histories and overlapping territories of the culture of imperialism should be seen as a secular critique of this irreducibly religious view, where Manichaean dualism invests the geography of East and West in an invidious way with cosmological significance, and maps those differences in ethical terms. This dualism also allows Austen to refer absentmindedly to Antiguan slavery, and allows Camus to be untroubled by the anonymity of his Arab characters, whether they are murdered or taken by the plague. Said disrupts the economy of light and darkness, the religious and metaphysically derived conception of social space, and the ethical dualism that it sustains, by joining at the head and the hip, as it were, Ohrmazd and Ahriman.

### ENTHUSIASM AND THE PURITAN ERRAND

The idea of Manichaeanism also informs Said's analysis of postcolonial (which is not to say postimperial) culture. T. S. Eliot's complex reflections on past, present, and future, each anticipating, presupposing, and mutually determining the others, underscore Said's notion of cultural imperialism as the presence of the imperialist past in the postcolonial present.

According to Said, the culture of imperialism has left a residue of attitudes and historically informed reflexes that, under certain circumstances, uncritically propel "the Western powers into action against ex-colonial peoples." Said characterizes this imperial dynamic in terms of its "separating, essentializing, dominating, and reactive tendencies." What Said describes here is the atavistic irruption of those Manichaean-derived elements that are constitutive of Western imperial identity. This identity expresses itself, domestically, in reactionary cultural politics, which represent an atavistic recovery of the imperial moment – what Mircea Eliade calls sacred time. Said construes this moment as replicating Matthew Arnold's notion of culture and of dovetailing with Francis Fukuyama's triumphalist reading of American liberal democracy as the "end of history." Fukuyama is part of an interpretive tradition in which culture and humanistic study are constructed as "the recovery of the Judeo-Christian or Western heritage." In some versions, American heritage is ethnically cleansed of Native American and other forms of cultural contamination (*CAI* 36–37, 320).

Internationally, the elision and denial of the relationship between Western imperialism and its culture is reproduced in "Strident journalistic debates about decolonization, in which imperialism is repeatedly on record as saying, in effect, You are what you are because of us; when we left, you reverted to your deplorable state." Said describes these journalistic debates as strident, "right-ward-tending," rhetorics of blame. They separate what they designate as the Western ethos from the non-white, non-Jewish, and non-Christian, which they herd together under the rubric of non-Western, and demean as terroristic and second-rate. To define the West by attacking the non-Western is a virtue:

Self-definition is one of the activities practiced by all cultures: it has a rhetoric, a set of occasions and authorities (national feast, for example, times of crisis, founding fathers, basic texts, and so on), and a familiarity all its own. Yet in a world tied together as never before by travel, environmental and regional conflicts that can expand with tremendous speed, the assertion of identity is by no means a mere ceremonial matter. What strikes me as especially dangerous is that it can mobilize passions atavistically, throwing people back to an earlier imperial time when the West and its opponents championed and even embodied virtues designed not as virtues so to speak but for war. (*CAI* 25, 28, 35, 37)

Such rhetoric, Said argues, leads "inevitably to mass slaughter," to rhetorical if not literal slaughter. Thus the Gulf War. As I suggested in chapter 2, Said was greatly disturbed by the dispatch and conformity that characterized the American decision to go to war against Iraq during the Gulf Crisis of 1990 and 1991. The Gulf War underscores Said's claim that there is a residual imperialism that manifests itself reflexively and uncritically in military action by the Western powers against so-called Third World people. The historical roots of this phenomenon lie in the peculiarities of America's historically persistent self-image of moral exceptionalism. Even though the American government has an unbroken history of imperial intervention into so-called Third World countries from 1945 to 1967, and many others before and after this period, its official self-image is that of the guardian of freedom and democracy. On this view, American interventions were not expansionist, nor was America trying to shore up Europe's crumbling empire. On the contrary, America was acting in the interest of freedom and democracy as international guardian, regent, and godfather. This self-image, Said argues, complete with "*a sense of mission, historical necessity, and evangelical fervor*" (emphasis is mine), insulates the United States, at least in its official mind, from the charge of imperialism. The idea that United States intervention into the Gulf was an imperial venture was never given a serious hearing. Those who made such arguments were viewed as raving ideologues who deserved to be shunted aside and marginalized as the stooges and "crackpots" that they were. A scattered and largely ineffective protest against United States intervention barely raised any doubts for a significant segment of the American public. America's moral exceptionalism remained an unquestioned article of faith. From the Puritan errand into the wilderness to the Gulf War – excepting a brief period of doubt and introspection following the Vietnam War and an even briefer period after the Mexican War of 1840 – this sense of manifest destiny was unbroken.

Said mocks the solemn talk of "principles, morality, and right" that occurred in many media outlets during the Gulf Crisis and War. It barely succeeded in concealing American-style *realpolitik* – a naked act of power, in pursuit of geo-imperialist interests (*CAI* 293). But more than this was going on. The "nationalist psychosis" that Said describes – if not on both sides of the imperial divide, then surely on the Western one, which produced the Gulf War and was engendered by the politics of national identity – can be interpreted, within the limits of Said's assumptions, as a post-Arnoldian analogue of Protestant enthusiasm:

Historically the American, and perhaps generally the Western media have been sensory extensions of the main cultural context. Arabs are only an attenuated recent example of Others who have incurred the wrath of a stern White man, a kind of Puritan superego whose errand into the wilderness knows few boundaries and who will go to any lengths to make his points. (*CAI* 295)

I shall address Said's reference to stern White men, Puritan superegos, and errands into the wilderness in a moment. But surely Locke's critique of enthusiasm, mediated, perhaps, by Said's reading of Swift's *Tale of the Tub*, underlies this critique? Enthusiasm was a one-word description of the fervor and zeal of the nonconforming church in England. It was a fairly common term. In *Leviathan*, Hobbes traces enthusiasm to an excess of passion. He calls it a form of madness and compares it to intoxication, fever, and demonic possession, which is madness under another description.[32] On this view, enthusiasm is an extreme, demonically inspired form of false consciousness. In 1655, Meric Casaubon wrote *A Treatise Concerning Enthusiasm* and the following year Henry More wrote *Enthusiasm Triumphatus* (1656). Perhaps best known was Locke's 1690 critique of enthusiasm in chapter 19 of *An Inquiry Concerning Human Understanding*. In good empiricist fashion, Locke regards enthusiasm as the refusal of evidence, disregard for rational argument, and deference to the authority of "inner light" – that is, an intuitive, God-given sense of the truth. Locke asks "Who can reasonably expect arguments and conviction from him in dealing with others, whose understanding is not accustomed to them in his dealing with himself?" He suggests that enthusiasm is a private form of revelation, "which, laying by reason, would set up revelation without it. Whereby in effect it takes away both reason and revelation, and substitutes in the room of them the ungrounded fancies of a man's own brain, and assumes them for a foundation both of opinion and conduct." Enthusiasm is a product of intellectual laziness, an unwillingness to engage in the tedium of strict reasoning. Neither reasonable nor revelatory, enthusiasm is anti-intellectualism in its purist form. "Their minds being thus prepared, whatever groundless opinion comes to settle itself strongly upon their fancies, is an illumination from the Spirit of God." Nor is error possible. "Reason is lost upon them, they are above it: they see the light infused into their understandings, and cannot be mistaken . . . they feel the hand of God moving them within, and the impulses of the Spirit, and cannot be mistaken in what they feel."[33]

This is the intellectual environment in which Swift wrote. He associated enthusiasm with self-induced madness, Dionysian sexuality, Gnostic heresy, and violence, all of which he saw as human artifice, a "mechanical operation." The artificial nature of religious enthusiasm is the primary theme of Swift's essay "The Mechanical Operation of the Spirit." Swift echoes Locke when he describes enthusiasm as neither divine inspiration nor demonic possession, nor "the product of natural causes, the effect of strong imagination, spleen, violent anger, fear, grief,

pain, and the like." On the contrary, in enthusiasm he discerns the bourgeois spirit of acquisitiveness. Enthusiasm, he says, anticipating Weber's
*Protestant Ethic,* is a trade. Working out one's "soul-salvation" looks a lot
like making money. Perhaps this reference to commerce refers to more
than money. Perhaps it refers to the trade in human bodies and their
pleasures? These questions are not far off the mark insofar as Swift's language suggests that enthusiasm is a collective orgasm.[34] Sexual impro-
priety was a standard criticism of dissenters. The ecstatic character of
Puritan liturgies, it was thought, suggested sexual orgy. Dissenters were
often suspected of strange and perverse sexual practices, which in turn
were associated with witchcraft. Swift assumed that there was a connection between the enthusiasm of the Puritan Revolution and devil
worship. In other words, he construes enthusiasm, as had his patron Sir
William Temple, as part of the same set of anxieties that produced a
witchcrazed society – the last such craze had occurred only two decades
before Swift's birth.[35]

This detour into the views of Locke and Swift is not aimless wander-
ing. On the contrary, Said has a high regard for Swift who exemplifies
the cultural anarchy that Said commends. Swift helps to illuminate
Said's self-image and his critique of imperialism as enthusiasm, a religious effect of culture. According to Said, Swift was "an extraordinarily
important organic intellectual because of his closeness to real political
power." His work shows a remarkable opposition to war, "conquest,
colonial oppression, religious factionalism, the manipulation of minds
and bodies, schemes for projecting power on nature, on human beings,
and on history, the tyranny of the majority, monetary profit for its own
sake, the victimization of the poor by a privileged oligarchy" (*WTC*
83–84). Said's praise of Swift, among other things, should be viewed in
relation to Swift's low regard for Calvinist enthusiasm and his anticolo-
nialism. Swift thought that Calvinism was a murderous creed, whose
advocates always committed villainy and cruelty "under the disguise of
religion and long prayers." He is just as crude in his description of
Calvinism as he thinks Calvinism is gross in its enthusiastic practices.
When referring to "Jack," the personification of Protestant enthusiasm
in *Tale of the Tub,* Swift notes his roguish behavior: how, when Jack had a
trick to play, would fall to his knees, lift-up his eyes, and pray as if in the
midst of a kennel. Those who knew better would get as far away as possible, knowing full well of his crude practice of "pissing" into the eyes
and spattering with mud curious and unsuspecting strangers.[36]

Said's reference to evangelical fervor presupposes all of this and undergirds his reference to "the wrath of a stern White man, a kind of Puritan superego whose errand into the wilderness knows few boundaries and who will go to any lengths to make his points." Behind Said's casual invocation of the "errand into the wilderness" lies a rich history of Puritan scholarship: from the monumental work of Perry Miller to the revisionary work of Scavan Bercovitch. These scholars refer repeatedly to the Puritan colonizers' self-image. They were the new children of Israel, conquering a new land of Canaan, where they would establish a New Jerusalem. This recalls what Said said in his dispute with Michael Walzer: "There is no Israel without the conquest of Canaan and the expulsion or inferior status of Canaanites – then as now." In the same vein, there is no America, no American Israel or New Jerusalem, without the conquest and extirpation of new world Canaanites. Thus the evocative power of the Puritan errand into the wilderness – Said's preferred trope for dispossession and empire.

# CHAPTER 5

# The responsibilities of the secular critic

In "Speaking the Truth to Power," the fifth of his six-part Reith Lectures, *Representations of the Intellectual*, Said poses the following question:

Is the intellectual galvanized into intellectual action by primordial, local, instinctive loyalties – one's race, or people, or religion – or is there some more universal and rational set of principles that can and perhaps do govern how one speaks and writes? In effect I am asking *the* basic question for the intellectual: how does one speak the truth? What truth? For whom and where? (*RI* 8)

Said has always been something of a Trojan horse in the poststructural-ist–postmodernist city. This passage is only one place among many where he expresses his suspicion of those who are suspicious of truth, of those who describe themselves as poststructuralist or postmodernist. Said is a high modernist, who is neither poststructuralist nor antipoststructuralist. He is ambivalent – an in-house critic, an exiled admirer. While skeptical of naïve notions of truth he is equally skeptical of the notion that truth is "endlessly deferred" or the notion that truth and power are the same thing or that the former is a mask for the latter. By proposing to speak truth to power, Said signals his rejection of a particular epistemological and ethical construction of truth, where Descartes' certainty and Nietzsche's radical skepticism are two sides of a single misunderstanding. But he takes a false step when he places universality and rationality in opposition to those things that he construes as "instinctive," especially religion. This step obscures the affinities between his notion of intellec-tual responsibility and what Nietzsche describes as the outcome of a two-thousand-year-old Christian tradition of truth-telling. I explore this affiliation through a triangular analysis of Said, Noam Chomsky, and Michel Foucault. From Said's current views, I work backwards through the Chomsky–Foucault debate of the 1970s, to Nietzsche's Christian-derived notion of promise-making and truth-telling. This trajectory partly underwrites Said's notion of intellectual responsibility.

## THE TRUTH-TELLING VOCATION OF THE INTELLECTUAL

"It is the responsibility of intellectuals to speak the truth and to expose lies." So writes Chomsky. That intellectuals have such responsibility may not be so obvious, given Martin Heidegger's 1933 Rectorship Address, where he wrote "that 'truth is revelation of that which makes a people certain, clear, and strong in its action and knowledge.'" This is the only kind of "truth," on Heidegger's view, "that one has a responsibility to speak."[1] Twenty years before it again became a scandalous affair in Western intellectual circles, Chomsky had already "sniffed out" Heidegger's foul air and denounced his collaboration with National Socialism. He opposed the conception of truth that Heidegger affirmed and that post-Heideggerian thinkers such as Foucault elaborated. This is a point to which I shall return.

To restate and slightly paraphrase Chomsky, the role of the intellectual is to speak truth to power and to expose lies. It matters little that these were Chomsky's words before they were Said's. They express succinctly Said's view of the intellectual's responsibility – to confront powerful liars with the truth and to expose their lies to public scrutiny. This is a risky business to be sure, but the responsibility of the intellectual nevertheless. Said's intellectual attempts to break down "stereotypes and reductive categories" that limit thought and communication. Cynical dismissals of the universal (always a sign of disappointed hopes and suppressed sentimentality) have no place in this intellectual's vocation. Nor is there a place for Pyrrhonic skepticism with its contemporary French accent, which often construes itself, against the *naïveté* of mitigated (or healthy-minded) skepticism, as a higher form of sophistication. The intellectual takes the risk of universality (knowing full well that he might be wrong and that his hands might get dirty), treating like cases alike, going "beyond the easy certainties provided us by our background, language, nationality." Under this description, universality is a radical form of iconoclasm[2] that abjures the worship of any god as idolatry (*RI* xi, xiv). Said's intellectual is something more and something less than Antonio Gramsci's intellectual, and should not be confused with, although she may very well be, an academic. The responsible intellectual of which he speaks is a marginal figure, who lives on the borders of power and respectability. An expatriate in her own country, she lives in internal exile. She is an "amateur" rather than a "professional." Serving no god, she speaks truth to power and exposes lies.

That Said's intellectual is more and less than Gramsci's intellectual becomes clear when we compare it to the intellectual that Julien Benda describes in *The Treason of the Intellectuals*. Benda distinguishes between "clerks" and "laymen." Laymen are practical men and women of affairs, the masses. They are realists and materialists. In contrast, clerks are intellectuals, who pursue art, science, or metaphysical speculation while disregarding practical, mundane, and worldly affairs. They are not interested in obtaining material advantage, as their "kingdom is not of this world." Clerks are idealists. They stand above the pandemonium of ordinary life and, through their transcendental witness to truth and justice, act to constrain class, racial, and national passions, which are the religion of the masses. The clerks began, however, "to play the game of political passions" toward the end of the nineteenth century; this was an act of treason, the betrayal of their sacred vocation. Not only did they play the game, but the game became their work, as the prevailing winds of political propaganda determined what they wrote. Indeed, propaganda insinuated itself into the very principles of the clerks. Following the racial, class, and nationalist passions of the laymen, the clerks denounced universal values and the transcendence of spirit.[3] The effort to put forth their "principles as valid in the practical order of things, as reconcilable with the safeguarding of the sword's conquests" was an act of betrayal. For:

As soon as the "clerk" claims that he does not disregard the interests of the nation or of the established classes, he is inevitably beaten, for the very good reason that it is impossible to preach the spiritual and the universal without undermining the institutions whose foundations are the possession of the material and the desire to feel distinct from others. A true "clerk" (Renan) says excellently: "The mother-country is a worldly thing; the man who wants to play the angel will always be a bad patriot." To be strong, and to avoid transgressing his principles or undermining the institutions that he supports, the clerk must self-consciously declare his principles: that *the grandeur of his teaching lies precisely in this absence of practical value, and that the right morality for the prosperity of the kingdoms, which are of this world, is not his, but Caesar's.* When he takes up this position, the "clerk" is crucified, but he is respected, and his words haunt the memory of mankind."[4]

The measure of Benda's intellectuals is their willingness to "risk being burned at the stake, ostracized, or crucified" (*RI* 3–7). Benda's expectations are strenuous and, perhaps, unrealistic. But buried in his combative, though conservative, rhetoric is "this figure of the intellectual as a being set apart, someone able to speak the truth to power, a crusty, eloquent, fantastically courageous and angry individual for whom no worldly power is too big and imposing to be criticized and pointedly taken to task" (*RI* 8). Said points to Benda's choice of a religious term "*clerics*" to describe intellectuals. In choosing this term, Benda reaccented a word that, in earlier usage, had a more restricted meaning. "It referred specifically to those churchmen who studied in monasteries as monks during the Middle Ages. Knowing how to read and write, and avowedly searching for truth, they were the intellectuals of their day."[5] Perhaps, with this knowledge in mind, Said mentions the fact that Benda's description of the intellectual's vocation presupposes the religious distinction between clergy and laity, but moves on much too quickly. Perhaps he senses a problem for his secular account of intellectual responsibility? Or maybe he is insensitive to what Benda acutely senses: that the Platonic–Christian idea of knowledge and virtue lies behind the notion of intellectual responsibility that Benda advocates. This is the same tradition to which Said, like Nietzsche, claims an ambivalent allegiance.

Said construes Gramsci and Benda as representing the extremes when it comes to identifying intellectuals as a class. For Gramsci, an intellectual is anyone who works with ideas. While everyone has intellectual capacities, not everyone functions as an intellectual.[6] In contrast, Benda describes the intellectual as a member of a knowledge and moral elite. Said recounts Gramsci's distinction between traditional and organic intellectuals, those who view themselves as autonomous from the prevailing power relations (or hegemony), and those who seek to elaborate the current hegemony or create a new one. As Said notes, intellectuals can be organic to reactionary or progressive groups, groups that elaborate the status quo or insurgent groups. In either case, organic intellectuals are partisans of a particular cause, which makes them very different from Benda's intellectuals who view themselves as "nonpartisans," serving pure truth and justice.

Said distances himself from Benda, somewhat, when he claims that Gramsci's notion of the intellectual is "much closer to the reality than anything Benda gives us, particularly in the late twentieth century." Most intellectuals can fairly be described as functionaries of various types: as academics, journalists, managers, government bureaucrats, and so on. Said does not view this development favorably; not so much, I believe, because such functionaries are not essential to a modern, complex society, but because of the narrow, "squint-eyed," and local character of those kinds of intellectuals. While Foucault speaks approvingly of this sort of intellectual who, with Robert Oppenheimer in mind, he calls "specific intellectuals" (*RI* 8–10), Said is far from impressed. He refers to such intellectuals disparagingly as "professional." He does not say, but one can imagine him saying, that the specific intellectual cuts a poor figure in comparison to universal intellectuals like Jean-Paul Sartre, whose time according to Foucault's Delphic pronouncement is over.[7]

Against this oracular pronouncement, Said asserts the following: "it is the intellectual as a representative figure that matters – someone who visibly represents a standpoint of some kind, and someone who makes articulate representations to his or her public despite all sorts of barriers." This includes the barrier posed by the arrogant and false modesty of those intellectuals who, having discovered that representation is often bad, conclude that it is necessarily (metaphysically) bad. Said will have none of the still too fashionable notion that representation is bad, and that we cannot and should not speak for others.[8] Nor is he embarrassed by the romantic undertones of the idea of the intellectual as a witness, whose vocation is to publicly testify to the truth (*RI* 12–13). "The purpose of the intellectual's activity is to advance human freedom and knowledge." Said holds to this unfashionable view, despite Jean-François Lyotard's claim that the heroic ambitions associated with modernity's "grand narratives of emancipation and enlightenment" are *passé*, an occasion for incredulity. Lyotard's bizarre use of Wittgenstein's notion of "language games," which supposedly have replaced grand narratives and their universal values of truth and freedom, does not impress Said. "I've always thought that Lyotard and his followers are admitting their own lazy incapacities, perhaps even indifference, rather than giving a correct assessment of what remains for the intellectual a truly vast array of opportunities despite postmodernism." Despite postmodernism, governments continue to oppress people, grave injustices still occur, and intellectuals are still susceptible to the allures of prestige and power and, thus, continue to betray their secular calling (*RI* 17–18). As this line of argument should suggest, Said's intellectual is a hybrid figure: part Gramscian organic intellectual, part Bendian cleric.[9] If we construe Lyotard as a representative of the Foucauldian line of thinking when it comes to the intellectual, then Said is clearly a representative of the Chomskian line.

## SPEAKING TRUTH TO FOUCAULT'S POWER

In 1971, Noam Chomsky and Michel Foucault met before a Dutch television audience and debated the question "Human Nature: Justice or Power?" The organizer and moderator of the debate was a Dutch philosopher named Fons Elders. The Chomsky–Foucault debate was the third in a series of one-time encounters between prominent thinkers: A. J. Ayer and Arne Naess, Karl Popper and John Eccles, Noam Chomsky and Michel Foucault, Leszek Kolakowski and Henri Lefebvre. The transcripts of the debates were later published as *Reflexive Water: The Basic Concerns of Mankind*. To read the transcripts of this debate more than a quarter of a century later, and after what Chomsky and Foucault have come to signify in critical circles, is enlightening. What are often cited as important differences between the two are not nearly as important as some commentators suggest. Where their differences matter is less on the philosophical issue of human nature than on the political question of utopia. This difference might be formulated as "What is the political significance of utopian ideas in subverting undesirable forms of hegemony?" This is not to suggest that the philosophical and the political issues are not related, but that practical politics is more important than abstract theory. In what is admittedly a "strong" reading, I construe Chomsky as inferring his notion of universal human nature from his political commitments. In contrast, Foucault derives his political commitments from an unacknowledged notion of human nature. I do not take Foucault's expressed suspicion of the idea of human nature as a serious obstacle to this reading. Just because someone says that they do not hold certain views (such as a working notion of human nature) does not mean that they do not have such a notion and that one cannot discern in their work assumptions about how people are. In line with my claim about what is most important in the Chomsky–Foucault debate, I shall begin with the second part, which focuses on the issue of politics.

After some preliminary questions about why Foucault was interested in politics and more interested in politics than philosophy, the debate really gets underway when, responding to the moderator's question, Chomsky describes his political ideal. He describes an anarcho-syndicalist or libertarian socialist society, where there is a permanent revolution against repression, oppression, destruction, and coercion. In this society, centralized autocratic control of markets (private ownership of capital), state regulation of various aspects of human life, and centralized and unaccountable institutions are replaced by a participatory workers democracy.[10]

For his part, Foucault politely demurs, saying that he is unable and unwilling to propose an ideal social model, and that the real political task "is to criticize the workings of institutions," unmasking their phony claims to neutrality and independence, and exposing their political violence. Chomsky agrees with Foucault's analysis, but insists on the necessity of constructing visionary, humanistic models of how "a future just society" might look. The intellectual has the dual responsibility of criticizing what is and imagining what might be.[11] It is here that Foucault begins to draw a sharp distinction between Chomsky and himself, which reveals the extent to which Foucault is simultaneously a vulgar Marxist and a disillusioned romantic.

Foucault sees danger in Chomsky's willingness to imagine ideal social models that presuppose an essential human nature. "[D]oesn't one risk defining this human nature – which is at the same time ideal and real, and has been hidden and repressed until now – in terms borrowed from our society, from our civilization, from our culture?" Foucault cites late nineteenth- and early twentieth-century socialism, which he argues reproduces the very bourgeois model of human nature out of which it was trying to imagine itself. From this vantage point, he concludes "that it is difficult to say exactly what human nature is," and that there is a risk of error.[12] What are we to make of a self-styled Nietzschean who finds the risk of error a reason for not being a "strong creator," for not making strong judgments about good and bad? For now, I will allow this to stand as a rhetorical question, but Nietzsche aside, how would Chomsky answer? "Well of course!", I imagine Chomsky responding. Since when did politics become a philosophical parlor game? Politics is not philosophy; it entails risks, which force us to acknowledge our susceptibility to error, the partial and fallible character of our imaginations, and the likelihood that our hands will get dirty. Where is the news in all of this? Why the excessive sensitivities of someone as eagle-eyed and hardheaded as Foucault? Marx was never so vulgar, when he wrote that consciousness does not determine social being but social being determines consciousness, as vulgar Marxists are accused of being or as the Foucault who asked the above question is. That we are subject to all sorts of constraints is undeniable. To suggest that constraints on the utopian imagination are so deterministic (far more deterministic than Marxist economism[13] ever was) as to make imagination and vision not merely difficult but dangerous in a perverse sort of way is, as

I suggested earlier, a bad mixture of vulgar Marxism and disillusioned romanticism.

Foucault opens a second front, so to speak, in his battle with Chomsky, when he asks the following question, which I shall paraphrase: "When you commit an illegal act in the United States, do you justify it in terms of justice, a superior legality, or the needs of the proletariat in their struggle against the ruling class?" Underlying this question is Foucault's allegedly Nietzschean view of justice and power, which characterizes his engagement with Chomsky during the remainder of their debate. According to Foucault, justice is how the victorious describe what they do. Chomsky does not agree. Not only does he deny that this is what justice is, he also denies that this is the way that victors view themselves. Chomsky does not doubt that there are some people who think this way; Trasymachus and Nietzsche[14] would be examples of this view, where "might makes right."[15] What Chomsky does reject is Foucault's claim that the proletariat (read: any revolutionary or oppressed class) "makes war to win, not because it is just."[16] Foucault appropriates Nietzsche's idea of the will to power, but strips it of the metaphysics of noble and slave forms of life, which give it some plausibility. Thus Foucault can give no account, however defective Nietzsche's account may be, of the "why" of these power relations. His silence only underscores his own, unacknowledged ontology of power, his minimalist and unargued view of human nature as a struggle for power.

Remarkably, Foucault expresses doubt about whether "we would still use this [the Nietzschean] notion of justice" in a classless society. This statement is remarkable, because Chomsky is never so utopian (in the bad sense) as to believe that a classless society is possible. As Foucault construes Nietzsche's view, justice is an invention that political and economic powers and the opponents of those powers use as a weapon against each other. Justice is the product of a class society and presumably will "wither away" when class is abolished. Chomsky rejects this notion of justice, that is, the equation of justice and "systems of class oppression," the claim that justice is a cynical mask for power devoid of intersubjective idealism, the view that there will ever be a society where the need for justice, like the state, has "withered away."[17] Sympathetic readers might argue that Foucault's account is "dripping" with irony. His references to the proletariat and classless society are merely strategies for "smoking out" Chomsky's obvious humanism. Or they might argue that this is a strategy driven by Foucault's misrecognition of who Chomsky is. Perhaps he thinks that Chomsky is an orthodox Marxist,

who privileges the urban industrial working class in his account of revolutionary social change. No doubt, this would be a sympathetic
reading, but one that ignores a constant throughout Foucault's work,
namely, his romance and disillusionment with Marxism.

The debate effectively ends with Foucault's summation of his views
and those points on which he and Chomsky agree or disagree. As he
notes, he and Chomsky do not disagree when it comes to a theoretical
account of human nature, but disagree strongly on the relations between
human nature and politics. According to Foucault, notions of human
nature, justice, and human essence have been constructed by our civilization, knowledge, philosophy, and class system. So, regrettably, these
notions cannot be used "to describe or justify a fight which should – and
shall in principle – overthrow the very fundamentals of our society."
There is no historical justification for such a claim.[18]

Chomsky provides his own post mortem on the debate in *Language and
Responsibility*. He and Foucault agree partially on the "question of human
nature" but "not as much on politics." He cites Foucault's skepticism
"about the possibility of developing a concept of 'human nature' that
is independent of social and historical conditions, as a well-defined biological concept." Chomsky does not share Foucault's skepticism. While
acknowledging the elusiveness of human nature, which continues to
elude "the reach of scientific enquiry," he believes that some areas, such
as linguistics, may provide information that allows us to speak in
significant ways about the cognitive aspects of human nature.[19] Both
Foucault and Chomsky confirm the claim that I made earlier: they disagree less about human nature than they do about the political value of
utopia and the role that ideas of human nature have in how or even
whether we construct it.[20]

Here I return to Said by triangulating what until now has been the
Chomsky–Foucault debate. I shall begin with a passage from the essay
"Traveling Theory," where Said gives his assessment of the
Chomsky–Foucault debate. I quote at length:

There is a more important criticism to be made of Foucault's theory of power,
and it has been made most tellingly by Chomsky. Unfortunately most of
Foucault's new readers in the United States seem not to know of the exchange
that took place between them several years ago on Dutch television, nor of
Chomsky's succinct critique of Foucault contained in *Language and Responsibility*.
Both men agreed on the necessity of opposing repression, a position Foucault
has since found it more difficult to take unequivocally. Yet for Chomsky the
sociopolitical battle had to be waged with two tasks in mind: one "to imagine a

future society that confirms to the exigencies of human nature as best we understand them; the other to analyze the nature of power and oppression in our present societies." Foucault assented to the second without in any way accepting the first. According to him, any future societies that we might imagine now "are only the inventions of our civilisation and result from our class system." Not only would imagining a future society ruled according to justice be limited to false consciousness, it would also be too utopian to project for anyone like Foucault who believes that "the idea of justice in itself is an idea which in effect has been invented and put to work in different societies as an instrument of a certain political and economic power or as a weapon against that power." This is a perfect example of Foucault's unwillingness to take seriously his own ideas about resistances to power. *If power oppresses and controls and manipulates, then everything that resists it is not morally equal to power, is not neutrally and simply a weapon against power. Resistance cannot equally be an adversarial alternative to power and a dependent function of it, except in some metaphysical, ultimately trivial sense* [italics mine]. Even if the distinction is hard to draw, there is a distinction to be made – as, for example, Chomsky does when he says that he would give his support to an oppressed proletariat if as a class it made justice the goal of its struggle. (*WTC* 245-246)[21]

## A POLEMICAL ENGAGEMENT

Perhaps the most compelling response to Said's account of the Chomsky–Foucault encounter is Paul Bové's *Intellectuals in Power*. What is most remarkable about his response is its tone. Reading Bové, one can easily get the impression that Foucault's genealogies of power and of the intellectual are so persuasive that only the foolish or the dishonest can view them as anything less. He speaks confidently about power, hegemony, and representation, all of which are supposed to be bad. That they are bad, he takes to have been shown by Foucault and before him by Nietzsche. Bové is a Foucauldian, a left-Nietzschean. Said is a left-wing critical humanist. Foucauldians are antihumanist, which means that they are suspicious of (weak version) or deny (strong version) the notion of a timeless and universal human nature. They reject the claim that one can infer from the idea of human nature what is right and just. To base one's view of what a just social order should be on the notion of human nature is utopian, and utopianism by any name is dangerous. It is against this backdrop that Bové reads the Chomsky–Foucault–Said debate. In parsing Bové's account of this triangular conversation, I shall contest the claim that Foucault's genealogies of power, justice, and the intellectual are persuasive, by questioning Foucault's Nietzschean ancestry. Foucault may be Nietzschean, but he is a bastard son, and the circumstances of his birth are important.

I shall begin with some of Bové's concluding remarks: "People who take Foucault seriously do so, not because they believe he has said the final word on social reality, but because they believe he has said a few words on the relationship between truth, intellectuals, and human misery." No doubt, but the important question, as Nietzsche would say, is the *value* of those words. Bové clearly accords great value to what Foucault says, which is evident in the way that he characterizes the reaction of other intellectuals to Foucault's "genealogy of the intellectual." According to Bové, these responses "can be seen, above all, as *defenses* of the discourses and practices that always and variously validate and extend the privileged social, political, and psychological positions of both *hegemonic* and *oppositional* intellectuals."[22] By hegemonic, Bové refers to those intellectuals who are affiliated with "the power structure," with the prevailing relations of power and knowledge. In contrast, oppositional intellectuals oppose the status quo. I italicize "hegemonic" and "oppositional" to underscore Bové's Foucauldian allergies to power and hegemony, which are neither Nietzschean nor Gramscian in derivation.

In contrast, Bové italicizes "defenses." I draw attention to this because an important element of Bové's account is a critique of Said's rhetoric. Bové objects to Said's use of "succumbed" and "hermeticism" to describe what he regards as Foucault's flight from intellectual responsibility. These metaphors signify "violence and competition" (but only non-Nietzscheans or those who misconstrue Nietzsche as an opponent of violence and competition will find this disturbing). "'Succumbed' suggests not only defect but guilt, an unnecessary giving in, a yielding to pleasure, desire, or temptation. There is a moral tinge to Said's critique of Foucault's theory of power."[23] Only a non-Nietzschean will find a moral or ethical evaluation of power disturbing. After all, that is precisely what *Genealogy of Morals* is. Nietzsche provides an ethical evaluation of different moralities: noble-aristocratic-master morality is good, base-plebeian-slave morality is bad. Bové's indiscriminate, Foucauldian-inspired suspicion of power is not a Nietzschean affliction.

All this is relevant to the question of rhetoric. When Bové describes Said's response to Foucault as "defense," he suggests that Said has something to be defensive about, which is true, but only if defensive has the right inflection. What Said is trying to defend, according to Bové, is his "privileged social, political, and psychological" position as a "leading intellectual." Bové is so convinced by his own account that he sees no need for argument. True, he does cite Foucault and what Foucault's genealogies supposedly show. But are Bové's claims as compelling as he thinks they are? Should we take Bové at his word when he says that Foucault's "genealogical research often subverts the social and cultural authority of traditional disciplines and discourses – the very means by which intellectuals (no matter what their 'politics' or 'intent') normally acquire power and identity?" What Bové takes Foucault's genealogies to show may be clear. Less clear is why he thinks that they show what he claims they do. Bové has a propensity for making bold assertions about what Foucault's work does without providing a supporting account. The claim that Foucault's work directly challenges the legitimacy of traditional and oppositional intellectuals is typical.[24] After Foucault, as Bové would have it, authorizing competitive quests "for power, authority, and identity" is more difficult. Foucault shows the complicity between the rhetoric of opposition and "the hegemony of power."[25]

These claims, especially the last, are curious. Do Foucault's disciples recognize his challenge to "leading intellectuals" because it is persuasive or is his challenge persuasive because they are his disciples? This is not a trivial question, as is evident by Bové's further claims about the complicity of oppositional rhetorics with the "hegemony of power." Complicity is an interesting choice of words. It is a lot like "succumbed," implying guilt, something bad, inappropriate, or morally defective. But since when, on a Nietzschean view, did hegemony or power become a bad thing? The idea that one can be in complicity with power is thoroughly foreign to Nietzsche's way of thinking. Like everything else, Nietzsche evaluates power in ethically discriminating and differential terms. Power is good or bad in relation to who exercises power and for what purpose. Foucault's vague and indiscriminate critique of an amorphous power that is unrelated to specific forms of life (noble or base, aristocratic or plebeian, master or slave) is absent in Nietzsche. In relation to Nietzsche's notion of power and in language Nietzsche would appreciate, Foucault's notion of power is ill conceived and misbegotten. Bové's Foucault moralizes power precisely in the manner that Nietzsche calls *ressentiment*. Resentment is at work when the weak try to disempower and devitalize the strong, by making them think that their competitive struggle for power and hegemony is evil. Of course, Bové does not use the word evil, but his Foucauldian account of power and of the leading intellectual carries that accusation.

When Bové finally does get down to the business of providing a supporting argument for the persuasiveness of Foucault's work, it becomes clear that he is not up to the task. He only provides "one specific and limited example of Foucault's critique of the leading intellectual." A curious example it is. Bové parses Foucault's easygoing if not ironic engagement with a group of Maoists in the piece "Our Popular Justice."[26] From this piece, Bové distills his Foucauldian wisdom, namely, that the masses do not need leading or even organic intellectuals, the masses being quite capable of carrying out acts of popular justice themselves. This insight is not as banal or reminiscent of the notion of "spontaneous revolution" as it sounds if Foucault's goals, as Bové describes them, are achieved. Those goals are "to discredit the authority of revolutionary rhetoric by revealing its historical and political *naïveté* regarding courts and justice," and to expose the will to power of those who envision an alternative society. [27]

The second goal – which from a Nietzschean perspective does not make sense, for why would a self-described Nietzschean object to the will to power? – brings us back, full circle, to the centerpiece of the Chomsky–Foucault debate. To restate the central point, Chomsky and Foucault disagree about the ethical–political implications of imagining an alternative social order, the role that notions of human nature should play in that act of imagination, and the role of justice. Chomsky thinks that imagining an alternative social order is necessary. Also necessary is a dialectical interplay between that act of imagination and the act of constructing models of human nature; imagining a better society and speculating about what it means to be human are inextricably connected activities. Finally, Chomsky affirms the relation between justice and revolution. Foucault disagrees with Chomsky on each of these points. To imagine the future is to extend the hegemony of the present. The notion of human nature only enables the colonization of the future by the present. Justice is an artifact of a class-stratified society and presumably will disappear in a future classless society.

Bové takes Foucault's argument as showing that leading intellectuals collaborate with power when they imagine sociopolitical alternatives and that these intellectuals, therefore, are "dangerous to people." He goes further, saying that "leading intellectuals are a tool of oppression and most so precisely when they arrogate the right and power to judge and imagine efficacious alternatives."[28] (This is like saying, and I do mean to trivialize, that parents are a danger to children or that generals puts the lives of their soldiers in danger. That parents are and that generals do is no doubt true, but that is not all they do, and is probably not the most important thing that they are or that they do.) Bové's Foucault has a purity-problem, which would be debilitating were it not amusing. He speaks as if knowledge should be without the effects of power, but since it is not, it should be disdained as dangerous to people. Well yes,

power is dangerous, but – and you would think that a follower of Nietzsche would know this – so is life. In contrast to Bové's Foucault, Nietzsche never confuses the hazards of power with an argument against power. To do so would be like despising life because it ends in death, or rejecting medicine because in high doses it becomes poison. (I might add in this regard that a little bit of Foucault may be a cure for what ails us, but too much Foucault is poison.) As I suggested earlier, Nietzsche's discussion of power is never this vague or abstract. I shall consider Bové's reading of Nietzsche in due course, but not before considering his account of Chomsky, Foucault, and Said a little further.

On Bové's view, Said does not take "Foucault's reasons for not agreeing with Chomsky" seriously enough. Had he done so, he would realize that Foucault does not say that our limited perspective makes action impossible. What he does say is that we should examine the grounds for our perspectives "critically and genealogically."[29] This claim is odd, because Foucault can be read as saying exactly what Bové says that he does not say: that action by leading intellectuals is impossible because it is constrained by the present "regime of truth," the politics that currently determine what we regard as true. This is what Foucault's objection to Chomsky is all about, and not merely the view that Chomsky is not critical or genealogical enough. This peculiar construction of Foucault's position may serve Bové's purposes, but he domesticates Foucault when he attributes that view to him. Ironically, Bové may be criticizing Said for an aspect of Foucault's own views that Bové is not willing to own. Contrary to Bové's construction, Foucault discounts the role of the leading intellectual and his "imaginings" because he views those imaginings as irremediably tainted. On his view, the intellectual has "dirty hands." Nor are their hands dirty because of historical contingencies. The "dirt" has to do with how intellectuals are, with human nature, with how knowledge and power work. So, contrary to Bové, I think that it is Foucault who does not take Chomsky's reasons for disagreeing with him seriously enough. Bové's claims to the contrary, Chomsky knows only too well that notions of human nature, justice, and better social orders are not absolute ideas. I am sure that Chomsky would reject Bové's tendentious reference to these ideals as "ideology." As Chomsky realizes, his concept of human nature is limited, socially constructed in part, and constrained by the moral and intellectual fallibility of its host culture. But the critic's reach, *pace* Foucault, should exceed his grasp; the impossible is essential to achieving the possible, to even knowing what it is. According to Chomsky, "We have to be bold enough to speculate and create social theories on the basis of partial knowledge, while remaining very open to the strong possibility, and in fact overwhelming probability, that at least in some respects we're very far off the mark."[30] This is as clear a statement of the falliblist perspective as one can find. Politics requires some general theory, which is irremediably historical *and* ideal. (This idealism is not subjective and transcendental but immanent and intersubjective.) Critics reflect on what has been and image what might be, constructing notions of human nature and revising them in light of experience.

The important difference between Chomsky and Foucault has everything to do with Foucault's inflated notion of the "regime of truth." Truth is this-worldly, according to Foucault. It is produced through various forms of constraint and has power-effects. Each society has a particular regime of truth, which determines what discourses are true, the procedures by which they are made true and who can say what counts as true.[31] Bové thinks that Said, like Chomsky, chooses to ignore Foucault's notion of the regime of truth, which apparently is so persuasive that acknowledging it or ignoring it are the only options. Bové takes the truth of Foucault's account as established and noncontroversial. He need merely invoke Foucault's name, mention the notion of the regime of truth, quote briefly from Foucault's account, and let the irresistible power of Foucault's logic do the rest. According to Bové, Said does not address directly Foucault's claim about the regime of truth because he is less interested in its truth or falsity than in its effects on leading intellectuals. I think that this is a misreading. Said understands all too well what Foucault's notion suggests. He also knows that to take this notion as more than a metaphor, an allegorical account of the complexities of truth and power is nonsense. To read Bové, one would think that Foucault invented the "analytic of power," or that his analysis represents more than a rich footnote to Marx and that huge tradition of "reader response" that he founded called Marxism. Unlike Nietzsche, Foucault cannot tell us why people crave power. Unlike Marx and Gramsci, he can give no account of why they fight for it. To repeat, Said understands Foucault well enough. He simply thinks that Foucault is wrong.

Following Chomsky, Said argues that power and resistance to power are not the same thing. Bové construes Said as making a metaphysical argument when in fact he is making an ethical–political argument. He construes Said as unwilling to see that intellectuals and their practices are "functions of their positions within a massive network" of political institutions and discourse. Bové adds that intellectuals are relays in a discursive circuit and thus are neither constitutive nor privileged subjects. Their visions and practices, therefore, "serve interests and structures" that they might not want to defend. Bové thinks that he makes a telling point when he argues that Said cannot risk a serious and open-minded examination of Foucault's claim that any alternative to the current regime that oppositional intellectuals might imagine is the product of the prevailing "regime of truth." If Said were honest, he would admit that there is no humanistic way out of the predicament that Foucault describes.[32]

One has to take this argument seriously because Bové does, but it is not a serious argument, more a parody of what a serious argument would be. This is obvious when one considers what Said actually says. *"Resistance cannot equally be an adversarial alternative to power, and also a depen-dent function of it, except in some metaphysical, ultimately trivial sense"* (*WTC* 228, emphasis is mine). This is the crux of the disagreement between Said's Chomsky and Bové's Foucault: Said and Chomsky are *political* radicals, Bové and Foucault are *epistemological* radicals. This distinction is simple but not simplistic. It captures well the important difference between these pairs. Foucault is an epistemological radical – a radical skeptic or even a cynic, that is, a disappointed sentimentalist – rather than a polit-ical radical because he is more obsessed with an impossible kind of intel-lectual object (the utopia that we cannot imagine and should not try imagining) than with the good but imperfect society that we might succeed in creating. His standards are precisely those of the starry-eyed but disillusioned dreamer and not those of the political militant. Chomsky and Said do not need a lecture on the irremediable limitations of imagination. They know that our judgments are fallible and error-prone; they also know that "it does not get any better than this." Only utopian thinkers – or, what is different and far worse, inverted utopians, dystopian thinkers – believe that our human-all-too-human limitations are reasons for "castrating" the political imagination. To pursue this Nietzschean line of metaphors a little further, Chomsky and Said can look into the "abyss" of intellectual faults, foibles, and failures and manage their nausea. They do not reject imagination and power because they are dangerous. Dangerous, the human condition is. In the end, Foucault is a jilted Cartesian, so to speak; having learned to distrust absolutes, he can no longer trust at all. Fortunately, Chomsky and Said refuse to scratch Foucault and Bové's metaphysical itch – their inverted (disillusioned) quest for certainty. Bové's Foucault is exemplary of so-called left-intellectuals who construe their fetish for "clean hands" as sophistication and the willingness of others to look into the "abyss" and still imagine a different future as naïve. Said is right when he describes Foucault's theory of power as Spinozist and describes well the

Foucauldian intellectual: who wants "to go beyond Left optimism and Right pessimism so as to justify political quietism with sophisticated intellectualism, at the same time that they wish to appear to be realistic, in touch with the world of power and reality, as well as historical and antiformalistic in their bias."[33]

Bové is exemplary of the Foucauldian intellectual that Said describes. The way he reads Nietzsche is also exemplary of those "left" intellectuals who adopt Nietzsche as their critical patron and in doing so think they are adopting a stance that is more sophisticated and progressive than the stance of oppositional critics such as Said. The short account that follows, where I read Bové reading Nietzsche, should be seen as a retrospective on the previous discussion and as an introduction to Nietzsche's account of responsibility and truth.

Bové's reading of Nietzsche goes badly from the very beginning when he construes Nietzsche as an opponent of the "dynastic order." The dynastic order refers to a perduring mimetic relationship between tradition and innovation. In his struggle for identity and authority, the sublime master of knowledge, or the genealogical intellectual, reproduces the very tradition he wishes to displace. His very will to power buries innovation beneath tradition reconfigured. The willfulness of the genealogical intellectual generates competition, "an endless and undesirable succession of displacements," as one intellectual attempts to knock over the other. Thus genealogists repeat "the pattern of repetitive displacement within humanism, the authority of which itself rests on the superior knowledge and interpretive power of its leading or representative intellectuals." The genealogist, Bové concludes, places himself within the very tradition that he opposes. By reaffirming the mastery of the leading intellectual in cultural formation and the control of knowledge, genealogists inhibit "the development of participatory democracy."[34]

This account is rife with misunderstanding, which exemplifies the ignorance of those on the "left" who think that Nietzsche is more than a "good enemy," who think that he is a friend. Bové's problem begins when he construes Nietzsche as a simplistic opponent of the ascetic idea and intensifies with his uncritical acceptance of Foucault's Nietzsche. According to Bové, Nietzsche authorizes a "competitive or agonistic" pursuit of authority that reproduces the ascetic idea as will to truth, which is the defining characteristic of humanistic knowledge. This makes it difficult for Nietzsche to distinguish genealogy from the nihilistic sciences. Since Nietzsche fails adequately to develop his own notion of genealogy, Bové turns to Foucault. This explains why we learn something about Foucault's notion of genealogy but little about Nietzsche's. They are not the same. In Bové's account, Nietzsche is a puppet for a Foucauldian ventriloquist. In this way, Foucault is able to cast far his very different notion of genealogy in Nietzsche's voice, with what he takes to be Nietzsche's authority. The Foucauldian Nietzsche is concerned not only with how knowledge is produced but also with how it can be repositioned within our culture. This Nietzsche casts "doubt on the value and desirability of 'knowledge' as it functions under the sign of 'will to truth' within the humanistic project, that is, as it is presumed to 'assure' liberty, progress, and human fulfillment."[35]

To construe Nietzsche as opposed to asceticism, especially its crowning achievement the will to truth, is a misunderstanding of the same order as the notion that Nietzsche opposes morality and justice as such. Alas, things are never so simple with Nietzsche, which is apparent when he claims that "Bad conscience is a sickness, there is no point in denying it, but a sickness rather like pregnancy." This paradoxical description of bad conscience sheds light on Nietzsche's view of the ascetic idea. Nietzsche's "highest type" (Dionysus, the free spirit, the genuine historian, Zarathustra, the "superman," or the philosopher of the future) is possible only through the sublimation or self-overcoming of the ascetic idea. The ascetic idea "is a sickness, there is no point in denying, but a sickness rather like pregnancy." This is why Nietzsche says, "Except for the ascetic ideal: man, the *animal* man, had no meaning up to now."[36] It is the ascetic idea that enabled man to become something more than an animal. This is not a lament, but high praise. Bové is wrong when he says that Nietzsche is antihumanist, if by this he means that Nietzsche refrains from saying what humans are and what constitutes the human good. I am not merely suggesting that Bové is crudely selective in his citation practices, but that his method of selection is driven by Foucault's mischaracterization and thus redescription of Nietzsche's idea of genealogy.

We see just how bad things can get when so-called left intellectuals are seduced (*interpellated*) by Nietzsche so that they forget his politics and their own. One would never know from reading Bové's account that Nietzsche is a protofascist thinker.[37] This is underscored by Nietzsche's esoteric semiotics in which forms of life (healthy and diseased) and human types (masters and slaves, aristocrats and plebeians, noble and base) are rank-ordered. This hierarchical ranking is maintained by the "pathos of distance" that masters, aristocrats, and nobles feel toward slaves, plebeians, and people of the baser sort. Bové, with an apolitical inattention to context that is astounding, attributes to Nietzsche the following: opposition to humanism, "the hegemonic order," originality, and the violence of the powerful. Only someone who has not read Nietzsche carefully could make these attributions. If Nietzsche opposes humanism, there is nothing salutary about that as he makes brutally clear in "The Greek State": "The misery of men living a life of toil has to be increased to make the production of the world of art possible for a small number of Olympian men." This necessity accounts for the hatred nourished by Communists, Socialists, and "their paler descendants, the white race of 'Liberals.'"[38] (Surely Nietzsche would add to this list the "sophisticated" critics of Communists, Socialists, and Liberals who call themselves Foucauldians. One can only imagine the wicked and humorous turn of phrase he would use to describe those who call themselves "left-Nietzscheans"!)

Bové throws around the notion of antihumanism as if Foucault and Nietzsche are talking about the same thing. Nietzsche's antihumanism has nothing to do with Foucault's often anarchic and (for the sake of argument) sometimes radical egalitarian view. This is why Bové's representation of Nietzsche as a democrat, whose intellectual practices inhibit the development of participatory democracy, is so alarming. Nietzsche is no democrat, least of all is he an advocate of participatory democracy. On this point, Nietzsche is brutally frank: "The masses seem to me worthy of notice in only three respects: first as blurred copies of great men, produced on bad paper with worn plates, further as resistance to the great, and finally as the tools of the great; beyond that, may the devil and statistics take them!"[39] Passages such as this one should give "left-Nietzscheans" pause. It challenges the unexplicated assumption that antihumanism is a leftwing position, by showing that there are rightwing and quasi-fascist (or fascoid) ways of being antihumanist too.

In Bové's account of genealogy, Nietzsche's is a bold but faulty precursor of Foucault's genealogical practices. But if Nietzsche is guilty of the things of which Bové accuses him, it is because the Nietzsche that he has in view is a puppet and Foucault is pulling his strings. Nietzsche does not help Bové's Foucault do what he wants to do. Bové's Foucault, Bové and Foucault must stand or fall by themselves. I have already suggested why I think that they fall and their notion of the intellectual fails. I argued that Nietzsche does not share Foucault's globalized condemnation of power, which is exemplary of the reactive disposition that he calls *ressentiment*. Nietzsche thinks that the hegemony of aristocratic forms of power is a good thing; the only people who matter to Nietzsche are great men, the works of great men "alone are of value."[40] It is these monumental men that Nietzsche celebrates and not their "anonymous, discursive construction." Nietzsche does not share the Foucauldian view, where the purpose of genealogy is to expose the complicity of various practices with power/knowledge, especially the practices of universal or leading intellectuals. I believe, therefore, that I have cast doubt on the view that Nietzsche provides a usable source of authority for Foucault and Bové's critique of the universal or leading intellectual. Their critique falls far short of undermining Chomsky and Said's claim that it is the intellectual's responsibility to speak truth to power and expose lies. I am done with Foucault and Bové, but not with Nietzsche, whose reflections on responsibility as promise-keeping and the will to truth as the highest manifestation of the ascetic idea merit further investigation.

NIETZSCHE ON PROMISE-MAKING AND TRUTH

In Nietzsche's regressive account, responsibility is an artifact of promise-making, which depends on memory, which emerged as an island from the sea of our active powers of forgetfulness thus enabling us to suspend forgetfulness "in those cases where a promise is to be made."[41] Responsibility is a late development, the "ripest fruit," of a long evolutionary process.

The consequences of this developmental history are certain character traits or dispositions such as future-oriented and causal thinking, calculation, reliability, regularity, uniformity, automatic, and predictable behavior. Nietzsche calls these traits the "morality of custom," which he argues is justified despite "the hardness, tyranny, stupidity, and idiocy" that it contains. Customary morality is justified because it made man (he is not interested in woman) predictable. Without predictability, there can be no responsibility. The meaning and end of predictability is the sovereign individual who as "an autonomous, supra-ethical individual" overcomes or self-sublimates the morality of custom. He willfully and independently seizes "*the right to make a* promise." Nietzsche describes this sovereign individual who has the right to make a promise and the strength to do so as an achievement. He judges according to his own standards of value. He respects "his peers, the strong and the reliable (those *with the right* to give their word)," and despises the rest. Because he is a strong man, he remains "upright in the face of mishap or even 'in the face of fate.'" This strong individual is always ready "to kick the febrile whippets who make a promise when they have no right to do so, and will save the rod for the liar who breaks his word in the very moment it passes his lips." Nietzsche's sovereign, responsible individual does not "speak truth to power," rather, as the personification of power he speaks the truth and exposes lies. Were the sovereign man to reflect on what has become his dominant instinct, he would no doubt call that instinct his conscience.[42]

Nietzsche supplements this genealogy of responsibility as good conscience with a genealogy of responsibility as "bad conscience." I shall work from Nietzsche's account of the causes of bad conscience to the implications of this idea for Said's notion of intellectual responsibility. Nietzsche gives a succinct account of the bad conscience in essay two, section 18 of *The Genealogy of Morals*. In Freud's language, bad conscience is a "reaction formation" by the weak when they find themselves crushed, so to speak, beneath the heel of the strong. Nietzsche describes these strong types as "involuntary, unconscious artists" who create something new through the very act of domination. Obviously, they are not the soil in which bad conscience grew, but they are the fertilizer. For:

this ugly growth would not be there if a huge amount of freedom had not been driven from the world, or at least driven from sight and, at the same time, made *latent* by the pressure of their hammer blows and artists' violence. "This *instinct of freedom*, forcibly forced back, repressed, incarcerated within itself and finally able to discharge and unleash itself only against itself: that, and that alone, is *bad conscience* in its beginnings."

Is bad conscience a bad thing? In an obvious sense it is. Bad conscience is bad because the will to power has been blocked and turned inward, deforming body and spirit. Bad conscience is a disease, a sickness, there is no point in denying. But it is "a sickness rather like pregnancy."[43] Here Nietzsche has made things shaky and uncertain for those who want to read bad conscience as merely a bad thing. It may be bad, but like asceticism it "hurts so good." As a reaction formation, bad conscience is the internalization of violence and cruelty, the instinct of freedom, the will to power, which is produced through grudging submission to superior power. Unable to construct external structures of height, the man of bad conscience digs a basement, he becomes deep. Subjective depth is the consequence of repression. It is this inward deepening that makes the man of bad conscience a *tertium quid* between Nietzsche's violent artists and the higher type of man that he variously envisions. It is through this sickness that is like pregnancy that Nietzsche's highest types will be born.

"'Bad conscience,' the most uncanny and most interesting plant of our earthly vegetation, did *not* grow in this soil." To what soil does

Nietzsche refer? He refers to the soil of punishment and guilt. This passage is near the end of Nietzsche's account of the moralization of punishment and guilt. Here we begin, or continue what has already become, an investigation of the consequences of bad conscience – where punishment and guilt are robbed of their amorality, their moral innocence. In former times, according to Nietzsche, punishment was viewed in a variety of ways: as a way of rendering harmless, satisfying a debt, isolating a social disturbance and preventing it from spreading; it was a way of inspiring fear, counterbalancing the ill-gotten privileges of criminality, and rooting-out degeneracy from the social body. Punishment was also viewed as a festive violating and mocking of enemies, an aid to memory, as "protection money" against revenge, an act of war against the enemies of peace, law, and authority.[44] Bad conscience, the moralizing of guilt and punishment, is a reaction to these healthy interpretations of guilt and punishment. It is what happens when these healthy interpretations become sick, when good responsibility and good conscience "go bad."

Bad conscience was born of suffering and the self-overcoming of suffering by decadent forms of the will to power. Pain is the most effective way of creating and sustaining memory, and memory, as I suggested earlier, is the "ground floor" of responsibility. No pain, no responsibility. No bad, no good – "how much blood and horror lies at the basis of all 'good things'!"[45] We should not be misled by the quotation marks around good things. Nietzsche is not trying to scare us away from the view that responsibility is a good thing, rather, he wants to drive home the point that responsibility or any good thing is not pure, but is alloyed with its opposite. Good and bad are born of and nourished by the other: bad conscience is a sickness rather like pregnancy; without the ascetic ideal, man, the animal man, has no meaning. Man, by definition, is a sick animal, but his sickness is constitutive of his creativity and superiority to other animals.

The moralizing of these complex relations is a consequence of bad conscience. Where, in the distant past, guilt referred to a debt incurred, an objective relationship between people of roughly equal power, guilt now refers to a state of consciousness. One feels guilty and that feeling devitalizes and makes one reactive. Likewise, where punishment was once meted out because its consequences (the whole litany that I recited earlier) were regarded as good for those doing the punishing, now punishment is regarded as what guilty people deserve. From what is good for me, guilt and punishment have become the state of consciousness and moral liability of the other. Consequently, we now view the criminal as someone who "deserves to be punished *because* he could have acted otherwise." But the notion of freedom, on which the moralizing of punishment is based, was absent, according to Nietzsche, in earlier times. It is "an extremely late and refined form of human judgment and inference."[46] To repeat, in the distant past we punished people because we thought that punishment was good not because we thought that those punished deserved it. Guilt and punishment were utilitarian calculations by and for the powerful.

How were debts discharged in the past, before the moralization of guilt and punishment? Nietzsche's answer is perhaps the most difficult, controversial, and misunderstood of his views. He claims that guilt is discharged through acts of compensation. These compensatory acts do not restore what has been damaged or destroyed. They are not financial. Nor do they entail obvious forms of barter: my ox for your damaged mule. These compensatory acts are not to the positive advantage of the injured party in any obvious sense. Compensation takes the form, rather, of making the other suffer, exercising power over the powerless, without measure. It is the sheer pleasure of violating the other. "To see somebody suffer is nice, to make somebody suffer even nicer."[47] As if anticipating that his views would be misread as a license for pessimism, the nihilism of those who refrain from creating, imaging or making judgments because they might be wrong, Nietzsche says plainly that such cruelty was a good thing. Then people were not ashamed of cruelty, and life was more cheerful. This was before "sickly mollycoddling and sermonizing" made man, the animal man, ashamed of his instincts, the instinct of freedom, the will to power. Nietzsche will have none of the nay-saying and hand-wringing (disguised as cold, eagle-eyed sophistication) of those who disdain power because it causes human misery. He regards this as testimony against life, which "functions *essentially* in an injurious, violent, exploitative and destructive manner." On Nietzsche's view, human misery is hardly a persuasive argument against the instinct of freedom, the will to power. Human happiness (in egalitarian terms) is not part of Nietzsche's discriminating, rank-ordered, notion of excellence. "Man's sacrifice *en bloc* to the prosperity of one single *stronger* species of man – that *would* be progress." Nietzsche is *not* interested in the genuine philosopher's path to happiness; he is interested in the path that leads to power, "action, the mightiest deeds, and in most cases, actually, his misery." "[A]nybody whoever built a 'new heaven,' only mustered the power he needed through his *own hell*."[48]

The pessimism that Nietzsche criticizes here is the product of bad conscience, and grows from the soil of the weak and subjugated. Nietzsche concludes his account of bad conscience by drawing a portrait of a redemptive figure, a man of the future, who resembles, but in exaggerated form, Said's notion of the responsible intellectual. From all that we know about Nietzsche's social and political views, his redemptive man of the future is no democrat, but a spiritual aristocrat, an elitist in the most troubling sense of the word. Nietzsche's redeemer will not be an advocate of the radical democratic, ethical–political future that Said imagines and for which his responsible intellectual speaks. But, in character terms, there are some striking similarities. Both are of Spartan disposition; they are "spirits which are strengthened by wars and victories, for which conquest, adventure, danger and even pain have actually become a necessity." They are acclimatized to "thin air" and "winter treks." Willful and self-assured of insight, they leave no doubt about what they love and hate, respect and despise. Both are opponents of "the great nausea, the will to nothingness," the nihilism of those who are afraid to make judgments or who worry endlessly because things are fundamentally "undecidable." If Said's responsible intellectual worships no god, then Nietzsche calls his redemptive figure *"Zarathustra the Godless."*[49] This account is given with tongue firmly in cheek, but not so firmly that I cannot defend the comparison. But it is time to raise another question. What is the relationship between Nietzsche's redemptive figure and bad conscience, between the man who is strong enough to make promises and the flower of the ascetic ideal, the will to truth?

I propose to address this question by first posing another: is Said an ascetic priest who reproduces the disease of humanism that he wants to heal by reinfecting the wound? This is what Bové, to return to him briefly, is really suggesting, but what does his notion of asceticism have to do with Nietzsche's? Nietzsche's ascetic idea, as I suggested earlier, is complex and paradoxical, which is evident in his ability to hold together extreme and contradictory claims in a single breath. Because he does not pause to catch his breath, it is easy to misread him. I have noted repeatedly, in this regard, Nietzsche's paradoxical view of asceticism as a sickness that resembles pregnancy. It is in this context that Nietzsche rails against the ascetic priest. As prosecutor, Nietzsche's indictment of the ascetic priest has several counts: the ascetic priest is the *representative of seriousness,* unparalleled *ressentiment,* a *negative man,* a sick doctor in a sickroom, the shepherd of the suffering herd, a surgeon whose tools are infected, a therapist who trades in the intensification of guilt.[50] Nietzsche

is also an attorney for the defense, although with friends like this . . .
Nietzsche does offer a qualified but important defense of the ascetic
priest and the ascetic idea. The ascetic priest is the "*direction-changer* of *ressentiment*," redirecting it away from the noble, the powerful, and the good
toward the suffering herd itself. Through the conceptual apparatus of
sin, guilt, and punishment, the ascetic priest provides "ointments and
balms" for the wounds of the suffering herd, but "*he poisons the wound at
the same time*" by telling them that they are responsible for their own
injury.[51] This is certainly not a good thing from a radical democratic perspective, and even Nietzsche, the *radical antidemocrat*, vacillates on this
point. His dominant, aristocratic view, however, is that this tendency to
reinfect the sick is a good thing because the weak are less likely to do what
they do best, which is make the strong weak and the healthy sick.

The ascetic priest has other virtues too. For my purposes, the most
important of these virtues is his role as *tertium quid*, the catalytic agent in
the emergence of the higher type of man. Nietzsche signals this seem-
ingly contradictory role early in his account. "To put it vividly and
clearly: the *ascetic priest* has until the most recent times displayed the vile
and dismal form of a caterpillar, which was the only one philosophers
were allowed to adopt and creep around in . . . Have things really
*changed?*"[52] This question is rhetorical. Its importance lies in what it
signals, which is the integral connection between the vocation of the
ascetic priest and the will to truth, which ranks a close second to what
Nietzsche values most, a healthy will to power. The ascetic priest is to
Nietzsche's "highest type" as the caterpillar is to the butterfly: vile and
dismal in form, but necessary to the metamorphosis of something higher
and more beautiful. The discipline born of weakness, self-sacrifice,
cruelty, and torture gives Nietzsche's highest types a spiritual and subjective depth that his "blond beasts" and noble barbarians did not have.
Unlike the ascetic priest, however, their depth is an active and
affirmative self-sublimating of instincts. Between the two, as *tertium quid*,
cocoon, and catalysis, is the ascetic priest. The ascetic priest (especially
the scientist) and Nietzsche's highest type (the philosopher of the future)
meet on the issue of truth – the will to truth. Here Said's commitment
to truth is at issue. If the will to truth leads to nihilism, as Nietzsche
claims, then what are we to conclude about Said's commitment to truth
and the necessity of speaking truth to power? The first thing that we
should note is that Nietzsche also believes in speaking truth, if not to
power. If this sounds strange it is only because for too long now we have
been reading Nietzsche through Foucault, and their views, as I have

argued throughout, are very different. Nietzsche's account of truth and power have the same paradoxical character that we have encountered before. Because Nietzsche distinguishes ethically between different kinds of power, he makes sense when he praises healthy and blames sickly wills to power. We know what he is fighting for and against and why. We understand, even if we reject, his fascoid metaphysics of sickness and health.

Sickly will to power runs counter to Nietzsche's notion of human excellence. He opposes it for this reason alone, but we should not suppose that this is a simple reason. Sick forms of the will to power are dishonest. They tell lies. This shows just how complex Nietzsche's notion of truth is, why he is not opposed to the will to truth in any simple way. As we saw in the second essay, Nietzsche regards the ability to make promises as a hard-won achievement; it is good, but not uniformly so. Only certain people have a "right" to make promises, namely, the strong and reliable. The weak and the rest lie the moment that they open their mouths. It is no surprise, therefore, when he criticizes those who lie poorly because they cannot tell the truth, least of all about themselves. These he calls dishonest liars, their mendacity is moralistic. They pretend to be innocent, when they are guilty of weakness. Nietzsche describes the intellectual's responsibility for exposing this mendacious innocence: "To have to rediscover this 'innocence' everywhere – that is, perhaps, the most revolting task among the somewhat dubious tasks a psychologist [read: intellectual] today has to perform."[53] A dubious – doubtful, uncertain, ambiguous, ambivalent, debatable, and disputable – task perhaps, but it must be done. It is precisely the dishonest mendacity of "innocent liars," their inability to tell genuine, resolute, "honest lies" that Nietzsche criticizes. When Nietzsche refers to honest lies, he has Plato's notion of the "noble lie" that I discussed in the previous chapter in mind. To recall that discussion, Plato knew that some people were naturally better than others and of superior rank. Based on this truth he told a lie: men are composed of different grades of ore (gold, silver, bronze, and iron), which determines their rank-ordering in society. Some are born to be philosopher-kings, some warriors, some artisans and farmers. It is these *hard* truths (the irremediable necessity for the rank-ordering of man and his virtues) that dishonest liars cannot handle.[54]

One truth that even higher types have difficulty handling is the truth about truth. They are especially susceptible to a pious, unconditional, absolutizing of truth. Where does it come from and what are the consequences of this will to truth? According to Nietzsche, the ultimate achievement of the ascetic ideal is the denial of God by an absolute will to truth. You shall know the truth and the truth shall make you free. Here the Christian notion of truth, underwritten by God, consumes itself by consuming God. Christian truth is the ascetic ideal in its last stage and final form – "it is the awe-inspiring *catastrophe* of a two-thousand-year discipline in truth-telling, which finally forbids itself the *lie entailed in the belief in God.*" The death of God is the birth of Godless truth – truth as absolute value, which represents the transfiguration and sublimation of "the confessional punctiliousness of Christian conscience . . . into scientific conscience, into intellectual purity at any price."[55] Is this what Said's notion of speaking the truth to power entails?

My answer is an equivocal yes and no. Yes, if the claim is that Said's notion of truth-telling makes greater sense in relation to the Christian history of the idea that Nietzsche sketches. No, if the claim is that Said prefers "intellectual purity at any price." On the contrary, it is intellectual purity as "sophistication" and "antihumanism" that Said opposes, in the face of which he is determined (no matter how naïve some might construe it) to speak truth to power. How much of Nietzsche's account of truth-telling and lying Said would subscribe to is an open question. Sometimes his notion of truth-telling has the absolutist tone of Julien Benda. At other times, he sounds more like Nietzsche, where life requires a judicious blend of truth-telling and lying. On these occasions, Said understands the necessity for telling the truth at the right time and lying at the right time, to paraphrase Nietzsche's comments on remembering and forgetting. He knows that truth is subject to ideological contention, which is not to say that one refrains from speaking the truth and exposing lies. This makes Said much more like Nietzsche than Nietzsche's supposed heir Michel Foucault, for whom the death of God means the death of man – the death, that is, of someone who can make strong evaluations (this is true and that a lie) based on provisional and contingent grounds, the only grounds we have.

# CHAPTER 6

# Marx, Said, and the Jewish question

## THE JEWISH QUESTION

Somewhere, I surmise, offstage and in the background of the Said–Walzer dispute, is Marx's critique of religious identity and political liberalism in "The Jewish Question." The great Zionist leader, Theodor Herzl, a younger contemporary of Marx, saw the establishment of a Jewish state as a solution to the Jewish question – a solution, that is, to the European tradition, several centuries long, of Jew-hating persecution. The same Jewish question on which many thinkers, including Marx, spilled much ink. Marx subordinates the Jewish question to the question of real emancipation, to which Jewish civil rights are, paradoxically, an obstacle and real Jewish emancipation is an effect. As I construe Said's view, Herzl's notion of Jewish emancipation won out, and in ways that Marx could have scarcely imagined. The resolution of the Jewish question, under the constraints of European imperial hegemony, created the "question of Palestine." It is appropriate that this study of Said concludes with his reflections on the question of Palestine and with Marx's reflections on "The Jewish Question." On these questions there is a convergence of the three interlocking themes of this study: the religious effects of culture, the religious seduction of the secular critic, and the return of repressed religiosity. This convergence underscores the importance of the questions that I posed in Preliminary Remarks and to which I have offered various responses throughout this study.

In "The Jewish Question," Marx's argument takes a controversial form. He uses the popular stereotype of Jews as hucksters ("Money is the jealous god of Israel, beside which no other god may exist") to make a larger point about political liberalism and real emancipation. In what is undoubtedly an offense, Marx describes Judaism as a religion of practical need and self-interest, which centers around huckstering, or the acquisition of money. Only by "emancipating itself from *huckstering* and

*money*, and thus from real and practical Judaism," can our age emancipate itself. In this sentence Marx confounds the "huckstering Jew"
with the general condition of man under the constraints of capital. He
goes on to say that the abolition of the conditions that make huckstering possible "would make the Jew impossible." "His religious consciousness would evaporate like some insipid vapour in the real, life-giving air
of society."[1]

Because of this essay in particular, Marx is often viewed as anti-Jewish
and even anti-Semitic.[2] Some call him a self-hating Jew because of his
criticism of specifically Jewish aspirations, and a few writers have
attempted to psychoanalyze him in this regard. Marx was anti-Jewish to
be sure, but he was also anti-Christian, antireligious in general. Whether
his anti-Jewishness took an anti-Semitic form or not is an open question.
(Some may want to question the distinction between anti-Jewishness and
anti-Semitism as a verbal sleight-of-hand. This is understandable since
in the mouths of some they are indistinguishable. For the same reasons,
blacks are often deeply suspicious of negative criticism by whites. As with
Jews, their paranoia is well earned. But, in each case, criticism that is not
simply anti-Semitic or racist is possible, even when difficult to recognize.)
The rhetoric of "The Jewish Question" is anti-Semitic, but we should
ask to what end? Jewish comics often use anti-Semitic stereotypes for
comedic purposes and, ironically, to criticize anti-Semitism. Whether
"The Jewish Question" is an ironic critique of anti-Semitism or not is
far from clear. What is clear is Marx's critique of liberalism, and here we
can attribute ironic intentions to him: he uses Jewish stereotypes to
tarnish liberalism's allure.

Marx's essay is a review of Bruno Bauer's *The Jewish Question*, the
general outline of which can be rehearsed quickly. According to Marx,
Bauer only goes part of the way toward a resolution of the Jewish question, which he construes as an interreligious dispute between a Jewish
minority that wants civil rights, political equality, or emancipation and a
Christian state that is intent on denying such rights. This dispute can be
resolved critically and scientifically, according to Bauer, by abolishing
religion, that is, by disestablishing the Christian Church and by preventing the establishment of any other religion. For Marx, this will not do,
as it only exposes a deeper and more intractable opposition between the
liberal state and real freedom, between *political emancipation and human
emancipation*. Bauer fails to consider the degree to which the Jewish question, as a religious issue, is a defective by-product of an alienation-pro-
ducing bourgeois state. Constraints on free citizenship are overcome,

according to Marx, only when theological questions are turned into secular ones, when religious constraints are exposed as the deceptive "appearing" of secular constraints. The political emancipation of religious man – Jewish, Christian, or other – is possible only when the state is emancipated from religion. The political emancipation of religious man and the religious emancipation of the state, however, are not enough. "To be *politically* emancipated from religion is not to be finally and completely emancipated from religion, because political emancipation is not the final and absolute form of *human* emancipation."[3]

Marx uses the Christian, Trinitarian idea to explain why liberal emancipation is not real, why it is formal and not substantive. Like Christ, the state is an intermediary. Where Christ mediates between man and his own alienated divinity (that is, human subjectivity in its highest form), the state mediates between "man and human liberty." Political emancipation is religious because it is indirect and mediated. It inverts the proper relationship between the maker and the made, the worker and her "objective spirit." This roundabout form of self-recognition[4] is symptomatic of several problems, not the least of which is a practiced sophistry. The liberal state abolishes private property as a formal, legal prerequisite for political participation, while leaving the substantive barriers – of *birth, social rank, education, occupation* – in place. The public–political self and the private–civil self are constantly exposing the sophistry of the other. Bauer's world is an "inverted world." He makes the mistake of focusing on the formal rather than the substantive, the virtual power of the political state rather than the actual power of civil society, religious expression rather than profane contradictions. The liberal state is only a half-step along the path to real emancipation. Political emancipation obscures the realities of civil society, which is a new state of nature, the new form that Hobbes' war of all against all assumes under the constraints of capital. Political emancipation is the bifurcation of man into public and private selves: citizen and Jew, citizen and Christian, citizen and religious man. Liberalism, that is to say, is a formalism that conceals the substantive operations of power and privilege behind notions such as equal rights. In the liberal state, Christianity is disestablished, divested of its formal privileges, but "on the ground," in civil society, its power is unchallenged. Thus Christianity's private ownership of "spiritual capital" is to other religions what the private ownership of economic capital is to the impoverished worker. Both social relations underscore the formal and abstract nature of political emancipation. Liberalism is religious precisely because it presupposes a dualism between individual and social life, civil society and political life; in short, liberalism is religious because it is an inverted world.[5]

The idea of inversion is important, I think, for getting a handle on Said's assessment of the Palestinian question. On my reading, Said recasts the Jewish question as the question of Palestine. The problem of emancipation, "who should emancipate? who should be emancipated?" (as Marx put it), is no longer a problem for European states and Jews but for the state of Israel and Palestinians. In the most direct way possible, the Palestinian question is the metamorphosis of the Jewish question, the ironic repetition of the Jewish question, the difference that repetition makes.

Is Said's notion of Palestinian emancipation defined by the either/or options that Marx sketches in his essay? It is not clear what Said's views are in this regard. He is painfully aware of the ways in which post-Zionist Palestinian history mimics Jewish history, especially during the period of European state formation and the rise of nationalist sentiment. Given the Marxist tenor of his thinking, one would expect Said to be wary of the sort of analyses that Marx condemns as liberal. This includes any analysis based on liberal notions of freedom, equality, and rights. One would expect Said to be well aware of the formal, abstract character of political emancipation. One would expect this to be the case, and mostly it is, as we shall soon see. But first I draw attention to just how prevalent the language of human rights is in Said's account of Palestinian liberation. From the very beginning, Said frames the question of Palestine in terms of fundamental human rights. The rights of self-determination, freedom of religion, freedom of movement, and the right to leave and return to one's country. The last two rights have to do with freedom of movement within and across national boundaries. These rights, as Said observes, are codified in "Article 13 of the Universal Declaration of Human Rights (1948)" and in "The International Covenant on Civil and Political Rights (1966)" (*QP* xvi, 47). By citing these documents, Said writes Palestinian liberation into the discourse of human rights whose ancestry includes the Rights of Man, which were espoused during the French Revolution, and in defense of which Thomas Paine wrote his famous essay *The Rights of Man*. These rights are the object of Marx's stinging critique of liberalism in "The Jewish Question." To restate that criticism briefly, the Rights of Man are formal and abstract, leaving things on the ground – the social relations of wealth and poverty, power, and powerlessness – pretty much as they are. The Rights of Man exemplify religion in its most insidious form, namely, the liberal state's inversion of substance and form, act and shadow, actual power and virtual power.

Said's account of Palestinian liberation is both this and more as his portrait of the Palestinian Liberation Organization suggests. He claims that perhaps the most novel and revolutionary aspect of the PLO is the idea of a secular democratic Palestinian state for Arabs and Jews. Unfortunately, according to Said, the idea of a secular democratic Palestine was undermined by Zionists and their American supporters who constructed that idea as genocidal. So, in a perverse reversal, the Palestinian question, which as I said earlier is the direct metamorphosis of the Jewish question, is recast as old-fashioned European anti-Semitism, Nazi-style genocide in "Arab-face" (*QP* 44, 139, 164, 220–221). Said writes with real pathos when he describes the complex struggle of the Palestinian people against Israeli oppression and against the ghost of European anti-Semitism and genocide, the burden of which Palestinians are unfairly expected to bear. All of this is part of the huge wall of denial that he calls Zionism. He is mindful of what Palestinians and Jews stand to lose with a human rights approach to the question of Palestine and what they stand to gain. They stand to lose and must abandon pan-Arab and Zionist constructions of Palestine. There can be no Israel without Palestinians, no Palestine without Jews. Gone would be notions such as a Jewish state or an Islamic state. Gone too would be civil distinctions between Palestinians and Jews and customary distinctions between European and non-European Jews. What Palestinians and Jews stand to gain by doing this is what each really wants: freedom from terror, oppression, insecurity, and social relations that make unjust domination possible. For Jews, this long-term goal "means freedom from the awful historical pressure of anti-Semitism whose culmination was Nazi genocide, freedom from the fear of Arabs, freedom also from the blindness of programmatic Zionism in its practice against the non-Jew." For Arabs, the long-term "goal is freedom from exile and dispossession, freedom from the cultural and psychological ravages of historical marginality, and freedom also from inhuman attitudes and practices toward the oppressing Israel" (*QP* 51–54, 230–231).

Said's recourse to human rights language is only slightly vulnerable to Marx's critique of capitalist liberalism, because what Marx criticizes are not rights but the formal, abstract, ahistorical character of liberal rights. Rights are not "a gift of nature" or a legacy, "but the reward of a struggle against the accident of birth and against the privileges which history has hitherto transmitted from generation to generation." Rights have a time and place, a history and specificity that liberalism obscures when it places birth, social rank, education, and occupation out of bounds, offstage, beyond the reach and discipline of the Rights of Man. It is precisely those things that are out of bounds and offstage that Said privileges in his account of Palestinian rights. Otherwise put, Said is not among those that Marx castigates as theologians. He does not invert and, therefore, distort the relationship between the secular and the religious, political emancipation, which is the formal proclamation of rights, and real emancipation. He knows, having learned from Marx, that real emancipation is the result of struggle against circumstances that the Palestinians did not choose and privileges that history has transmitted from the generation of insurgent Zionism to the triumphant generation of post-1967 Israel, post-PLO insurgency, and the 1993 Declaration of Principles – the "Palestinian Versailles" (*POD* xxxiv).

Said realizes that Palestinian rights are only virtual. These rights can only become actual through struggle, but not armed struggle, the feasibility of which he has long since abandoned, and to which he says that he has always been opposed. But he also opposes a unilateral Palestinian cease fire. This is why Said regards the Oslo Declaration of Principles as "an instrument of Palestinian surrender." His anger is kindled by the fact that the agreement that Yasser Arafat negotiated secretly – without the consent of the Palestinian National Council (PNC), of which Said is a former member – fails to meet the standards of political emancipation, much less real emancipation. Of the Palestinians, Said writes: "We received no acknowledgment of self-determination, no certainty of future sovereignty, no right of representation, no mention of reparations (and this from a state which received billions of dollars from Germany for the Nazi Holocaust)." The flames of his anger are only stoked by the "vulgar and distasteful" celebration of the agreement by Arafat and the Palestinian leadership, which pretends that the Oslo Accord represents a great Palestinian victory. According to Said, the Israeli novelist Amos Oz is closer to the truth, when of the Oslo Accord he says: "This is the second biggest victory in the history of Zionism." The size of this victory is underscored by the Accord's national security state premise, where primary consideration is given to Israel's security, with no provision for Palestinian security against Israeli incursions. Even more startling is the dramatic transformation that the Accord entails. It effectively transforms the PLO from a national liberation organization into a prosthetic arm of the Israeli police forces. In Said's language, "[t]he PLO will become Israel's enforcer," "an instrument of the Occupation."

Comparing the PLO unfavorably with the African National Congress (ANC), Said claims that the PLO is the only modern anticolonial movement that "capitulated to the colonial occupation *before* that occupation had been defeated and forced to leave" (*PD* xxiv, xxx, xxxiv, xxxviii, 8–9, 12, 23, 74, 177).

Not that forcing the Israelis to leave is feasible, as he acknowledges in a 1995 interview. Since the mid-1970s, according to Said, he has gradually come to the conclusion that a war of liberation is practically impossible. It imposes a leadership burden on Palestinians and Arabs that is too heavy to bear. He has also come to the conclusion that Palestine is not Algeria. The historical peculiarities of Israeli existence impose different conditions from those in the Algerian liberation struggle or the South African struggle. "I go so far as to be convinced by Rosa Luxemburg's statement," he writes, "that one cannot impose one's own political solution on another people against their will. As a Palestinian who has suffered loss and deprivations, I cannot morally accept regaining my rights at the expense of another people's deprivation" (*PD* 175).

This is Said in one of his more reflective moments, thinking about the peculiarities of the Palestinian struggle for emancipation and why in the end it is not simply one more anticolonial struggle. The Algerian liberation struggle can no longer serve as a proxy for the Palestinian struggle, as it did in his dispute with Walzer. The Palestinian question is a different sort of Jewish question, which is too complex for proxies. Although there is a sense in which the extraordinary events unfolding in South Africa provide a new model of what the possibilities are in an anticolonial struggle where there is a large settler community. I get the sense that Said is, paradoxically, both more pessimistic and more optimistic than this. Indeed, he consoles himself by invoking Gramsci's notion – pessimism of the intellect, optimism of the will (*PD* 16). This notion is constitutive of Said's idea of secular criticism. This conception of the secular vocation accounts for his willingness to break publicly with the PLO (of which he has never been a member) and with Arafat, both of whom he often defended against Israeli and American vilification. Said went from being their defender to their bitter critic when they betrayed the principles of Palestinian national independence and self-determination. The loyalties and solidarities of secular critics, in his view, are always principled. Those principles sometimes demand that the bonds of loyalty and solidarity be broken. To break these sacred bonds is preeminently a secular act. But, as Said well knows, the religious seduction of the secular

critic is always a possibility. Religion sometimes "returns" and in the
most unexpected places.

THE RETURN OF REPRESSED RELIGIOSITY

In *The World, the Text and the Critic*, Said criticizes the "return of repressed
religiosity" in contemporary critical theory. As he notes ruefully, evidence of this trend can be found in the vogue for texts such as *Kabbalah
and Criticism, Violence and the Sacred, Deconstruction and Theology*. He laments
the valorization of "the private and hermetic over the public and social"
in ostensibly radical movements such as Marxism, psychoanalysis, and
feminism. He notes the triumph of uncritical religiosity, which is underscored by the growth of special languages, "many of them impenetra-
ble, deliberately obscure, willfully illogical." What concerns him most
about this "curious veering toward the religious" are its political implications. "Political neoconservatives and the religiously inclined critics"
converge when they forget the realities of capital accumulation. They
forget that capital accumulation, and the globalization of labor and cultural markets that result, are presuppositions if not *the* presuppositions
of robust cultural critique. Against this religious trend, he calls for critical, secular renewal. "Once an intellectual, the modern critic has
become a cleric in the worst sense of the word. How their discourse can
once again collectively become a truly secular enterprise is, it seems to
me, the most serious question critics can be asking one another" (*WTC*
291–292).

The return of repressed religiosity is a loose reference to Freud's
psychosexual theory and to the notion of repression in particular. The
return of the repressed is the irruption into our mature present of our
infantile past. We become children again, if only momentarily. Religion
is symptomatic of our immaturity, evidence of our failure to deal
effectively with the temptations of infantile sexuality and the challenges
of mature sexuality. It suggests that we have regressed. Can there be any
doubt that this is what Said has in mind when he criticizes the return of
repressed religiosity in contemporary critical theory? Is he not asserting
that academic-Left theory is a form of regression? But a regression from
what? Obviously he refers to a regression from secular criticism as
exemplified by Marx, where the criticism of religion is the premise of all
criticism.

Said's work and public pronouncements are full of references to
sacred history and Gentile history, religious criticism and secular criti-

cism, the text and the world, the professional and the political, the abstract and the concrete. In each pair, the first term refers to religion or the sacred and the second to the secular or profane. He uses all these terms and others to identify what troubles him about the state of Left theory. Take the first pair of terms. Said's sacred history–secular history distinction presupposes "the notion of *beginning* as opposed to *origin*, the latter divine, mythical, and privileged, the former secular, humanly pro- duced, and ceaselessly re-examined." From this basic distinction, Said makes several claims: that beginning is a secular displacement of divine originality. That to begin is to transgress a divine intention and disrupt a sacred order of meaning. That beginning is not some irrational or "absurd" gesture, but a rational and enabling intervention into an order of meaning that has always already begun. That beginnings inaugurate new orders of meaning, by displacing God's original text (the book of nature) with the human work of history (*B* xi–xiii). That beginning is secular work, outside the text,[6] in the world of history and circum- stance.

"Origin" and "beginning" signify different attitudes toward meaning and authority, one religious the other secular. Or, as Said describes it, "Beginnings inaugurate a deliberately *other* production of meaning – a Gentile (as opposed to a sacred) one." They are repetitive rather than mimetic, producing new meanings, not copying old ones (*B* xvii). Beginnings are transgressive, blasphemous. Origins, in contrast, estab- lish mimetic relationships that ritualistically re-enact what God has done. We might gloss Said's account by saying that the mimetic relation- ship is one of mindless *re-presentation*. Like the stereotypical believer before the authoritative pronouncements of the church, it signals pros- tration before the claims of divine originality. Said calls this attitude toward origins religious or sacred. To displace the religious is to begin. Or as Marx put it, "the criticism of religion is the premise of all criti- cism."[7] Criticism requires the rejection of the servile, mimetic character of religion. But Said's critique of mimesis is different from René Girard's. The object of Girard's critique is mimetic rivalry and its violent-scapegoating denouement, which lies at the heart of the sacred. Thus, Girard accents the chaos-producing character of mimesis. In con- trast, Said gives mimesis a Marxist gloss – it is a form of alienation. This is an important difference. Girard's notion of mimesis serves to natural- ize (make necessary) this bloody form of rivalry. Structurally, it is indis- tinguishable from what Christians call Original Sin. Said's account, on the other hand, is a form of ideology-critique that attempts to unmask the historical as opposed to the cosmological character of mimesis and the human-all-too-human interests its serves.

Said attributes the notion of beginning as repetition and transgression to Vico. He claims that Vico "is the first philosopher of beginnings . . . because for him a beginning is at once never given and always indefinite or divined and yet always asserted at considerable expense." Here he underscores Vico's anti-Cartesian point. Beginning ideas are never "clear and distinct," but crude acts of imagination and divination, the products of an indefinite mind. More importantly, Vico underscores the costly nature of beginning; beginning transgresses the status quo, which those committed to it construe as sacred. According to Said, Vico construes beginning as a Gentile act that inaugurates a *secular* order of meaning that is other than the *sacred* order of meaning characteristic of Hebrew religion. He claims that Gentile history is predicated on the transgression of God's prohibition of divination, the observance of which constitutes Judaism as sacred. To be Gentile is to displace origins with beginnings and the given with imagination and invention, to "divine or imagine divinity," in one's own image. To be Gentile, in short, is to be done with sacred time and sacred narratives, "to live permanently in history, in an order other than God's" (*B* 349– 350). Beginnings, therefore, are the emancipation of the secular subject, the history-making subject. This is the subject that Marx imagined engaging in a ruthless critique of everything existing. The subject for whom the criticism of religion was now complete and for whom Marx could not imagine that religion would again be an issue. With the benefit of history and hindsight, Said sees things differently. For him, there is a return of repressed religiosity at the heart of contemporary critical theory.

Michel Foucault and Jacques Derrida are exhibits A and B in Said's case against repressed religiosity; they re-imprison the secular subject in sacred categories such as "power" and "*différance*." Between Foucault and Derrida is American postmodernism – a redundant formulation, if ever there was one. This triangular configuration, with sundry contributions from other sources, is the object to which Said refers when he speaks of a return of repressed religiosity. But why religion? For an answer to this question, I turn to what I take as Said's account of the linguistic turn in philosophy and theory, that is, the ascendancy of the notion of "textuality." On Said's view, textuality is a denial of history, a flight from circumstantial realities, a descent into the abyss of meaninglessness, paradox, and "undecidability." As the preferred metaphor of the postdiscourses (whether postmodern, poststructuralist, post-Marxist, or postphilosophical), textuality is the antithesis and displacement of history (*WTC* 3–4). According to Said, contemporary literary theory (that intellectual movement of the 1970s and 1980s that sublated, transfigured, and disfigured philosophy and social theory) operates in an ahistorical labyrinth of intertextuality. Theory has "isolated textuality from the circumstances, events, the physical senses that made it possible and render it *intelligible as the result of human work*" (*WTC* 4, emphasis mine). In contrast, secular, worldly, reality-based forms of critique foreground the circumstances under which agents produce texts, exposing the affiliation between texts, relations of power, and structures of meaning. In short, S*ecular Criticism* accents history.[8]

Said wants to distinguish the worldliness of *Secular Criticism* from the otherworldliness of poststructuralism–postmodernism, from "the aporias and unthinkable paradoxes of a text," from the religious practices of "a priestly caste of acolytes and dogmatic metaphysicians" (*WTC* 4–5). Obviously, Said regards the concept of religion as especially evocative of what he deplores in postmodernist and poststructuralist discourses. By invoking reality or history (Said uses them interchangeably), he can highlight the otherworldliness of postdiscourses, where the transactional relations of textuality and the world are denied. Said's genealogy of these discourses includes the fierce parochialism of the American New Critics and the cosmopolitan abandonment of the French "new New Critics," which is his terminology for structuralists and poststructuralists (*WTC* 142). Whether parochial or cosmopolitan, these forms of criticism (American, French, and "French Fried" American) have strong *otherworldly* tendencies.

Said acknowledges the contributions of the French-inspired critical discourses. They helped American critics challenge a university system dominated by positivism, determinism, bourgeois humanism, and the rigidities of disciplinary specialization (*WTC* 3). Unfortunately, these theories never took well to American soil, but mutated into degraded forms. Said calls this phenomenon (the transformations that theory undergoes when transplanted from one set of historical circumstances to another) "traveling theory." Theory is degraded by "dissemination" when the inevitable process of transplantation is carried out without proper attention to the local climate. This has been the fate of most French theory in America. The distinctive circumstances of post-World War II France that made structuralist and poststructuralist theories seem appropriate were different from those in the United States. The American appropriation of French theory took place against a cultural

backdrop that lacked historical memories of the specific intellectual and
social struggles that made these theories seem natural, if not effective, in
the French context. Consequently, American appropriations of French
theory seem artificial and dismally ineffective. Whether the master theorist is Deleuze, Derrida, Foucault or Lacan, this appropriation is often
little more than a bewildering and embarrassing series of intellectual
fads. This explains the worldlessness and weightlessness of much
American criticism. In this disconnection between the particularities of
French theory and the specificity of American history, Said sees a
descent into textuality, where critical theories are severed from worldly
transactions. The results are methodologies and systems that Said
describes as dogmatic, mystifying, otherworldly, and religious.

To underscore this point, textuality can be viewed by analogy to biblical fundamentalism, where overriding authority is assigned to canonical texts and authors. Said describes a logic of displacement, where the
canonical authorities of the New Critics (for example, Donne and
Dante) are displaced by the authority of the new New Critics – that is,
by "Rousseau, Artaud, Bataille, Saussure, Freud, and Nietzsche." Said
might have also noted the irony of the subsequent displacement of this
canon, within American postmodernism, by none other than Deleuze,
Derrida, Foucault, and Lacan. "These authors are employed as principles beyond which texts as texts cannot and need not go. To return to
them, as Lacan returned to Freud, is to establish them as a canon whose
legitimacy is maintained with loyal devotion" (*WTC* 143). Collectively,
these texts constitute a new holy writ, a sacred canon for the acolytes of
the new critical discourses. These authors are accorded the deference
usually reserved for religious gurus, and their work is constructed as
scripture, even as it is used to debunk scripture.

The newer critics pour over these new New Critical sacred texts with
the exegetical enthusiasm and conviction of biblical fundamentalists.
Rather than argue a point, they merely drop names, usually Nietzsche,
Freud, Artaud, or Benjamin, as if name dropping was sufficient "to over-
ride any objection or settle any quarrel" (*WTC* 143). What Said says
about these figures can now be said about Lacan, Foucault, Derrida, and
Deleuze in spades. In summary, Said accuses the proponents of recent
French theory, especially in its domesticated American varieties, of
engaging in the secular equivalent of "proof-texting," of behaving like
fundamentalists before the authority of sacred scripture. Thus they
reproduce the canonical practices of fundamentalist Christianity. Is
there not more than a little irony here? For Said is as responsible as

anyone for introducing French theory to an American audience. Furthermore, I am not sure that Said avoids the tendencies that he criticizes. Can anyone? Do not we inevitably and necessarily construct something as scripture?[9]

If textuality, as Said sees it, is the problem, then worldliness is the solution. Worldliness, which means roughly the same thing as reality and history, is a set of constraints on interpretation and reference such that "the closeness of the world's body to the text's body forces readers to take both into consideration." Said contrasts this notion with the claim that interpretation is limitless (*WTC* 39). He regards such talk as evidence of the religious attitude, a kind of monkish inwardness that refuses to truck with the world outside the church, the academy, the text. To speak of worldliness is to enter into an antagonistic relationship with academic and professional insularity. Said "tropes" on an important theme in Christian discourse, where worldliness signifies an order that is in open rebellion against the Christian God; it is the refusal of divine sovereignty, "the Kingdom of God." Worldliness signifies "this worldliness," secular hopes, secular forms of solace, secular forms of meaning. It signifies, in short, the loss of one's critical bearings, blindness, captivity to sin, the devil's ideology. Said inverts the normative codes of the worldly–otherworldly distinction, with worldly as a positively charged term for a secular disposition and otherworldly as a negatively charged term for a religious disposition. Otherworldliness is characterized by a flight from circumstantial realities that constrain interpretation, provide a referent, and confer meaning. In contrast, worldliness is a skeptical disposition situated within the cultural and systematic cross-currents of its historical conjuncture, between the religious effects of culture and the return of repressed religiosity in contemporary critical systems. *Secular Criticism* regards both culture and critical theory with suspicion. Critical theory is (or becomes) a form of religious seduction; it is as seductive as a religious wolf in the sheep's-clothing of secular critique and thus is especially pernicious. Said does not believe that critical theory is religious in a literal sense, but religious is the most appropriate naming of what cannot properly be named – it is a *catachresis*.

*Secular Criticism* avoids both the mindless conformities of culture and the otherworldliness (abstraction and reification) of system. It is criticism between culture as transfigured religious thought and system as the return of repressed religiosity. This brings us, again, to Derrida and Foucault who illustrate this point. Said's position toward Derrida and Foucault has become less enthusiastic and increasingly negative over the last decade or so. I think it is fair to say that he has moved from skeptical sympathy to qualified hostility. Where he once saw them as revolutionary critics, he now sees them as antirevolutionaries, whose work is a counsel of cosmological pessimism or otherworldly-messianic hope. Where he had once favorably distinguished Foucault's notion of discourse from Derrida's notion of textuality, he now sees them as pretty much the same thing.[10] During that earlier period, when he was decidedly more sympathetic to Foucault's notion of discourse than to Derrida's notion of textuality, his argument was this: that Derrida's work fails "to accommodate descriptive information" that would give his notion of Western metaphysics a meaning that is more than repetitive and allusive. Derrida's work, he adds, has shown little interest in actually "dissolving the ethnocentrism of which on occasion it has spoken with noble clarity." This is an instance of Said's criticism of political quietism, of Derrida's failure to politicize the text, to show how ethical–political judgments can be made "inside the text," that is, in a world without transcendence. Neither has Derrida's critical work, he continues, "demanded from its disciples any binding engagement on matters pertaining to discovery and knowledge, freedom, oppression, or injustice." This continues the previous charge that Derrida fails to politicize the "inside text" (the network of language and everything else), having argued that there is "no outside text." The prominence of this charge, now a commonplace in critical circles, owes a great deal to Said, who turns up the intensity in this passage: "If everything in a text is always open equally to suspicion and to affirmation, then the differences between one class interest and another, one ideology and another, are virtual in – but never crucial to making decisions about – the finally reconciling element of textuality" (*WTC* 214). This is not the clearest passage. But I take Said to be making a simple point: that the skeptical play of textuality does not allow us to make the political–ethical distinctions that we want to make. Said's criticism of Derridian textuality is an analogue to his later criticism of Foucault's all-encompassing, Spinozistic notion of power, which also resists a politicized inside – that is, an immanent critique of the discourse, text, plane of immanence, or community of language users of which we are part.

Thus, on his mature or developed view, Said refuses to make a politically significant distinction between textuality and discourse. We see this refusal in his attitude toward the entire range of poststructuralist and postmodernist theory. Said chooses to be "unfair," rejecting distinctions among poststructuralists or between poststructuralists and neopragmatists that others find relevant. Despite their theoretical hairsplitting, Said finds few practical political differences between them (as opposed to abstract theoretical differences) that truly make a difference. In an interview, he takes Occam's razor, now Said's razor, to a broad swath of postmodernist and poststructuralist theory. The context is the aftermath of the Gulf War. Said is responding to the interviewer's question about the relevance, given the contemporary context, of Noam Chomsky's idea of intellectual responsibility. To be intellectually responsible, Said argues:

One would have to pretty much scuttle all the jaw-shattering jargonistic postmodernisms that now dot the landscape. They are worse than useless. They are neither capable of understanding and analyzing the power structure of this country, nor are they capable of understanding the particular aesthetic merit of an individual work of art.

This is true of such discourses across the spectrum: of deconstruction, postmodernism, poststructuralism, and so on. All represent forms of the post-1968 retreat by political radicals throughout the West, but especially in France. As a response to this collective retreat, Said calls for critical renewal. This means returning to old-fashioned scholarly virtues and to the premise that men and women make their own history and that what they make they can always remake (*POD* 316–317).

Said's razor is equally sharp in *Culture and Imperialism*. His comments there are so similar to those in the interview that one could easily imagine them as components of a single chain of thought. Of contemporary critics, Said says this: "Jargons of an almost rebarbativeness dominate their styles. Cults like post-modernism, discourse analysis, New Historicism, deconstruction, neo-pragmatism transport them into the country of the blue; an astonishing sense of weightlessness with regard to the gravity of history and individual responsibility fritters away attention to public matters, and to public discourse." The results of this treason of the intellectuals are truly dispiriting, when issues such as racism, poverty, ecological devastation, disease, and ignorance "are left to the media and the odd political candidate during an election campaign" (*CAI* 303).

Notice the themes in these passages, the explicit correlation between religion and critical theory, their jargons, otherworldliness, and cultic practices. On Said's view, too few posttheorists are willing to pay the personal and professional price of an engaged, worldly criticism, for criticism as a secular enterprise. The jargons of the various postdiscourses signify retreat from the realm of public discourse to the privacy of the

monastery, the cloister, the academy. This explains the unseemly spectacle of an academic struggle for position that shows little interest in its
extra-academic purchase and that has even less to do with politics.
Gramsci's useful idea of a struggle for position within civil society
between the ruling (or hegemonic) class and insurgent (or subaltern)
classes has been reduced to a size that is proper to these theorists. Thus
academic politics becomes the most important form of politics, if not
politics as such. What the postdiscourses signify, Said concludes, is a
religious retreat from the power and politics of the secular world, the
quotidian, ordinary, and everyday world. These discourses, that is to say,
represent a retreat from what most people mean most of the time by politics. The very claim to sophistication by poststructuralist, postmodernist, post-Marxist, and postphilosophical critics is a form of mystification.
Or as Said remarks regarding Foucault's American followers, and this
charge can be generalized to all advocates of the postdiscourses, they
"wish to go beyond Left optimism and Right pessimism so as to justify
political quietism with sophisticated intellectualism" (*WTC* 245).

### REPRESSED RELIGIOSITY WITH A FRENCH TWIST

No one exemplifies the sophisticated intellectualism that Said criticizes
more than Foucault and Derrida – except, perhaps, their American followers. Foucault and Derrida's legacies to American theory are a secular
notion of "Original Sin" and a messianic notion of justice. In both cases,
something beyond this world, larger than we, and other than human
capacities in their natural circumstances, determines our fate and is the
source of whatever hope we have.

Foucault is the dark prince of contemporary theory, the hypersophis-
ticate who ostensibly knows things that most of us do not want to know.
If Foucault's major claim is that nothing occurs outside relations of
power, then his claim is trivial. Foucault's followers do not take his claim
to be trivial, nor apparently does he. Thus there is good reason to suspect
that he is saying more than what the bare-faced claim that there is
nothing outside relations of power, no outside power, would suggest.
What he is saying, and many commentators have understood this from
the beginning, is that power cannot be morally qualified. There are not
any nonfraudulent ways of distinguishing good power from bad power.
Power is beyond good and evil and beyond good and bad. Thus Foucault
one-ups Nietzsche in the stringency of his "immoralism." I should
amend this claim just a bit. Foucault's view of power is really amoral

rather than immoral; Nietzsche's immoralism, in contrast, is thoroughly ethical in character. Foucault's sphinx-like response to those who questioned his amoral view of power partially gave way in his later work to a qualified view. But, even there, he does not give us any reason to regard what he says as true – or false. He clearly believes, however, that his assertions are true, even if he does not, and I think cannot, say why. For many of his followers, this is not a problem. The attraction of Foucault is not the cogency and meticulous care of his arguments but the revelatory power of his pronouncements. Despite their cold dispassion, his pronouncements sound more like inscrutable revelation than reasoned argument and the citation of evidence. Undoubtedly, Foucault's followers would denounce this characterization as evidence of an Enlightenment hangover or Enlightenment blackmail. So be it.

Foucault's notion of power where there is no outside is like Original Sin without redemption. Foucault can look down his nose with an air of superiority on those benighted souls who still believe in redemption or in its secular analogues of liberation and emancipation. He has accepted a truth that they cannot accept, that even Nietzsche could not accept: that there is no Christ or Dionysus; that there is no Zarathustra, Superman, or philosopher of the future. But there is the Original Sin of power, the human condition in its indelible reality, which he has dared to look in the face. Foucault is not as explicit in his later work as he was in earlier work, but there is little reason to believe that he ever amended the view that we move from one morally unqualified domination to another. We have no grounds, and I do not mean metaphysical grounds, but historically contingent grounds, for saying "Yes" or "No," for preferring this power to that power. We are in the position of waiting for Godot, but can give little more than an idiot's reason for doing so.

This is a view that Derrida has never bought, which has become increasingly evident in his recent "political" phase. If his goal is not liberation and emancipation, then it is justice. Unlike Foucault, Derrida does not give up on this notion. The question, however, is what does Derrida mean by justice? Justice is not law. In any case, it is not identical to law or reducible to what is legal. Justice is an ideal, an "ought" that surpasses every "is." Nor is justice merely the higher law of Socrates or the natural law that Paul says is written in our hearts. Justice is a Levinasian call to infinite responsibility. It is not here or there, was not yesterday, but may be tomorrow. Justice is a Benjaminian messianism. But what does that mean? Derrida describes a "desert-like messianism (without content and without identifiable messiah) . . . the coming of the other, the absolute and unpredictable singularity of the *arrivant as justice.*[11] As is true of most incantations, how he speaks is more important than what he says. Justice is a revelation – beyond nature and reason, beyond language. Justice is the one thing that cannot be deconstructed, which escapes the destabilizing and skeptical play of *différence*. This means – and his American readers will be surprised – that there is something outside the text after all.[12] Justice is the experience of the impossible, of what Kierkegaard says is humanly impossible, of the absurd. Derrida does not use this language, but there should be little doubt that this is what he means.

From Marx's notion of justice as a difficult and precarious human achievement, we move to Derrida's neo-Jewish, neo-Christian notion of justice as eschatological promise. Derrida counterpoises justice as messianic to the messianic eschatologies that dominate the contemporary Middle East, the three religions of the Book – Judaism, Christianity, and Islam. Marxism is indispensable but inadequate to a radical understanding of these eschatologies and the violence that they unleash. Marxism, as a species of modernism and postmodernism, as the eclectic ideas that dominate American high theory, denies the necessity of a messianic eschatology. Therein lies the common inadequacy that Marxism shares with its modernist and postmodernist kin. It simply will not do, according to Derrida, for critics of Marxism to criticize messianic eschatology as the ideological-and-theological common ground of Marxism and religion. They ignore the "*epokhe* of the content," the suspension and evacuation of a determinant content, which he claims is "essential to the messianic in general." I should add here, that this sounds more like Kant's moral "ought" than Jewish or Christian notions of messianism, even on Benjamin's idiosyncratic view. Given this idiosyncratic view, Derrida makes the startling claim that:

> what remains irreducible to any deconstruction, what remains as undeconstructible as the possibility itself of deconstruction is, perhaps, a certain experience of the emancipatory promise; it is perhaps even the formality of a structural messianism, a messianism without religion, even a messianism without messianism, an idea of justice – which we distinguish from law or right and even from human rights – and an idea of democracy – which we distinguish from its current concept and from its determined predicates today . . .[13]

I will address the implications of this passage in a moment, but first some preliminary remarks. I cannot imagine Said objecting to Derrida's qualified endorsement of Marx. Who on the Left, after all, would disagree with the notion that "one may still find inspiration in the 'spirit' of

Marx – the spirit that reveals 'the *de facto* take-over of international authorities by powerful Nation-States, by concentrations of techno-scientific capital, symbolic capital, and financial capital, of state capital and private capital.'"[14] Said no doubt would agree with the claim that there is little reason to celebrate the "end of the great emancipatory discourses," given the innumerable sites of suffering, subjugation, starvation, and extermination in the world. But he would pull out his hair and gnash his teeth when Derrida supplements and displaces Marxism with messianic eschatology, deconstruction-as-justice, which is what Derrida does in the passage above and in many others. On Derrida's view, deconstruction is what was always most important and what is still living in Marxism! Derrida provides the most brutally sophisticated evisceration of Marx by an ostensibly sympathetic critic that I have read. He removes from Marx's corpse and corpus what is most important, the very heart of his work – the idea of justice as humanly achievable, and replaces it with a quasi-Levinasian, quasi-Benjaminian idea of revelation and messianic promise. This promise of justice is from another time and place, beyond time and space, a future time that we cannot calculate, a space that we cannot map. If the proponents of Jewish emancipation, against whom Marx inveighed, confused civil emancipation with real emancipation, then Derrida confuses justice with revelation. Justice is a political project, not a messianic hope. This is what makes Marx's appropriation and repetition of Jewish and Christian notions of historical messianism different and more significant than Derrida's.

Derrida's notion of justice as messianic eschatology and Foucault's notion of power, which I read as Original Sin, are dominant themes in contemporary American theory. It is precisely otherworldliness of this sort that is the object of Said's critique – his critique, that is, of the return of repressed religiosity, the religious seduction of the secular critic, and the religious effects of culture. Said errs, however, to the extent that he construes secularism as the other of religion. Secularism is incomprehensible without religion; it is often an aspect of religion and always a product of a religious culture. There is no Marx without Judaism and the complex reality of being a second-generation Christian convert in a Jew-hating culture. There is no Nietzsche without Christianity, no Antichrist without Christ. There is no Said, the secular critic, the Palestinian Christian by birth, without the contending messianic eschatologies – Jewish, Christian, and Islamic – of which Derrida spoke. I contend that religion makes Said's project more comprehensible, especially his scattered but persistent reference to religion and secularism.

This highlights the many meanings and complexities of secularism, which Said never explicates. One can be religious and thoroughly secular or secular and thoroughly religious. Secularism as secularization means the political disestablishment of churches and other religious institutions and traditions. Sometimes it refers to the critique of traditional religious belief. Thus those who regard witchcraft as a false belief, or deny the existence of an immaterial essence called soul or spirit, or dispute the biblical account of the Battle of Jericho in which the sun stood still, are secular in this second respect. Said's secular criticism suffers from his failure to explicate the varieties of secularism. In turn, his critique of religion as a cultural effect – a temptation for the secular critic and a piece of repressed infantilism that threatens to "return" – misfires when it takes religion as something that can be completed or terminated. *Pace* Said and Marx, the criticism of religion, as far as we can see, is interminable.

# Concluding remarks: religion, secularism, and pragmatic naturalism

Art is the sole alternative to luck; and divorce from each other of the meaning and value of instrumentalities and ends is the essence of luck. The esoteric character of culture and the supernatural quality of religion are both expressions of the divorce.

Fidelity to the nature to which we belong, as parts however weak, demands that we cherish our desires and ideals til we have converted them into intelligence, revised them in terms of ways and means which nature makes possible. When we have used our thought to its utmost and thrown into the moving unbalanced balance of things our puny strength, we know that though the universe slay us still we may trust, for our lot is one with whatever is good in existence. We know that such thought and effort is one condition of the coming into existence of the better. As far as we are concerned it is the only condition, for it alone is in our power.

(John Dewey, *Experience and Nature*, pp. 372, 420)

But human power is extremely limited, and is infinitely surpassed by the power of external causes; we have not, therefore, an absolute power of shaping to our use those things which are without us. Nevertheless, we shall bear with an equal mind all that happens to us in contravention to the claims of our own advantage, so long as we are conscious, that we have done our duty, and that the power which we possess is not sufficient to enable us to protect ourselves completely; remembering that we are a part of universal nature, and follow her order. If we have a clear and distinct understanding of this, that part of our nature which is defined by intelligence, in other words the better part of ourselves, will assuredly acquiesce in what befalls us, and in such acquiescence will endeavour to persist. For, in so far as we are intelligent beings, we cannot desire anything save that which is necessary, nor yield absolute acquiescence to anything save to that which is true: wherefore, in so far as we have a right understanding of these things, the endeavour of the better part of ourselves is in harmony with the order of nature as a whole.

(Benedict de Spinoza, *On The Improvement of The Understanding, The Ethics, Correspondence, The Ethics*, Part VI, Appendix XXXII)

Throughout this study I have collaborated with Said's invidious distinction between religion and secularism. I took this distinction as a rhetorically effective, if not persuasive, way of criticizing various currents in contemporary critical thought. But now it is time to bid farewell to Said, to distinguish between him and me, to consider my personal stakes in these matters, and show why the invidious distinction between religion and secularism is besides the point of radical critique.

One spirit of radical critique is captured well by a proponent of the French Revolution who reputedly looked forward to the day when the last king was strangled with the entrails of the last priest. The arbitrary and antidemocratic power of church and state is the object of this critique. It is a view for which, in my darker moments, I have some sympathy. But closer to my considered view is a statement by Thomas Jefferson, the most important representative of the American Enlightenment: "It does me no injury for my neighbour to say that there are twenty Gods or no God. It neither picks my pocket nor breaks my leg."[1] Except where it causes positive harm, religion is something that we can benignly neglect. Where religion does cause harm, that harm is indistinguishable from injuries that occur in secular life. The object of radical critique, therefore, is neither religion nor secularism but those things that are common to both – dogmatism, illiberalism, scapegoating, arbitrary power, antidemocratic authority, and the propensity to dissemble and lie.

Stanley Cavell's comments on the difference between Marx and Emerson – their different accounts of the relations between religion and cultural critique – help to illustrate the perspective that I call pragmatic naturalism. Cavell is puzzled by Gershom Scholem's blindness and insight where Emerson and the lineaments of American philosophy are concerned. Scholem shows great insight when he praises Walt Whitman whose writings, like those of the cabbalists, speak to both the private and the public individual. In their ability to produce forms of obligation in both spheres and even to erase the boundaries between the two, these writings overcome the divisions that characterize modern secular life. "Walt Whitman revealed in an utterly naturalistic world what cabbalists and other mystics revealed in their world." Why, Cavell, wonders, is Scholem unable to "recognize Emerson behind Whitman"? He is puzzled but not completely stumped. Scholem's reference to Romain Rolland's[2] condescending description of Emerson as Whitman's intellectual underlaborer provides the interpretive opening that Cavell needs:

In Rolland's account, Emerson is unable to appear as a thinker with his own relation to establish between philosophy and religion, call this his own continuation of philosophy's mission in the critique of religion. It is a mission, roughly simultaneous with Marx's claim that the philosophical critique of religion is completed, that shows Marx's claim to be premature. I assume this mission provides a reasonable ground for Nietzsche's undying debt to Emerson. It also seems to me precisely pertinent to Scholem's central quarrel with Benjamin over the relation of Marx and theology. Shall we think of Scholem's passing up of Emerson as an intellectual near miss?[3]

And what of Said? Shall we think of his passing up of Emerson, of Emersonianism and pragmatic naturalism, as an intellectual near miss? I think that we should. And I shall begin that argument by rewriting, in an Emersonian vernacular, Marx's first and eleventh "Theses on Feuerbach":

Thesis I. The chief defect of most notions of secularism – that of Said included – is that secularism is conceived as other than religion as even the opposite of religion. But secularism is not the other of religion; it is a particular way of *not being religious* and an equally particular (if not peculiar) way of *being religious*. Secularism, so conceived, is specifically available (perhaps exclusively available) to those who have been exposed to liberal and Enlightenment ideas.

Thesis XI. The idea that one can be both religious and secular would never occur to Said. That secularity could be the chief modality of some forms of religiosity would be equally incomprehensible. To construe religion and secularism as opposites, as Said does, is to be blind to some of the most interesting ways of being religious or secular. From an Emersonian-pragmatic naturalist perspective, about which I shall say more in a moment, religion and secularism are an economy, an ongoing process of exchange. From this perspective, religion and secularism must be thought about together rather than singly. It makes more sense, therefore, to speak of religion-secularism. What is criticized as religious – dogmatic views, obscurantist language, uncritical forms of solidarity, and violent dispositions – are often reproduced in what is praised as secular. These nasty aspects of our common life are found, always and already, in the secular world. The Emersonian-pragmatic naturalist, therefore, is not satisfied with the notion of a return of repressed religiosity in secular form or the notion of religion as the inverted and fetishized appearance of the secular world. The language of self-incurred immaturity and Enlightenment or decadence and health doesn't quite work either. Those things that we criticize as religious are simply human-all-too-human. Thus our susceptibility to dogmatism, mystification, and violent forms of solidarity is a mark of our finitude and fallibility, of our status as homo sapiens, not *Homo religiosi*. For these things there are no deep philosophical or theoretical solutions, only the art of politics. If the point of criticism is to change the world, then the criticism of religion and secularism is an indeterminate if not interminable critique.

Pragmatic naturalism is a historically contingent strategy for coping with finitude. That is the negative description. Positively speaking, it is an awe-filled and grateful acceptance, in the face of tragedy, of our place in the natural process.[4] Pragmatic naturalism is post-Darwinian. To invoke Darwin's name is to conjure up a host of disagreeable ideas – crude biologism, genetic arguments for the cognitive inferiority of black people, social Darwinism, and so on. That much nonsense has been written and continues to be written in Darwin's name, and that he like all epochal thinkers sometimes said stupid things,[5] does not make Darwinism nonsense. I chose an affirmative approach to Darwin, concentrating more on his insight, less on his stupidity. Thus Darwin's views, properly qualified, set the terms of my response – and ought to be our response, as self-conscious and linguistically equipped mortal beings – to natural finitude. These views trouble dualities such as nature/human and human/machine. Humans and their machines are part of the natural world. Machines/technology may be the *being* (even the species being) of human beings, but we pragmatists think that Heidegger "questions technology" in a dark and one-sided way.

On our view, *Homo sapiens* are one more species, however complex, doing the best it can, responding to the pressures of natural selection like the amoeba or the coral reef. We mortals do our best within the orders, disorders, and accidents of the natural process. Were we to ascribe intentionality to that process, we would say that nature is indifferent to our beliefs, desires, hopes, and fears. But strictly speaking such anthropomorphic language, while generally harmless, is a mischaracterization. Nature, apart from our attributions, is not cold and indifferent. It just is. To think otherwise is to anthropomorphize. On the other hand, if nature has the quality of serendipity, it is only because we have the language to imagine it so. There is no goal, destiny, or *telos* other than those we have imagined. Our imaginative investments are often sublime, but they are our investments. We should not imagine that some One else or some Thing else is paying interest. Pragmatic naturalists do not think less of these investments because they are ours, rather than God's, Being's, or Nature's. We are not disturbed by a cosmos forever mute, which is indifferent (not hostile or sympathetic) to value and truth. We do not begrudge the fact that we share a common fate with the amoeba, although we can understand why animals such as us might be tempted.[6] That our life cycle is only a complex variation on the simplest form of animal life is a source of wonder and awe. Wonder, awe, dependence, and gratitude come close to exhausting our religious affections; beyond these, we feel no desire to worship, which is not to say that this is not another way of worshiping.

Pragmatic naturalists are skeptical (not dismissive) of every form of panpsychism, including Charles S. Peirce's "metaphysics of evolutionary love," William James' radical empiricism, and Alfred North Whitehead's process thought, of every effort, that is, to supply the natural process with subjectivity, with the qualities of mind, spirit, and intention. We are skeptical of naturalized forms of metaphysical humanism – that is, the attempt to make human being ontologically unique, the view that humans are something more than complex animals. Where panpsychics find psychic, spiritual, mind-like relations throughout nature, the pragmatists whom I commend find causal relations.[7] What connects "man" and amoeba is not mind, divine or otherwise, but relations of cause and effect. And here, we are willing to admit, though not necessarily own, all of the problems and paradoxes that constitute the very idea of cause and effect.

My account of pragmatic naturalism is indebted to Henry Levinson.[8] Levinson is a "Princeton pragmatist," a group that includes Richard Rorty, Jeffrey Stout, Cornel West, and Victor Anderson. He is the eccentric in this group in that his views are deeply influenced by George Santayana, who is absent from, or appears as an antagonist in, most accounts of classical pragmatism. Levinson retrieves certain aspects of Santayana's work, especially his thoroughgoing naturalism, poetic understanding of religious traditions, and festive or comic understanding of criticism (that is, his Nietzsche-like abandonment of the spirit of gravity). Along the way, he cast a wary eye toward Santayana's racism, patriarchal sensibilities, and imperial conception of democracy. Levinson gives a pragmatic reading of the more troubling aspects of Santayana work, reinterpreting where he can and discarding what he must.

Levinson describes West as a member of the pragmatic naturalist club (a club that includes Santayana, Dewey, and Rorty) but I wonder. West strikes me more as an ambivalent fellow-traveler than as a stalwart party member. His position, which presupposes a core-Christianity, "stripped of static dogmas and decrepit doctrines," reads as little more than a Protestant liberal manifesto. I do not think that this is a ruthless and overly aggressive reading. For if pragmatic naturalism is post-Darwinian, then it is also post-Protestant. My doubts about West's naturalistic "bona fides" are inspired by the relative paucity of references to natural existence in his work. The relative frequency of statements that presupposes something beyond natural existence only enhances my suspicions. For example, West has a great deal to say about the Hegelian side of his philosophical hero John Dewey, but little to say about his Darwinian side. Perhaps this explains why West is attracted to Kierkegaard, whose peculiar but brilliant perspective has influenced several generations of Protestant thinkers. Kierkegaard occupies a rather prominent place in West's religious thinking, which casts doubt on Levinson's claim that he is a pragmatic religious naturalist. What does it mean to describe him as such in light of the following:

> Like Kierkegaard, whose reflections on Christian faith were so profound yet often so frustrating, I do not think it possible to put forward rational defenses of one's faith that verify its veracity or even persuade one's critics. Yet it is possible to convey to others the sense of deep emptiness and pervasive meaninglessness one feels if one is not critically aligned with an enabling tradition. One risks not logical inconsistency but actual insanity; the issue is not reason or irrationality but life or death. Of course, the fundamental question remains whether the Christian gospel is ultimately true. And, as a Christian prophetic pragmatist whose focus is on coping with transient and provisional penultimate matters yet whose hope goes beyond them, I reply in the affirmative, bank my all on it, yet am willing to entertain the possibility in low moments that I may be deluded.[9]

West's Dewey-inspired prophetic pragmatism is different from the Santayana-inspired pragmatic naturalism that Levinson describes. On Levinson's account, religious traditions answer some questions and not others. What questions people take their religious traditions to answer has a lot to do with how they construct those traditions. Within a pragmatic naturalist account, Kierkegaardian answers – however brilliant and thought provoking – do not make any sense. They are answers to questions that pragmatists do not find a compelling reason to ask. So when West speaks of hope that goes beyond "transient and provisional penultimate matters," we are left scratching our heads. It is not clear to us what it would mean, on a pragmatic naturalist account, to be that sort of "desiring subject."

With provisos I think that we can assimilate Kierkegaard with Protestant liberalism. When we do so, some interesting similarities become evident. Both are reactions to Enlightenment critiques of religion and to modern biblical criticism. Both Kierkegaard and liberals concede crucial ground while placing the authentic kernel of the tradition – faith and subjective truth, for Kierkegaard, morality, for liberals – beyond criticism. Protestant liberalism demythologizes, dumping overboard anything that offends Enlightened reason, including the better part of its symbolic and imaginative riches. Kierkegaard (or at least his pseudonymous personae) pursues a different strategy. He acknowledges the force of Enlightened reason and historical consciousness by embracing Enlightenment judgments of Christianity's fundamental absurdity. Kierkegaard makes Christianity a strenuous quest (the most difficult imaginable) suitable only for aristocrats of the spirit. On Kierkegaard's view, an irrational "leap of faith" sublates rational possibility as the very definition of what it means to become a Christian.

The liberal option leaves pragmatic naturalists cold. We refuse to "thin-out," denude, or otherwise desiccate the imaginative, mythic, symbolic, and liturgical richness of our respective religious traditions, however eccentric, idiosyncratic, and heterodox our relations to those traditions may be. Nor is there much that commends the fideism of Kierkegaardians and postliberals.[10] Thus we reject the stance of the spiritual aristocrat: the stance of a Kierkegaard or Nietzsche, for whom the riches of the religious life are available only to the virtuoso, the knight of faith, the "superman." Pragmatic naturalists do not reduce religious traditions to morality or mistake them for alternative sciences or metaphysical accounts of the really-real. Religious traditions may be "pathetic fallacies." They may have emerged, at least under one description, in response to our hopes and fears, but it would be a mistake, a genetic fallacy, to suggest that this explains what they do. As pragmatists, we agree with William James; we do not confuse origins with consequences, the roots of the tree with its fruits.[11] That religious traditions are "transparent fictions" is no objection, much in our lives are such fictions, which does not make them any less valuable.

If religious traditions are not representations of the really-real, of the way things really are, of the way things infallibly ought to be, perhaps they are sublime products of the human imagination. On this post-Protestant view, God is the greatest character (at least in some narratives) ever imagined. Religious institutions (with all their faults) are among the best schools of virtue conceivable. Fasting and prayer (despite the allure of superstition) are among the most effective forms of spiritual discipline ever invented. Will fasting and prayer help us to get what we want?[12] Perhaps, but not because they produce the desired state of affairs. Not because they solicit, seduce, coerce, or otherwise presuppose powers greater than we mortal beings in our natural circumstances, as organisms transacting with other organisms, body to body, idea to idea. Fasting and prayer are best regarded as technologies of the self (in Dewey's rather than Foucault's sense of the term), as experimental responses to problematic situations. Thus fasting and prayer may help us cope with our finitude. They may help us cope with difficult circumstances until help comes. More important, they may help us cope with the all-too-human probability that help is *not* forthcoming. For some of us, fasting and prayer are not useful technologies, but we do not begrudge those for whom they are.

Pragmatic religious naturalism, unlike Protestant liberalism and post-liberalism, "is *imaginative, unrealistic,* seriously *playful,* and *symbolic.*"[13] Neither homeless nor nomadic, pragmatic naturalists are both in and out of the tradition, the community, the religious institution. Our conception of tradition is relational and dynamic. That which lies outside the tradition – the other and the different – is essential to what we are. This distinguishes us both from liberals and postliberals, from those who presuppose the Enlightenment's prejudice against prejudice and from those who construct tradition as a windowless monad. Some would call us postmodern, but we would gladly do without that description. We are tired of the endless, often mindless, circling of the "post"; after a while, it loses its novelty and ceases to amuse. We are tired of the pushing and shoving as American intellectuals struggle, lemming-like, to get a whiff of the latest poststructuralist–postmodernist flatulence. There are too many "French-fried" American intellectuals for our tastes. That pragmatic naturalists find fast food disagreeable, should not be confused with their taste for fine French cuisine.

Closer to home, we are often amused by the theological literalism of our fellow communicants, the insipid, infant formula, meatless quality of their religious diet. During our worse moments, we pragmatic naturalists succumb to feelings of amused contempt. At our best, however, we accept and even celebrate our differences and theirs. Still, we often wonder rather wistfully, "Why cannot they be like us?" But we know that being like us is not easy. It is an acquired taste. Unlike the spiritual aristocrat, we are mindful of not reducing "authentic" spirituality or versions of the religious life to what we have achieved. We do not believe that religious traditions are a ladder in the spiritual and intellectual ascent of *Homo sapiens* that can easily be kicked away. However, ladders are subject to all sorts of contingency. Sometimes they fall into disrepair or collapse of their own weight. Or we may simply lose interest in going where they might take us. As religious naturalists, we can only offer pragmatic reasons why it might still be worth going there, why it would be a good thing if religious traditions were conserved. What we cannot offer is the kind of "true believer" commitment that may account for those

traditions being built in the first place.[14] If we face a dilemma as pragmatic religious naturalists, and I am not convinced that we do, that
would be it. I think that it would be wrong, however, to view us as *merely*
parasites on the imaginative riches of the religious life. We pay our own
way through our attention to the tradition, our celebration and critical
elaboration. In this way, we make peace with those of our communicants
who have difficulty recognizing us as one of them, who are blind, so to
speak, to the religious features of our face.

Between the political life and the religious life: we believe that there is
an irremediable tension between the two, which is appropriately
described as a tension between the public and the private.[15] The
public–private distinction, like gender, is trouble, irremediable trouble.
But some version of that distinction will always be drawn and redrawn.
That distinction, or one like it, is something that we cannot do without.
Drawing that distinction is a perennial and interminable activity. We
cannot get rid of the public–private distinction, despite its complicity
with gender hierarchy, any more than we can "the universal and the particular" or "the one and the many," any more than we can affirm the
inviolability of our persons without appealing to bourgeois property
rights. This is true not because these ideas describe the way things really
are, but because they are intuitively persuasive ways of thinking, because
try as we might, we have not found better language, because though we
banish these ideas, they return. Our questions, therefore, should relate
to how the public–private distinction is drawn and under what conditions it can be redrawn. From this perspective, the famous feminist
slogan "the personal is the political" is read as a call for redrawing rather
than abandoning the distinction. That, at any rate, is how it should be
read. If the watch words of public life are duty and responsibility, then
the religious life, at least in part, is an escape; it is a utopian space where
"irresponsibility" is embraced, honored, and celebrated, where duty and
responsibility are sublated by love. The religious life, like the heart, has
reasons of its own; thus seduction and love are better analogies for this
aspect of life than are duty and responsibility. We live religious lives not
because we *ought* to but because we cannot *imagine* living otherwise, less
because we fear, more because we love.

Here I return to Cornel West, for whom the religious life is sublated,
taken up, canceled, preserved, and transformed by democratic faith.
Democracy is realized Christian eschatology. It is what Christianity
would look like after pragmatic reconstruction. In this way, West satisfies
his desire to hold Christian commitments and radical democratic

commitments as a single, comprehensive vision. I should say that there is much here with which I sympathize. However, West downplays, too much for my tastes, the irremediable tensions between public and private life. I refer to the tension between those things that are legitimately subject to majoritarian scrutiny and those things that enjoy a countermajoritarian privilege, which trump if not silence the hectoring claims of the majority. I refer to those things that are subject to the prying eyes of others and those that enjoy an antivoyeuristic privilege, the privilege of secrecy, of nondisclosure, of nonsubjection and nonconformity to public opinion.[16]

Here, perhaps, as elsewhere, West shares Dewey's expansive view of democracy as more than a political theory or form of government.[17] According to Steven Rockefeller, Deweyan democracy was at once an ethical ideal and the source of deep meanings of a psychological, social, and religious sort. Democracy is a source of enchantment in a disenchanted world, a "sacred" canopy in a world without God. For Dewey, God is a trope (that he used with circumspection, if not fear and trembling) for human creative intelligence, for our ability to transform problematic situations into those that meet our morally mediated standards of satisfaction. I must admit, however, that West's Kierkegaardian God is much more than this. Nevertheless, West shares much of Dewey's expansive view of democracy, where democratic norms would "govern all human relationships and all institutions – the family, the school, and factory as well as the town meeting and governor's office."[18] Nowhere are the ambitions of Deweyan democracy more clearly stated. In modern secular culture, democracy sublates and, thus, transfigures Christianity's pastoral role.

If I have spoken of Levinson and West, it is not merely because I split their differences, but refashion, hopefully in a more satisfying way, the "problematic situation" as they variously describe it. I embrace the broad outlines of Levinson's account of the religious life and I commend the political spirit of West's prophetic pragmatism. I cannot help thinking, however, that were West to abandon his desire to hold justice and the religious life in a single vision, he would no longer find himself between a political rock and a religious hard place. He would no longer feel the need to speak of an "Afro-American Revolutionary Christianity" or a "prophetic pragmatism." He would no longer have to vigorously resist the view that religion is the opium of the people. West could stop looking over his shoulder at Marx and others on the left who sneer at religious life. He could take his religion "straight no chaser." Indeed, he might rethink Marx's classic statement and redescribe what it means to call religion opium. Perhaps opium is not always a bad thing. Perhaps it provides that serious levity or comic spirit that allows us to push aside temporarily and forget momentarily desperate and irremediable circumstances. Surely the objection to opium cannot be that it anesthetizes: that after all is what opium does. Religion (again, under a particular description) is a pharmacopeia for pain that cannot be treated otherwise. It becomes a problem only when it gets in the way of us getting what we want, when it turns our attention away from more effective diagnostics and therapeutics, when it does not allow us to forget what we cannot master, when it tries to do what politics, medicine, or technology can do better. On this interpretation, there is no reason why one cannot have one's Marx and one's opium too. If Raymond Aron is correct when he says that Marxism is the opium of the intellectuals, then perhaps we can have our opium and our opium too. Perhaps opium comes in a variety of flavors – Marxist, postmodernist, and the good old-fashioned religious kind – in which case we can choose our poison-cure.

What I have tried to say, as I put a period on this point, is that our politics and our religious views may hang together well but they do different things. Once up on a time, we looked to religion for liberation. While this concept still bears religious traces and, perhaps, always will, we now look, or should look, to politics. Politics is where we turn when bad metaphysics – God, Nature, and the Kingdom of Ends – fail. Politics is what we can do, what our bodies can do, what thinking organisms encountering problematic situations can do. Thus, if art – invention, engineering, creative intelligence – is the sole alternative to luck, then Marxism, or something like it, something we have not yet imagined, will continue to have its place. Let us call this place, which *is* nowhere – with its good and its bad, and each the condition for the possibility of the other – utopia. But even the best arts, the best utopia that we can imagine, run head-on into the unmovable object of death and its various intimations called dread, despair, disease, and defeat. Death and forgetfulness run faster, further, and have more stamina than our most heroic efforts. And this is where Kierkegaard's perspective, when kept in proper perspective, remains powerful. Spinoza, no doubt, is even more powerful when he asserts that these (death and its intimations) are things about which free men and women should think least.[19] But these "sad passions," about which Spinoza warns us, on occasion must be thought. And how we think about them is as important as the infrequency and short duration of those thoughts.

As there are aspects of the human condition that are beyond remediation, about which a body can do little, so shall there always be a place (granted a small, narrow, and closely guarded place) for stoic resignation. Clearly, I disagree with Nietzsche's *amor fati*. We need not love our fate to accept it without resentment. And I can find nothing in Spinoza, Dewey's great naturalistic precursor, that suggests that we should. Here, I think, some commentators blur the differences between Spinoza and Nietzsche.[20] Thus, from a pragmatist perspective, there is something dishonest about Nietzschean affirmation when it purports to be something more than the "flipside" of revenge. On this view, Nietzsche needs love of fate to discipline his fear of death in the same way that *his* Socrates needs reason to discipline his unruly erotic passions.[21] If there is something "smelly" about Nietzschean-heroics, then there is something refreshing and profoundly true about laughter. I refer not only to nervous laughter or contemptuous laughter but to full-throated and belly-shaking laughter: to that laughter that is a close cousin of life-preserving forgetfulness. As there will always be things that can only be forgotten, we pragmatists count ourselves fortunate when we find a place (and there is always a place) for comic relief. By comic relief, I mean the ability to experience joy even when one knows that things are unlikely to get better. That, it seems to us, is the "joyful wisdom" at its best.

I like to view myself as in solidarity with the party of the weak, the poor, and the powerless. Nevertheless, I am often unsure about what specific action this solidarity entails. (Although everything I know, my every instinct, suggests that Marx will continue to be a better guide than Nietzsche, who would gleefully push the weak, poor, and powerless over the edge of a suicidal abyss, or retain them as the dull gray background for the improvisations of his noble-higher-supermen, or reduce them to pulling the plow of his slave-based political economy. This explains why I am alternately amused by or contemptuous of many of my friends on the so-called poststructuralist–postmodernist "left," who "work themselves up into a lather" over Rorty's relatively innocuous postmodern bourgeois liberalism, while remaining sanguine toward the dangers of Nietzsche's virtual-fascism, with its exoteric–esoteric semiotics of "masters and slaves," "order of rank," and "pathos of distance."[22]) That solidarity with those on the underside of the modern–postmodern project has much to do with cultural politics, I do not doubt. Thus I have a great deal of sympathy with "the new cultural politics of difference," but decidedly less sympathy when it degenerates, as it too often does, into fratricidal silliness. Power may corrupt, but so does impotence. And there is a great deal of corruption on the academic left – from a gnostic retreat on issues that affect the lives of ordinary people to irresponsibility, dogmatism, and careerism of the worse sort.

I am comfortable with self-descriptions (Marxist progeny all) such as social democrat, democratic socialist, or radical democrat. But what these terms mean – and whether they have a referent other than my own sense of "high-mindedness,"[23] my desire to be something other than a reluctant bourgeois male,[24] an academic at an elite university that is financed by the largess of the ruling class – is an open question. This fear of being merely a minstrel, vaudeville Marxist, or bourgeois in "socialist-face" is unavoidable in a time when Marxism has become a way of reading texts or conjuring specters. If Marxism is too often a form of nostalgia, then leftist commitment in non-Marxist sectors is too often a form of academic posturing, a veritable fashion industry, where theoretical fashions change as frequently and capriciously as those of the Parisian garment industry. "Whither the left?" is a question that is unavoidable when that venerable tradition called political radicalism, which once involved personal and professional risk-taking, has become a vehicle for self-promotion, self-aggrandizement, and even outright cynicism. Why is radical politics too often merely a textual politics – a little politics relegated to small, obscure journals, written for an audience that is hyperliterate in a culture that is postliterate? This is as much a question for me as for others. It is about these issues, to put a different spin on Said's words, that radical critics should be questioning each other. But we shall not find answers so long as we imagine that religion (apart from secularism) is the premise or the object of radical critique.

## Appendix A: Whose exodus, which interpretation?

The Said–Walzer dispute recalls an earlier dispute between Jean-Paul Sartre and Albert Camus. These giants of twentieth-century French letters disagreed about much – the Cold War, Algeria, and the nature of political obligation. Their friendship eventually collapsed under the weight of their disagreements. Sartre and Camus first met in the French Resistance. Sartre, we might say, was a "fellow traveler," Camus a deeply engaged participant. In her widely influential and thoroughly pro-Camus account, Germaine Brie describes them as:

anti-fascist, against the Franco forces in the Spanish civil war; and after Camus's short adherence to the Communist Party, non-communist left-wing men. They were on the side of the Resistance against the policies of Vichy and both, in the decolonialization period, were opposed to the repressive policies of the French government with regard to the national liberation forces in its former territories.[1]

How, then, to account for their famous "break" in 1952? The short answer is that philosophical differences latent in their relationship surfaced frequently and intensely, especially as regards Algeria. While recent history has been kinder to Camus, I think that Sartre was right on the question of national liberation. And I think that Conor Cruise O'Brien provides the best account of their estrangement.[2] On this account, Sartre became increasingly critical of Cold War-inspired anti-communism (only a month earlier, he had explicitly embraced the Communist party in "The Communist and the Peace"), while Camus' retreat from his early embrace of the Communist party accelerated. To put this differently, Camus was well on his way to becoming a cold warrior, who distinguished between good violence, such as the Resistance, and bad violence, such as revolutionary, national liberation movements. While Camus became the darling of Cold War liberals, Sartre was staking out a middle position between Stalinism and Gaullism. He was on his way to becoming a communist "fellow traveler" (a term that I use without a sneer), who was critical of both Stalinism and anticommunism. He rejected Camus' enthusiastic embrace of Cold War ideas, in which national liberation movements were construed as pawns on the Soviet chessboard. Over time, Sartre's early ambivalence toward violence was replaced by a resolute belief in its necessity in national liberation struggles. Meanwhile, Camus' lack of qualms about violence against the Nazi Occupation contrasted sharply with his opposition to the prophets of revolutionary, anticolonial violence in French colonial territories, such as Frantz Fanon in Camus' native Algeria.

The occasion for the break between Sartre and Camus was a harsh review of Camus' philosophical study *The Rebel* by a little-known writer named Francis Jeanson. The essay appeared in Sartre's journal *Les Temps Modernes* and precipitated a bitter exchange of open letters between Camus and Sartre. In simple terms, Camus accuses Sartre of toeing the Marxist line and Sartre accuses Camus of intellectual treason. Both play fast and loose with the other's position. While their disagreement never ceased being what it was from the beginning, over time it ramified into a disagreement about Algeria. Should France stay or go? Sartre said that France should leave Algeria and signed the "declaration on the right of insubordination in the Algerian War, called the 'manifesto of the 121.'"[3] Camus, in contrast, said that the French should stay and maintain their colonial strangle-hold, only not so tightly as to make the natives rebellious. Said construes Sartre and Camus' responses, respectively, as secular and religious. In contrast, Walzer construes their responses as exemplary of connected and detached forms of criticism, where the former is good and the latter bad.

Said and Walzer's disagreements about Sartre, Camus, and Algeria are the subtext of their differences on the Palestinian question, which in turn are the subtext of their dispute in the pages of the journal *Grand Street*. The occasion for their public dispute, which took the form of a review essay and an exchange of open letters, was the publication of Walzer's *Exodus and Revolution*. In Preliminary Remarks, I referred to the broad outline of Walzer's argument; here, I provide some details. Walzer's thesis holds that the Exodus story, when properly secularized, provides a paradigm for revolutionary politics. As evidence of the Exodus story's paradigmatic status, Walzer cites the sermons of Savonarola, "the pamphlets of the German peasants' revolt," John Calvin and John Knox's political tracts, "the radical contractualism" of French Huguenots and Scottish Presbyterians, "the self-understandings of the English Puritans," the "errand into the wilderness" of the

American Puritans, and the beliefs of Boer nationalists and black South African nationalists. Said sneers at this list. What about the vast majority of radical movements that make no reference to the Exodus story at all? He is flabbergasted when Walzer claims that the Exodus story, in the cases he cites, was central to their radical character (which Walzer attributes to the "this-worldly" character of the story), and when Walzer says that the "Exodus is an account of deliverance or liberation expressed in religious terms," but also a secular, historical account.[4] This claim is important if Walzer is to succeed in what he wants to do, namely, to deduce from the Exodus story a paradigm for revolutionary politics and the lineaments of liberal consent theory, a human-centered account of legitimate political authority.

Is the Exodus story revolutionary? That depends on what one means by revolutionary. What we can say without reservation is that the Hebrews were oppressed and, thus, were candidates for revolution. Walzer implies that their oppression was even greater than chattel-slavery, because it was absolutely arbitrary, and lacked ethical norms. I think that this claim is exaggerated. Said certainly thinks so. He suggests that Egyptian bondage was more akin to serfdom than to chattel-slavery. I think that this claim, on the other hand, has the opposite defect; it minimizes conditions that were, as far as the story goes, probably closer to chattel-slavery than to serfdom. I think that Walzer is surely right when he says that "Egyptian bondage is paradigmatic for abolitionist politics," but less right when he speaks of revolution. He rightly underscores the psychology of the oppressed, the distinctive subjectivity formed under oppressive circumstances. Oppression is both repulsive and attractive, its "fleshpots" look and smell good. The "luxuries and sensual delights" of, among other things, a meat-rich diet can easily tempt one to believe that oppression is not so bad after all.[5] To see and smell the fleshpots of oppression sometimes seems preferable to the milk and honey of freedom. This sort of slavishness is a consequence of oppression, and was addressed, on Walzer's interpretation, through the pedagogy of the wilderness years.

The wilderness years are especially productive for Walzer. There he states his view, derived from the historian Stanley Elkins, about the "psychological effects of oppression." There he tackles the thorny issue of when deadly political violence is justified. There he distills a liberal, social democratic theory of political consent from the Sinai covenant and the golden calf episodes. Walzer claims that what most Hebrew "slaves learned in Egypt was servitude and slavishness." He uses Elkins' controversial thesis about American slavery to illuminate the Hebrew experience of bondage. According to Elkins, slavery produces a slave mentality: an abject, childish, irresponsible, Sambo figure, the slave who panders to his master. Ironically, Elkins derived this notion from studies of the Nazi holocaust, which, in turn, Walzer uses to illuminate the conditions of the newly liberated Hebrew slaves. Walzer quickly modifies this account with an alternative interpretation. He says that conflict between the idealism of leaders and the materialism of followers, the present and the future, is common in political endeavors. Therefore, the liberated Hebrews should not be seen as simply cowering, slavishly before the difficulty of freedom, but as disagreeing with their leaders about what liberation meant. To some degree, the Hebrew slaves *had* learned slavishness. So the purpose of the wilderness experience was to destroy their slave mentality. The negative conditions for freedom (freedom from) had been provided when God liberated them from Egyptian bondage. The positive conditions for freedom (freedom to) was something that they had to do for themselves. The spirit of slavishness had to be broken by collective effort and strong leadership.[6]

Rather than construing the Abrahamic covenant as the beginning of the story, which, according to Said, would require Walzer to acknowledge Egypt as the prototype of the promised land, he takes the Egypt of Hebrew bondage as his starting-point. Were I to speculate on Walzer's motives, they would have something to do with the kind of story that he wants the Exodus to be – namely, linear and progressive. The sequence of Egypt, wilderness, promised land satisfies that purpose. The sequence that begins with the Abrahamic covenant, where the land of Canaan is promised and that proceeds through Egyptian bondage and the wilderness experience to the promised land episode, does not. This latter sequence makes the Exodus story look like the "pagan," cyclical accounts of history from which he wants to distinguish it. He can then explicitly suggest, and this is part of Said's critique, how Western the Exodus story is and how Oriental the "Canaanites" are. By making this distinction, Walzer can assimilate the Exodus story, with some rough edges no doubt, to liberal and social democratic political theory. In another move of separation and distinction that is sometimes taken to characterize Western modernity, Walzer can also construe the Exodus story as moral rather than cosmological. That is to say, the Exodus story is about the creation of moral subjects in a recognizably liberal, Kantian sense.[7] Whether Walzer's starting-point and his distinctions are persuasive or not is a question that I leave open, but, for Said, the matter is closed and settled.

For Walzer, matters are not closed or settled. And so, on his account, the education of this protoliberal and proto-Kantian moral subject begins in the wilderness. The high (or low) moment in the "reeducation" of the liberated Hebrews was the golden calf episode. The "new school of the soul," as Walzer calls the wilderness, was hard. People began to murmur, to remember how well they had it in Egypt or, nostalgically, to misremember how things really were. Briefly, the Hebrews, in Moses' absence and with Aaron and Miriam's approval, constructed a gold calf, a visible god to assuage their fears and anxieties in the face of freedom and the Invisible. Upon his return from Sinai, Moses was outraged, determined who the guilty parties were, and subjected them to summary and gruesome execution. The "counter revolutionaries," on Walzer's reading, were purged; the murmuring was stopped; the "red terror," as Lincoln Steffens would have it, had succeeded; the revolution was saved. The golden calf episode is especially thorny for Walzer, a self-described man of the left, a social democrat, who is decidedly anti-Leninist. What to do? What Walzer attempts to do is to show how a social democratic reading of the golden calf episode is possible, without denying the merits of a Leninist reading *à la* Lincoln Steffens. Said is hardly persuaded by Walzer's social democratic reading. And things do not get any better when Walzer "deemphasizes the story of the golden calf," while highlighting Moses' role as the people's pedagogue and advocate before God. Walzer does not dismiss Steffens' conclusion about the political lesson of the Exodus ("The grown-ups must die") so much as offer other texts that suggest that the moral of the story is pedagogy rather than "purgegogy." Walzer accomplishes this in part by supplementing if not expunging Elkins' notion of the "slave mentality." The Hebrew slaves were not merely slavish, but "stiff-necked" too. What is traditionally read as slavishness, as "the Egypt in them," should be read as the irascible spirit of a free, ordinary, and democratic people.[8]

Democratic relations are covenant relations, that is, they entail promise-making and promise-keeping, common deliberation, conclusions, judgments, and forms of accountability. The Sinai covenant is Walzer's model for the radical, social democratic account that he wants to give of the Exodus story. A people in bondage is cast by an act of God into the state of nature (the condition of natural liberty devised by liberal political theorists), where they make a covenant with God and with each other. To his credit, Walzer acknowledges a difficulty: natural liberty is not really natural; there are always relations, hierarchies, and norms. But then he smooths over this difficulty when he writes that, despite its lack of sociological plausibility, the account of natural liberty, where everyone freely accepts the covenant, makes moral sense. This is not a case, he says, of elders speaking for the people, husbands for wives, men for women. He cites a Midrash to support his case, but his citation of Deuteronomy 29 does not persuade me.[9] This citation does not overcome the problems associated with his effort to derive from the Exodus story the antecedents, if not the actuality, of liberal consent theory.

For Said, the conquest of the land of Canaan vitiates the entire story and precludes any democratic reading. My conclusions are similar to Said's. So I shall present them here, out of order, and in the middle of Walzer's interpretation of the Exodus story and Said's critique, before resuming Walzer's narrative and Said's counternarrative.

I agree with Said – the legacy of the Exodus story is far more complicated and problematic than Walzer's reading would allow. I also agree with Jonathan Boyarin who says that the story is more complicated than either Walzer or Said's readings will allow.[10] To be sure, Walzer acknowledges the selective nature of his reading, as every reading is selective, as every interpretation highlights certain themes and excludes others, and is adequate or inadequate relative to certain purposes. But, if the purpose of *Exodus and Revolution* is to affirm and encourage the revolutionary politics made possible by the Exodus story, then those parts of the story (for example, the conquest of the land of Canaan) that vitiate its revolutionary potential must be exposed and criticized. Those who would argue for its revolutionary significance must meet a high standard of proof. Walzer does not meet that standard when he distinguishes between Leninist and social democratic, messianic and revolutionary readings of the Exodus story. Still, he attempts to confirm these distinctions in his account of the promised land episode and in his concluding remarks on Exodus politics. He speaks of the entanglement of Exodus politics and political messianism in Zionist thought, which is no doubt true. It is also true that messianism and "revolutionary politics" are integrally connected in the Exodus story itself. Exodus politics *is* this connection. Messianism and revolution are, to use a biblical metaphor, like wheat and weeds. Kill the weed and you kill the wheat also; their roots are intertwined. It is hard to tell the two apart, so familiar and familial is their likeness. Thus the Exodus is an inspiring story about the potential for progressive politics. But it is also a depressing story about a progressivism that was aborted, which miscarried and continues to miscarry in the triumphal politics of divinely sanctioned war and mass killing.

Walzer does not endorse these conclusions. Nor, perhaps, would Said and Boyarin endorse them completely, but their reasons no doubt would be different. That Walzer does not accept these conclusions is evident in a chapter that he devotes to the promised land episode, where, as he dryly observes, the strength of the Exodus story is its beginning not its end. Thus he speaks less of an aborted revolution than of a revolution grown old and conservative, where memories of what God has done (Walzer would prefer to say what the people themselves have done) have dimmed amid the abundance of milk and honey. Said sees things very differently. He speaks of genocide as the founding act of the emergent kingdom of Israel. These starkly differing perspectives, especially given their roles as proxies for contemporary Israeli–Palestinian relations, could not help but lead to a bitter dispute.

Walzer accents the twofold character of the Sinai promise: God would lead the children of Israel to "a land flowing with milk and honey," and he would be their God and they would be his holy nation. Walzer's insights are striking as he replays the issue of split consciousness – the materialism of the people, who emphasize the first part of the promise, versus the idealism of the leaders, who emphasize the second part. Again, he cites the Leninist reading of Exodus, where the first promise appeals to the trade-union mentality of the masses, and the second promise to the socialist aspirations of the vanguard. Walzer questions the distinction between materialism and idealism, not so much for what it affirms but for what it denies: that there is "an idealism, a spirituality, a high theory of milk and honey." Against this view, Walzer theorizes the materialism of common people, proclaiming an integral connection between material plenitude and the absence of oppression. Milk and honey are the materiality of justice and freedom, justice and freedom are the ideality of milk and honey.

Walzer develops his position in "Albert Camus and the Algerian War," where he responds to Camus' critics, specifically those who impugned Camus' character because of his solidarity with the *pied noir*, the community of French settler-colonials. Walzer characterizes the differences between Camus and his opponents as the difference between a well-justified moral ambivalence and ideological rigidity. Unlike his opponents, Camus can see the many shades of gray. "Before taking a stand one must find a standpoint. Where? Too close, say Camus' opponents, and one becomes an apologist; too far, Camus responds, and one becomes a terrorist."[11] This is a fine formulation. But does not Walzer "gild the lily" here? For surely Camus' opponents would rejoin: stand too close and one becomes an apologist for *state sponsored colonial terror*. Apologist and terrorist are adjectival nouns that work best when they are further modified. The absence of such modification is important because what Camus' opponents, Fanon for example, object to are apologists for French colonial terror. *Pace* Walzer, the choice is not between the ordinary vice of apologetics and the extraordinary vice of terrorism, but the historical specificity and moral perspectivism of what he describes as apologetics and terrorism. The central issue is not critical distance, connectedness or detachment, but the moral quality of that distance. Camus' opponents, that is to say, do not criticize him because he loved his mother, but for what he took that love to mean and for the conclusions that he drew. I think that Walzer is right when he highlights what Camus understood as an antinomy between love and justice, his mother and Algerian liberation. And I am sympathetic to his sympathetic reading of Camus' position, where justice without love is injustice. But does not this let Camus off too easily? Were there no options between retrenchment against Algerian liberation forces and the annihilation of the *pied noir*? What about exile? Wasn't the *pied noir* community a classic example of a minority that, as Walzer has argued elsewhere (see Appendix B), should be helped to leave?

I do not want to suggest that Walzer ignores these questions. He acknowledges the last point, tentatively and subjunctively. Perhaps the exile of the *pied noir* community was not the moral equivalent of genocide. Perhaps exile was a better option than continued colonial domination. Perhaps French violence made it impossible, politically and morally, for the *pied noir* to remain in Algeria. Would not victory by the FLN (The Algerian National Liberation Front) make their stay impossible anyway? Said takes Walzer's tentative and subjunctive mood as a mask for disingenuousness. Is Walzer serious? one can imagine him asking. Did it never occur to him that the apocalypse that he associates with an FLN victory would be the consequence of 130 years of French colonial violence? He does not consider that question, but does consider the question "Should Camus 'have broken his silence and told his people that the struggle was over, that they had to leave?'" His answer is maybe. But then again, maybe not. Perhaps that is too much to ask of a writer, of someone like Camus. Walzer's Camus is a connected critic who refuses to abandon his commitments when things "go bad." Solidarity is his first principle. And Walzer can hardly imagine a circumstance that would demand that a specific form of solidarity be broken. Thus he construes the act of breaking solidarity, prototypically, with abandoning one's mother to terrorists.[12]

Walzer makes things easy on himself, but at the price of a weak argument, when he writes that the detached critic sides with the oppressed for abstract universal reasons, being blind to particular men and women. The detached critic that he constructs is a straw man. There is no absolute or necessary opposition between universality and particularity as Walzer supposes. The specificity of particular cases of oppression may lead one to make general claims (claims that mediate between the universal and the particular) about those things to which persons as persons are entitled. In any event, Walzer's alternatives of connection versus detachment – defined as an absolute, outside, ideal point of view – is phony. But Walzer is determined to make things easy for himself. So, without the least bit of charity or qualification and with no sense of irony, he takes Sartre and de Beauvoir's rhetoric of disgust, which was provoked by what they took as the moral and political myopia of the French people, as the evocation of an outside, abstract, and detached point of view. With evident distaste, Walzer cites de Beauvoir's disgust at the celebration of Charles de Gaulle's re-election in 1958: "'All those people in the streets . . . they were all murderers. Myself as well. "I'm French." The words scalded my throat like an admission of hideous deformity.' But it is not *her own* deformity that de Beauvoir is describing in these passages."[13] But as de Beauvoir, speaking for herself and Sartre, might rejoin "'I am French.' The words scalded my throat . . . because *I am* French." *Pace* Walzer, de Beauvoir is doing what all great critics do, especially when they are part of the privileged class; she speaks not from the outside, as a stranger, but as a marginal insider, who sees what others do not want to see. It is precisely because she and Sartre are not strangers and cannot easily abandon their French ties of loyalty that they experience disgust at the policies of *their* government and at the behavior of *their* fellow citizens.

Walzer, apparently, never entertains this thought. Thus he portrays Camus as the archetypical connected critic – a critic, as Said would have it, who puts solidarity with ethnicity, race, or nation before criticism. A connected critic is committed to a particular community, and this solidarity colors (and is the first moral principle of) her critique. Camus is a connected critic, Sartre a detached critic. Sartre and Simone de Beauvoir's expressed contempt for the French people, on Walzer's view, is an example of detachment. Walzer's point, and he uses de Beauvoir to illustrate a position that Sartre shares, is how distant, abstract, and easy this perspective is. There are no hard choices because the very thing that makes choices hard such as solidarity, a genuine commitment to a particular people, is cast off so casually. When the self is disencumbered of its traditional and sentimental connections of family and nation, then moral concepts of a thin, abstract–universal character are the result. But concepts without the precepts of traditional connections are morally empty. Are precepts without concepts morally blind? Walzer does not say. But he does think that Sartre is morally blind. Thus Sartre was a likely "candidate for ideological discipline" because there were no moral sentiments to restrain and discipline his abstract principles. In a back-handed gesture of generosity, Walzer notes that Sartre avoided the discipline of the Communist party, even though his critical faculties were otherwise in ideological "deep freeze." It is to Sartre and de Beauvoir's credit, Walzer argues, "that party hacks, whose alignment was really unconditioned, always thought them to be petty-bourgeois intellectuals." The case of the Algerian War, however, is different. There, Sartre is at his abstract, disencumbered worst, detaching himself from the French people, giving aid and comfort to her enemies, supporting, without dissent, the Algerian National Liberation Front. Sartre was not a terrorist setting off bombs, but his detachment robbed him of the moral vision necessary to condemn what he saw, to even see it as something worthy of condemnation.[14]

In contrast to Sartre, detachment was not a problem for Camus, who committed himself to the survival of the *pied noir* community even as he condemned the excesses of colonial domination. Walzer presents a compelling portrait of Camus as a Solomon-like figure, weighing the pros and cons of two claimants, holding the extremes at bay, while privileging in a morally commendable way the claims of his own community. Camus advocated a negotiated peace, which would preserve the interests of the *pied noir* community as symbolized by his mother. I think that Walzer's argument becomes especially strained at this point, which has a lot to do with the role of Camus and the *pied noir* as proxies for his engagement with the "question of Palestine." This strain, which Said recognizes, is especially evident when Walzer draws a moral equivalence between the Algerian nationalists' desire for independence and the desire of the settler-colonial *pied noir* to retain its status in Algeria. Walzer construes the Algerian national liberation movement as the annihilation (let us be explicit here, the genocide) of the *pied noir* which was struggling for its very survival. Thus he commends Camus' refusal to choose between the equally disastrous alternatives of colonial "repression" and revolutionary "violence." And he wonders why partition, a two-state solution, never occurred to Camus. It makes perfect sense to him, given the "fact" that there were two nations in question – the indigenous Algerians and the *pied noir*.[15]

The Algerian situation is clearly a proxy for Palestine and the State of Israel – for both Walzer and Said. But Said rejects Walzer's assumption that critical distance and intimacy with one's people are mutually exclusive. But what if they are? Might not intimacy with one's people "be less valuable an achievement," under certain circumstances, than risking isolation, as Sartre did, for condemning the evil that intimacy underwrites?[16] Walzer defends his portrait of Camus as an intellectual who, under difficult circumstances, did not toe the official party-line, while depicting Said as toeing the official Palestinian line, without a murmur of dissent, in the face of Palestinian terror.

To Walzer's characterization, Said rejoins:

> He's even less accurate when he tries to characterize my position within the Palestinian community. They're in trouble, he says correctly, and then makes the, for him, habitual mistake of connecting Palestinian trouble with the trouble of Camus' people, the French *colons* of Algeria. There it is, in all of its characteristic idiocy, Walzer's inability to mark the difference between a dispossessed, tragically victimized nation of Palestinian Arabs on the one hand, and on the other hand, the French settlers who for one hundred thirty years battened themselves by force on an overseas possession whose natives were abused, exploited, repressed until those natives rose up and sacrificed one million dead in the process of liberating themselves from French settlers. So infected is Walzer with blind loyalty to Israel that he sees replicas of Jewish settlers in Palestine everywhere he looks, and fails to see their victims![17]

"Michael Walzer," according to Said, "makes Camus an exemplary intellectual, precisely because he was anguished and wavered and opposed terrorism and loved his mother." But Said will have none of this; Camus, to his discredit, is no Sartre. His novels, though canonical, are not anguished reflections on the human condition, but cultural interventions in "the contest between Algerian nationalism and French colonialism" (*CAI* 93, 175, 348). Camus is to the Algerian liberation struggle what Walzer is to the Palestinian struggle for national liberation – a smooth-talking apologist for settler-colonialism. Thus Said's stinging review of Walzer's *Exodus and Revolution*. Thus his bitter exchange of letters with Walzer. Thus his determination to play Sartre to Walzer's Camus.

# Appendix B: an exchange of letters between Michael Walzer and Edward Said

THIS IS A REPRODUCTION OF "AN EXCHANGE: MICHAEL WALZER AND EDWARD SAID," *GRAND STREET* 5:4 (1986), 246–259. (REPRODUCED WITH THE PERMISSION OF EDWARD W. SAID)[7]

To the editor:

I

People don't always get the political enemies they want. Edward Said seems particularly unsatisfied in this respect, and so he has set out to make up his enemies to suit himself ("Walzer's *Exodus and Revolution*: A Canaanite Reading," *Grand Street*, Winter 1986). His materials are my own books and articles, everything I have written, in fact, since the watershed year of 1967. I am willing enough to play the part that Said assigns me, but I am not willing to play it according to his script – even if the script is put together out of bits and pieces of my own sentences. I prefer my sentences whole; my politics too. The enemy Said wants is the precise opposite of the self he would like to be: as he is in his mind's eye cool, detached, skeptical, alienated, secular, and universalistic, the very model of a modern intellectual, so I am to be warm, sentimental, mystical, complacent, religious, and parochial, a case study in the treason of the intellectuals. But I won't play.

Rereading Said's *The Question of Palestine*, I am inclined to think that he is his own best enemy: he doesn't need me. But I do make it possible for him to recognize a problem, even if he can't acknowledge that it's his problem too. The effort to maintain some degree of commitment to a group of people and some degree of independence from that same group continually runs into difficulties. The same could be said, of course, about love for individual men and women; that's not an argument against love, nor against commitment. But it is important to be

187

able to talk about the difficulties. Said obviously can't do that in his own case, and he can't do anything more than caricature mine. Even so, he raises hard questions, even touches some sore places. So I will try to engage his arguments – whenever I can find them beneath the bad faith of his polemical attack. But first, I'm afraid, I have to respond to the attack. Just for the record, I have to set the record straight.

II

A word first about methods: how does one go about constructing a portrait of the enemy one would like to have? I will take a small but entirely representative example of Said's approach. "In 1972," he writes, "[Walzer] argued that in every state there will be groups 'marginal to the nation' which should be 'helped to leave.'" He goes on to say that this discussion "coolly anticipates by a decade Kahane's bloody cries of "They must go,'" and so provides evidence for my parochial nationalism and triumphalism, the extent to which I have forgotten the "Canaanites" of the world. The reference here is to an essay that I published in *Dissent* (Summer 1972) on "Nationalism, Internationalism, and the Jews." This is the most substantial piece I've ever written on the national question, and so the example, if small, isn't trivial. I will have to quote from my own essay at some length so as to set out my argument and place the two phrases (italicized below) out of which Said makes up the argument he would have liked me to make.

The immediate issue is this: "National liberation is threatening to all those minority groups who find themselves trapped within the boundaries of a new nation-state, face to face with a community mobilized for action, eager to affirm its collective identity." Because of such groups, I wrote, "it is not enough to call for the independence of this or that oppressed nation, though that is surely the right thing to do. One's political virtue is always tested by the nation that comes next. Each act of liberation makes the next more necessary, if crime and cruelty are to be avoided . . . The freedom of Iraq, then, requires the freedom of Kurdistan; the freedom of Nigeria, Biafra; the freedom of Pakistan, Bengal. Similarly, the freedom of Israel requires that of Palestine; and conversely, for those leftists already committed to Palestinian liberation, Palestine requires Israel."

So it is necessary to draw new lines on the map: "Here is the maxim of a chastened humanism: good borders make good neighbors. And a good border, in a time of growing national antagonisms, is a line so drawn that different people are on different sides. I don't want to pretend that this is very much more than a minimal moral position. There is, in fact, no acceptable way of getting everyone on the right side of the line." It follows, then, that "having established boundaries, it remains to fight for minority rights, equal protection, and all the liberal safeguards within them, and then for economic and political cooperation across them."

But honesty and realism require something more than this, for "whatever we do, nation building in new states is sure to be rough on groups *marginal to the nation* (and too small and scattered to secede from the nation) – those archetypal aliens of the third world, for example, Jews, Levantines, Indians, and Chinese, or settlers like the French of Algeria. For them, very often, the roughness can only be smoothed a little; it cannot be avoided. And sometimes, it can only be smoothed by *helping people to leave* who have to leave, like the Indians of Kenya and Tanzania, the *colons* of North Africa, the Jews of the Arab world. No doubt this is a defeat for socialist internationalism, as it is for ordinary liberalism, but the refusal to help only leads to a worse defeat."

That was my argument and still is: I was a defender of the partition of old Palestine before 1967, and after, and still am. Helping people to leave is something I defend only as a last resort, the sad aftermath of, never a replacement for, national liberation. Said doesn't make any serious effort to report this argument. Is he interpreting it? Not unless interpretation is an activity entirely distinct from reading, even Canaanite reading. No; using the italicized phrases, he constructs an argument radically at odds with what I wrote. What else can he do, since what I wrote doesn't fit the model of the enemy he would like to have? I call this the method of hostile invention.[1]

Said's second method is perverse attribution: he repeatedly credits me with the opinions I oppose – as if he can't believe, given my intellectual treason, that I really oppose them. Since I can't oppose them without repeating them, the necessary quotations are always available. So, when he says that in *Exodus and Revolution*, I bestow "redemption" on "Exodus insiders" and elevate them to "the status of divinely inspired moral agents," readers who don't know the book will hardly guess (unless they know Said) that its central purpose is to oppose redemptive and messianic and divinely inspired politics. There is, of course, a sense in which the Israelites are redeemed: they are brought out of slavery – that is the word's original meaning. I try to work out a reading of the story according to which that is the only sense in which they are redeemed. I don't pretend, however, that this is the only possible reading of the text; it certainly isn't, among religious Jews or Christians, the dominant one. It is an alternative, though not an idiosyncratic, reading, used in the past, and intended by me, to draw out of the tradition some ideas and arguments that support a limited and this-worldly politics. Said may think this a worthless or hopeless enterprise; he ought nevertheless to acknowledge what the enterprise is.[2] But he insists on pretending that I have adopted a politics that "relies upon God" and that anticipates "triumphs in the extra-historical world." A bad joke – since those political militants who do rely upon God and anticipate such triumphs think that I have written an evil and dangerous book.

Another example: Said begins by arguing that I don't acknowledge the full significance of the conquest of Canaan. I avoid the implications of the fact that the Canaanites are "explicitly excluded from the world of moral concern." The quoted sentence is indeed my own, and it reports accurately the meaning of the Biblical text. By the end of his review, Said attributes this meaning to me – a bit ambiguously: I either believe it myself or I am sympathetic to those who do. In fact, I am the political opponent of those who do, as he certainly knows. In the book I try to show how later rabbinic interpreters of the text contrived (with ingenious and implausible arguments) to readmit the "Canaanites" to the world of moral concern, and I attack contemporary fundamentalists who would exclude them again. I don't "upbraid" these contemporaries "for being too fundamentalist" (as if there is a right way of taking the text literally as a guide for action) – of course, the fundamentalists read the text correctly. The question is whether it is the text, which reflects the earliest form of Israelite religion, or the later interpretive tradition, which gives shape to what we now call Judaism, that is most to be trusted and defended. That's not, obviously, a question for Edward Said; nor should it be. It is part of my disagreement with other Jews. I only ask that he acknowledge the disagreement. But, again, he can't do that; he insists that his enemies, all of them, are avowed or unavowed fundamentalists, intent on removing the Canaanites/Palestinians from the sacred soil. For Jewish supporters of Israel, there is only one politics, and we cannot design it for ourselves; Said designs it for us in the image of his rage.

III

There is a more serious point here, which Said might have made more effectively without denying me my own political position. Perhaps I am not sufficiently alert to the dangers of Exodus politics; perhaps I don't stress enough the "triumphalist" character of the Biblical story; perhaps I don't acknowledge the presumption and cruelty of men and women who think that God is on their side. Perhaps. Curiously, charges very much like this have been directed against Said's *Orientalism* by leftist and secularist critics in the Arab world (see Emmanuel Sivan, "Edward Said and His Arab Reviewers," the *Jerusalem Quarterly*, Spring 1985). They argue that Said radically underestimates the significance and the dangers of religious belief in contemporary Arab politics and in the Islamic world generally. (His early support for the Ayatollah Khomeini suggests that they may be right.) Now he has taken that criticism and passed it along to me. I'm not grateful. It was, after all, tailored for him. For he has made no effort to engage the religious fervor of contemporary Muslim Arabs, while *Exodus and Revolution* is at least an effort at engagement with the religious fervor of contemporary Jews.

But maybe the only appropriate engagement is absolute opposition, a rejection not only of fundamentalism but of the entire religious tradition. As a member of the Palestinian Christian minority, face to face with an increasingly militant Islam, that is a natural, perhaps an unavoidable, course for Said – though I don't know that he has ever urged it publicly upon his Muslim comrades in the PLO. But it isn't a natural cause for me because of the way in which Judaism intersects with and partly determines the culture of the Jews. The religious tradition is a battleground, and since I am concerned about the outcome, it makes sense to join the battle. Saying that is utterly different from saying, as Said does again and again in his books and in his review of my book, that Zionism was "primarily" a religious movement. It was, as every student of its history knows, primarily nonreligious and often, among its leftist cadres, fiercely antireligious. But it did create a Jewish state, in which the historic texts of the Jews have become the objects of interpretation and debate – exactly as the historic texts of the Arabs are in every Arab state.

The battle over the Jewish tradition is my battle; in that sense I am a parochial intellectual. But it is also a *battle*: it doesn't involve, as Said charges, "just going along with one's own people for the sake of loyalty and 'connectedness.'" Said must be writing here with a guilty conscience, remembering his own book on Palestine, whose first chapter ends on this melodramatic note: "In other words, my aim here will be to open the discussion of the question of Palestine to a much-denied, much-suppressed reality – that of the Palestinian Arabs, of whom I myself am one." The rest of the book is an example of how one can, even with skill and passion, just go along with one's own people. Said is critical of everyone else in the world, but not of the PLO and its core leaders, "chief among them Yasir Arafat, a much-misunderstood and maligned political personality." Said knows his people are in trouble, and for the sake of loyalty and connectedness, he toes the official line.

It is not this sort of behavior that I set out to recommend in my essay on Camus (*Dissent*, Fall 1984) and my defense of the "connected critic." A connected critic is a *critic*; the adjective modifies, it doesn't abolish, the noun. Camus is a useful example, since his people, the Algerian French, were really in trouble, and yet he didn't toe the line. We have "the right and duty," he wrote in 1958, "to state that military combat and repression have, on our side, taken on aspects that we cannot accept. Reprisals against civilian populations and the use of torture are crimes in which we are all involved. The fact that such things can take place among us is a humiliation we must henceforth face . . . The moment [such methods] are justified, even indirectly, there are no more rules or values; all causes are equally good, and war without aims or laws sanctions the triumph of nihilism." Camus' language is a bit stiff, and his argument not as sharply political as I would like. Still, I have searched for a similarly clear-cut statement on terrorism in Said's *Palestine*, and the best I could find was this equivocal sentence, which comes in the middle of a paragraph of apologetics: "Stripped of its context, an act of Palestinian desperation looks like wanton murder – as in fact, I have thought, many acts of individual adventure (highjacking, kidnapping, and the like) *were* acts of unbalanced, finally immoral, and useless destruction." The next sentence, predictably enough, begins with "But . . ." I'll begin the same way: But what about all those acts of terrorism, by far the larger number, that weren't "individual adventures" but parts of the systematic strategy of the PLO? About these, Said has nothing to say; he pretends that there has never been such a strategy. Who is guilty here of "lamentable waffling"?

So connection has its dangers; they can be illustrated out of Camus' career (or mine, for that matter) as well as out of Said's. But, as he must know, there are times when connection, for all its dangers, is morally necessary. The real question, then, is how one works out the connection. No, says Said, the real question is, to whom is one connected? The only morally safe course is to be one of the "Canaanites" – as if oppression always made for virtue. "If Jews were still stateless, and being held in ghettoes," writes Said, "I do not believe that Walzer would take the position he has been taking." Again, he may be right, though I don't see anything I would want to change in the argument about nationalism that I made in 1972 and quoted extensively above. I had not forgotten the long statelessness of the Jews when I wrote those lines; nor do I wish statelessness upon anyone else, now that the Jews have a state of their own. I can, however, pose a harder question to myself: suppose that the Jews were still stateless and the Zionist movement was led by men like Arafat, Habash, and Abu Musa, and committed to policies like those of the PLO. Would I be able to sustain a posture of internal criticism? I don't know; I don't feel all that confident of my virtue in such a case, and so on this score I am not disposed to be too critical of Edward Said. When national liberation is represented by a figure in a stocking mask, what can nationalist intellectuals say? Even the oppressed need their critics, but the role is a difficult and painful one. It is much easier to blame everyone else for not opposing the oppression with sufficient energy and zeal.

But let me return to my actual condition: the Jews have a state, and I still believe in the rights of "the nation that comes next." But Jewish statehood is more precarious than Said admits, and so the belief is more tentative than I would like. I support the peace movement in Israel (Peace Now) – and keep looking for a similar movement among the Palestinians. I criticize Israeli reprisals – and look for a Palestinian critique of terrorism. I defend national liberation – but insist at the same time that the stocking mask be removed. I want to be sure – and Said's insistence that all Zionists are (really) the same is no reassurance – that the face of "liberation" is not the face of a new oppressor.

Michael Walzer
Institute for Advanced Study
Princeton, NJ 08540

*Edward W. Said replies*:
Michael Walzer says that I have made him up as an enemy in order to suit myself. He's right. I was trying to debate a Zionist who was serious and to some degree intellectually responsible, someone prepared to look closely at the consequences of Exodus as a founding text for a "this-worldly," "limited," and yet "radical" politics in twentieth-century Palestine and elsewhere. Walzer proves that I was wrong by producing a maundering response that is neither serious, not responsible, nor knowledgeable. A good deal worse than the fiction I created, this "real" Walzer does not answer a single one of the many criticism to which his book *Exodus and Revolution* is vulnerable, and he does not add to his early affectations as a political thinker.

Far from suggesting that he was too consistent in his views, I had in fact pointed to a series of contradictions in *Exodus and Revolution* that make it unintelligible as the apparently general political philosophy offered, but that do make sense as a retrospective cover for Israel's military triumphs. What is the real meaning of a secular radical politics heavily dependent on the notion of redemption (whose first meaning is delivery from *sin*) as well as on the authority of priests and a divinity? How can one exit Egypt for an already inhabited promised land, take that land over, exclude the natives from moral concern (in his book Walzer *never* suggests that he has any difficulty with that exclusion; he says in his response that I certainly know he does, but I know exactly the opposite, as we shall see), kill or drive them out, and call the whole thing "liberation"? Is it true that Exodus is *the* great Western text of liberation, or that the ancient Hebrews in Egypt were a slave people who, alone in antiquity, fought for liberation? Walzer tried to have it too many ways, wishing to appear reasonably critical and radical while refusing to admit the complicity between Exodus politics and an altogether more sanguinary and exclusionist politics of the sort that Israel stands accused of. Could it be that Walzer's brand of "connected" criticism, which had already rehabilitated Camus' refusal to condemn French colonialism, was now appropriating Exodus as an in-house community text so as to excuse Israel's ideology of ethnic or religious separation and systematic oppression of the Palestinian people entailed by that ideology?

No one would deny that critics belong to a community, work in a sphere, are connected to a people. What Walzer cannot see is that there is considerable moral difference between the connectedness of a critic with an oppressing society, and a critic whose connection is to an *oppressed* one. In Walzer's case, it has made a difference that as an unskeptical Zionist he has programmatically allied himself with ideas, principles and actualities prolonging Israel's persecution of its "non-Jews," even as he occasionally pretends otherwise. That's the point, and it is Walzer's fantastic moral blindness to this difference that constantly ruins his efforts.

I kept my review of his book to a fairly serious level of discourse; it seemed to me to raise important unresolved problems about the role of intellectuals, about contemporary realities and ancient ideologies. Yet Walzer ignores all this and rests his entire case first on a single instance of what he calls my method, and second on a slew of undignified and largely incoherent countercharges against one of my books, my background, my character. He thus forces me to the distasteful task of dealing with him at what is, alas, a more appropriate level of analysis.

Since he attaches so much importance to it, let's examine his attempted refutation of the charge that his views in 1972 anticipate Rabbi Kahane's message to the Palestinians that they must be evicted from Israel. Walzer alleges that I misrepresent his views, that I fail to report his various complexities, etc., so he trundles it all out again: people on the wrong side of new borders, the marginality of some ethnic groups, the detritus of nation-building after liberation, and so on. But having quoted himself at tedious length, he prudently stops quoting just at the point where, in his 1972 essay, he got specific and made his real point: "I have been talking about Jews and Arabs all along, though I have used other names and attempted a more general argument." Excellent, he has really been speaking about the new Jewish state and the old Palestinian inhabitants who just happened to be caught on the wrong side of the new border and are marginal to Israel. In Israel, which group in 1972, or in 1986 for that matter, has the power "to help" the other group to leave, Israeli Jews or Palestinian Arabs? Whereas Rabbi Kahane puts it forthrightly, "They must go," Walzer puts it in a little cotton wool, "They must be helped to leave." As a last resort, of course!

Partition is what he believes in, Walzer says, as if once again to dignify his conquer-and-divide exclusivism with a slightly nicer word. But what, other than divine injunction and military strength, gives him the right to recommend the partition of Palestine, against the wishes of its majority inhabitants? Are binationalism and pluralism so contemptible as goals to be fought for that we ought to revert to religious millets? What is so magically effective about partition except that in twentieth-century Palestine it allowed European Jews to arrive there and kick the natives out, a type of behavior for which Exodus provides an edifying prior model?

To give dispossession a new Biblical pedigree is of course to elevate it somewhat, but from the victim's standpoint such a forced "partition" remains usurpation. And partition doesn't, never did, stop at that. There are all the discriminating laws against non-Jews that keep the partition partitioned, the racist immigration policies embodied in the Law of Return, the radically prejudiced landholding, housing, and school policies – and on and on. All this has in fact been part of what Walzer calls the redemptive, this-worldly politics of Exodus, which I connected with his defense of Israel's triumphs, but which he prefers to leave disguised in the wholesomeness attached to the friendlier parts of a Biblical myth.

There is no Israel without the conquest of Canaan and the expulsion or inferior status of Canaanites – then as now. Walzer says absolutely nothing in his book or elsewhere to distance himself in principle from that fundamental Zionist reality. Once you legislate that Israel is the state, not of its citizens, but of the Jewish people, and that only Jews can immigrate there, you consign native non-Jews to separate lower rank. Partition proceeds from that Ideology and is quite a different thing from equality of rights, or true community.[3] There are indeed disagreements within Zionism (I said so right at the beginning of my review), but on the basis of his actual record with regard to those disagreements, Walzer cannot pride himself on very much. Thus he proceeds to *imply* his virtues, even as in a series of ludicrously misinformed and intemperate accusations against me, he denounces my evils. Let's set the record straight.

Since 1967, Walzer has had ample opportunity to dissociate himself publicly from:

1.  The closing of schools and universities on the West Bank; censorship and curricular intervention by Israeli military occupation forces.
2.  Collective punishment, curfews, blowing up of thousands of Arab houses.
3.  Torture; deportation; the jailing of thousands of Palestinians on ad-ministrative detention; the use (by the Peres Labor government) of the Emergency Defense Regulations.
4.  In Lebanon, the iron-fist policy of Peres, the systematic bombing since the early 1970s of refugee camps in Sidon, Tyre, Nabatieh, Beirut, Baalbek, Badawi, Nahr el Bared; bombing of schools, hospi-tals, churches and mosques by the Israeli Air Force, Army and Navy; the uprooting of hundreds of thousands of Palestinians and Lebanese in South Lebanon.
5.  Israel's support for Saad Haddad and Basheer Gemayel, Somoza, the Shah and nearly every oppressive right-wing régime in the Third World, including South Africa. Has he ever signed a petition, joined protests objecting to a single atrocity, raised his voice, as so many have, to oppose the principle of discrimination against Palestinians? Has he said audibly that he believes West Bank Palestinians should be allowed, for instance, to manufacture their own cement, instead of being forced to import it from Israel, or that their land shouldn't be confiscated, or that whole villages shouldn't be made to endure twenty-four hour curfews for weeks on end?

He has been formally associated in the United States with a maga-zine, the *New Republic*, whose routine *racist* attacks by its owner (to whom

Walzer, interestingly, I think, dedicates *Exodus and Revolution*) on Arabs, Arab and Islamic culture, Islam as a religion, Palestinians as a people, are attacks that belong in the gutter, and yet Walzer has made no known sign of the slightest discomfort or demurral.[4] As advisor to various large and prestigious American–Jewish organizations (United Jewish Appeal, the American Jewish Congress, etc.) he's had nothing to say about the blacklisting of academics by the Anti-Defamation League, or slanders against individuals by the American–Israel Public Affairs Committee. He has the gall to say that I am represented by "Arafat, Habash, and Abu Musa," mixing together the one acknowledged symbol of Palestinian nationalism with two of his bitterest, most implacable enemies. Well, now, who represents Walzer, the Israeli pilot who drops cluster bombs on children in Beirut, or Generals Sharon and Eytan? I am a "Palestinian Christian," he tells us, deducing my world view from that ethno-religious fact; what would he say if I drew conclusions from his family background? Is this the kind of political analysis we are to expect from a professor at the Institute for Advanced Study?

What does he know of Arabs or the Muslim world? He depends on Emmanuel Sivan for his information, the Israeli author of an article[5] about me which gets all its emphases wrong because, as is the case with most Israeli Orientalists, he writes with that peculiar combination of hostility, ignorance and knowledgeability that characterizes their school, as from its anxious little enclave it peers out over the walls into a wide Islamic world of which none of them has any direct experience at all. Walzer assumes that I've "rejected" but not engaged Islam because I'm a Christian. Evidently he cannot imagine the principled antireligious position I hold, one that rejects Christianity and Judaism as well. I needn't chronicle here the number of times (including my review of Walzer's book) in which I challenge the nasty wave of Christian, Jewish and Islamic Ayatollahs that he so clearly venerates.

He's even less accurate when he tries to characterize my position within the Palestinian community. They're in trouble, he says correctly, and then makes the, for him, habitual mistake of connecting Palestinian trouble with the trouble of Camus' people, the French *colons* of Algeria. There it is, in all its characteristic idiocy, Walzer's inability to mark the difference between a dispossessed, tragically victimized nation of Palestinian Arabs on the one hand, and, on the other hand, the French settlers who for one hundred thirty years battened themselves by force on an overseas possession whose natives were abused, exploited, repressed until those natives rose up and sacrificed one million dead in the process of liberating themselves from French settlers. So infected is Walzer with blind loyalty to Israel that he sees replicas of Jewish settlers in Palestine everywhere he looks, and fails to see their victims!

Walzer, in short, cannot really know much about the politics of oppression: he can only display attitudes of petulance and dismissal in one direction, while offering the standard "liberal" formulae in the other. He's not even big enough to avoid the Reaganite–Israeli clichés about terrorism. Edward Said, he says, doesn't denounce terrorism. Does Walzer really want a comparative body count? Between 1967 and 1982, two hundred eighty-two Israelis killed by Palestinians violence versus twenty thousand Palestinians killed in the summer of 1982 alone. Does he dare to make explicit what he suggests – that Palestinian deaths by the thousands are less estimable than the few Israeli victims of Palestinian violence? Where, in Walzer's arithmetic of injustice, does he place the deliberate Israeli *state* campaign against the Palestinian people, a campaign about which some Israelis (e.g., Tom Segev and Benni Morris) but no American Zionists are beginning to reflect, as its horrendous scale becomes more widely known: the mass expulsions, the disenfranchisements, the razing of hundreds of villages, the legalized dispossessions of 1948 and 1949, all the way up to the crimes of occupation, the destruction of Lebanon, the systematic rejection of peace? As against this record, Walzer wheels out his *idées reçues* about terrorism and "the men in the stocking cap" as representatives of Palestinian liberation, knowing full well that among the authorized representatives of the Jewish people there are men like Shamir and Begin. In fact, Walzer knows exactly who represents Palestinians: their identities have never been hidden. But Walzer has fought our representatives on every occasion, especially when they have put forward detailed peace plans for negotiations with Israel. Will Walzer say outright what we have said, that we support negotiations between the PLO and Israel? Of course not. Today the Jewish state is led by cabinet ministers like Sharon (the hero of Kibya, Gaza and Shatila) and Rabin (he has at least fifty thousand homeless Palestinians to his credit): Walzer says he doesn't feel confident of his virtue if Jews were stateless and led by "Arafat, Habash, and Abu Masa." It is evident that his virtue isn't up to statehood either. Which takes more confidence for a Jew today, to denounce Palestinian terrorism along with Reagan and Shultz, or to denounce Israeli state terrorism with Chomsky and Shahak?

It is worth mentioning perhaps that I've been execrated repeatedly and in public by Abu Musa for supporting Arafat and his peace initiative with Jordan, and that Habash and I are in opposite camps. Nationalist intellectuals, despite Walzer's timidity, can say things that retrospective moralist professors in Princeton prefer not to. Oh yes, he's for Peace Now: a very brave position indeed, especially since it's accompanied by all that dreadful rubbish about there being no Palestinian Peace Now. I wonder if Walzer really could stomach a Palestinian Peace Now that says what the Israeli one does – that we should have peace with Israel because the Jews present a demographic threat, they breed too fast and are likely to be too numerous in a decade.

Instead of pressing hectoring demands on a people that Walzer's favorite state and movement have already persecuted mercilessly, he should express compassion and atonement. Yes, compassion and atonement. For only among American Zionists is the readiness for peace with Palestinians articulated with such hatred and distaste for Palestinians as a people. It reminds me of the character in a Jane Austen novel who "prepared for matrimony by an hatred of home, restraint, and tranquility; by the misery of disappointed affection, and contempt of the man she was going to marry."

Walzer's extraordinary myopic and ungenerous *envoi*, with its string of false equations between his wise caution and our dastardly terrorism, is little more than a catalogue of his qualifications for prolonged servility to a strong Israel. A courtier, an amateur mythographer, a champion of the strong. A small frightened man who is completely unequal to the question of Canaan–Palestine, and barely adequate for the easier bits of Exodus.

# Notes

## PREFACE

1 Robert C. Tucker (ed.), *The Marx-Engels Reader*, 2nd edn. (New York: W. W. Norton & Company, 1978), p. 53.

2 Ibid.

3 See Paul Bové, *Intellectuals in Power* (New York: Columbia University Press, 1986); James Clifford, *The Predicament of Culture* (Cambridge: Harvard University Press, 1988); and Robert Young, *White Mythologies* (New York: Routledge, 1990).

4 Bové and Clifford, though ambivalently, make the first claim, Young the second.

5 See Bryan D. Palmer, *Descent into Discourse* (Philadelphia: Temple University, 1990) and Aijaz Ahmad, *In Theory* (New York: Verso, 1992).

6 A partial exception is Aamir R. Mufti's "Auerbach in Istanbul: Edward Said, Secular Criticism, and the Question of Minority Culture," *Critical Inquiry* 25:1 (1998), 95–125. Also see Gauri Viswanathan, *Outside The Fold: Conversion, Modernity and Belief* (Princeton, New Jersey: Princeton University Press, 1998), pp. 45–49. She also makes limited use of Said's religious thematics, especially the notion of "worldliness."

## PRELIMINARY REMARKS

1 Michael Walzer, *Exodus and Revolution* (New York: Basic Books, 1985), p. 149.

2 Ibid., pp. 23–27.

3 This is a reference to Hegel's famous description of history in *Introduction to The Philosophy of History* (Indianapolis, Indiana: Hackett Publishing Company, 1988), p. 24. There he describes history as a "slaughter-bench, upon which the happiness of nations, the wisdom of states, and the virtues of individuals" are sacrificed.

4 Edward Said, "Michael Walzer's *Exodus and Revolution*: A Canaanite Reading," *Grand Street* 5 (1985–6), 87. Jonathan Boyarin, "Reading Exodus into History," *New Literary History* 23 (1992), 523–554, is critical of both Said and Walzer's interpretations of the Exodus story: "In this exchange, both Said and Walzer seem to need to cast the question of Palestine in typological

terms, as a reenactment or fulfillment of an archetypical narrative. Otherwise why would they need to read the Old Testament narrative in ways that so closely match their respective visions of Israel, Palestine, and 'Western' politics?"

5  Said, "Canaanite Reading," 89–91.
6  Ibid., 89, 92–93.
7  I am sure that Walzer provides a thorough definition of social democracy elsewhere in his writings. But, in *Exodus and Revolution*, I take social democracy to refer to a social and political system where citizens govern themselves and markets have broad but restricted freedom. Market values such as efficiency or the direct relation between risk and reward must compete with political values such as an equitable distribution of opportunities, which cannot be properly measured without some correlation to equitably distributed outcomes and a minimal standard of living.
8  Said, "Canaanite Reading," 88, 93–95.
9  Walzer, *Exodus*, p. 142.
10  Said, "Canaanite Reading,"102–103.
11  Michael Walzer and Edward Said, "An Exchange: Michael Walzer and Edward Said," *Grand Street* 5 (1985–6), 248.
12  Said, "Canaanite Reading," 98–99.
13  See Victoria Neuseldt (ed.) *Webster's New World College Dictionary* (New York: A. Simon & Schuster Macmillan Company, 1997).
14  René Girard is the most influential proponent of the notion of sacred violence. This is the notion that a violent, scapegoating syndrome lies at the heart of sacred traditions – Christianity excepted. See *Violence and the Sacred*, trans. Patrick Gregory (Baltimore: Johns Hopkins University Press, 1977).
15  Discursive refers to the relation of words and things, to the way that words produce and not merely reflect reality, to the way that things presuppose language. Language is "material"; it matters as much as things.
16  Said, "Canaanite Reading," 86, 92–95.

I  CULTURAL CRITICISM AS THE TRANSFIGURATION OF RELIGIOUS THOUGHT

1  On the relevance (actually the lack of relevance) of verification for religion, F. H. Bradley, *Ethical Studies* (Oxford: The Clarendon Press, 1927), p. 318, writes: "We hear the word 'verification' from Mr. Arnold pretty often. What is to verify? Has Mr. Arnold put 'such a tyro's question' to himself? If to verify means to find in outward experience, then the object of true religion can not be found as this or that outward thing or quality, and so can not be verified. It is of its essence that in this sense it should be unverifiable."
2  William Robbins, *The Ethical Idealism of Matthew Arnold* (University of Toronto Press, 1959), pp. 77–80.
3  Matthew Arnold, *Literature and Dogma*, ed. James C. Livingston (New York: Fredrick Unger Publishing Company, 1970), pp. 2, 27, 31.

4 Language-game is Ludwig Wittgenstein's term for the circumstances that govern the use of language, so that "[d]escribing the appearance of an object," "[s]peculating about an event," and "[m]aking a joke" belong to different language-games. Our expectations are different in the three cases. They have different kinds of propriety. You do not correct a person for a factual error when they are telling a joke. To do so would be a profound misunderstanding of what game she was playing – namely, the game of "let us have some fun" and not the game "just the facts ma'am." See Ludwig Wittgenstein, *Philosophical Investigations* (New York: Macmillan Publishing Co., Inc., 1953), pp. 11–12.

5 Arnold, *Literature,* pp. xvii, xx, 22.

6 Arnold's view of religion was and remains inadequate for many critics. See Henry Sidgwick's powerful critique in Carl Dawson and John Pfordresher (eds.), *Matthew Arnold, Prose Writings* (London: Routledge and Kegan Paul Ltd., 1979), p. 216.

7 Robbins, *Ethical Idealism,* p. 42.

8 Matthew Arnold, *Culture and Anarchy,* ed. J. Dover Wilson (Cambridge University Press, 1988), pp. 6, 43.

9 Raymond Williams, *Culture and Society* (New York: Columbia University Press, 1983), pp. 111–112.

10 Arnold, *Culture and Anarchy,* p. 44.

11 Ibid., pp. 11, 46–48, 52, 55, 211.

12 Arnold was a product of the racial ideology of his day which attributed the qualities of Hebraism and Hellenism to the distinctive "racial" characteristics of Semitic and Indo-European people respectively. It is this same racial logic that undergirds contemporary discussions of the humanities – what they are, and what kinds of people and traditions can be the bearers of humane values. Thus Arnold can write that: "Science has now made visible to everybody the great and pregnant elements of difference which lie in race, and in how signal a manner they make the genius and history of an Indo-European people vary from those of a Semitic people. Hellenism is of Indo-European growth, Hebraism is of Semitic growth; and we English, a nation of Indo-European stock, seem to belong naturally to the movement of Hellenism" (ibid., p. 141).

13 Ibid., pp. 14, 21, 130–132, 139.

14 Ibid., pp. 135, 143.

15 Lionel Trilling, *Matthew Arnold* (New York: Harcourt Brace Jovanovich, 1939), pp. 244–245.

16 Ibid., p. 302.

17 Arnold, *Culture and Anarchy,* p. 203. Arnold had no qualms about a brutal and decisive use of state power to repress public expressions of dissent, no matter how innocuous the expression or worthy the cause. There is an interesting convergence, when it comes to democracy and the virtues of majoritarian politics, among Arnold, *Culture and Anarchy,* Alexis de Tocqueville, *Democracy in America,* trans. George Lawrence, ed. J. P. Mayer (New York:

HarperPerennial, 1988), and John Stuart Mill, *Considerations on Representative Government* (London: Longman, Green, Longman, Roberts, and Longman, 1865). Also see Edward Alexander, *Matthew Arnold and John Stuart Mill* (New York: Columbia University Press, 1965), p. 241.

18  Edmund Burke and Thomas Paine, *Reflections on the Revolution in France/The Rights of Man* (Garden City, New York: Anchor Press/Doubleday, 1973).

19  Williams, *Culture and Society*, p. 11.

20  Arnold, *Culture and Anarchy*, p. 202.

21  James Livingston, *Matthew Arnold and Christianity* (Columbia, SC: University of South Carolina Press, 1986), p. 173.

22  Edward Said, "Nationalism, Human Rights, and Interpretation," *Raritan* 12:3 (1993), 27, 29– 31.

23  Arnold, *Culture and Anarchy*, p. 97.

24  Joubert was a French religious philosopher whom Arnold much admired and cited frequently. He lived from 1754 to 1824.

25  Trilling, *Matthew Arnold*, p. 218.

26  Alexander, *Matthew Arnold and John*, p. 240.

27  Arnold, *Culture and Anarchy*, p. 166.

28  Said thinks that it is wrong to blame Arnold, retrospectively, for racism and imperialism. This does not diminish the force of the following point: "Arnold's ideas about culture share with nationalists and patriots of the time a sort of reinforced sense of essentialized and distilled identity, which, in a much later context of twentieth-century genocidal wars and wholesale persecutions, Adorno saw as leading to 'identitarian thought.'" Nor does Said's desire to be fair diminish the force of this claim: "behind Arnold's disquisitions on English versus French or German cultural identities was a very elaborate set of distinctions between Europeans and Negroes, Europeans and Orientals, Europeans and Semites whose history is pretty constant and pretty unchanging from the 1840s till World War II." See Edward Said, *Raritan*, 31–33.

29  Theodor Adorno, "On the Fetish Character in Music and the Regression of Listening," in J. M. Bernstein (ed.), *The Culture Industry* (London: Routledge, 1991). pp. 28–35.

30  Ibid., pp. 43, 46.

31  Sigmund Freud, *Totem and Taboo* (New York: Vintage Books, 1946), p. 24.

32  Sigmund Freud, *Future of an Illusion*, trans. James Strahey (New York: W. W. Norton and Company, 1961), p. 55.

33  Bernstein, *Culture Industry*, pp. 86–87, 92.

34  Hegemony refers to the grudging acceptance by subordinate (subaltern) classes of a set of social relations that serve the interests of the ruling class, while satisfying some of the desires of subaltern classes. Hegemony also refers to the attempt by subaltern classes to establish a different hegemony, to renegotiate the balance of power.

35  Bernstein, *Culture Industry*, p. 35.

## 2 THE RELIGIOUS EFFECTS OF CULTURE: NATIONALISM

1 I am not suggesting that Zionism is racist, although, as a form of national-ism, it does have currents that are.

2 Edward Said, "Nationalism, Human Rights, and Interpretation," *Raritan* 12:3 (1993), 26–51.

3 Said resists the notion that there are not significant differences between Western and non-Western nationalisms. There is an element of self-criti-cism in so-called Third World nationalisms that is largely absent from so-called First World nationalisms. Ibid., pp. 38, 41.

4 Bani-Sadr is the "Alexander Kerensky" of the Iranian Revolution. Like that early, moderate leader of the Russian Revolution of 1917, Bani-Sadr was rendered obsolete by more radical forces in the revolutionary leadership. When he became an obstacle in their radical path, he became expendable. Like Kerensky, he fled to Paris, the inspiration if not the birthplace of polit-ical radicalism.

5 Carlton J. H. Hayes, *Essays on Nationalism* (New York: The Macmillan Company, 1928), pp. 94–95.

6 This claim may require some explication given Otto's criticism of Schleier-macher. On even a cursory reading of Otto's critique, it is apparent just how Schleiermacherian he is, and just how Kantian both are. Schleiermacher's influence is evident when Otto distinguishes his notion of "the Holy" from Kant's metaphysics and morals, which is precisely the move that Schleier-macher makes in *On Religion* (1799). Otto's criticism can be read as register-ing his disagreement with what Schleiermacher does with their common Kantian inheritance. Schleiermacher rejects Kant's distinction between the noumenal and the phenomenal, the "thing-in-itself" and its "appearing." In this respect, he is in accord with other post-Kantian thinkers such as Fichte and Hegel who also reject the distinction. According to Schleier-macher, we intuit the universe, the infinite, *immediately* and not its appearing. Otto, in contrast, holds onto the thing-in-itself-appearing distinction. The thing-in-itself, the Holy, the wholly other, has to be given to us; it has to impinge from without, objectively, upon our "faculties of receptivity." Only then do we have what Schleiermacher takes to be primary: "creature feeling," the notion of absolute dependence. For Otto, religious experience is an innate, universal capacity of humans as it is for Schleiermacher. They simply accent their views differently. On Otto's notion of religious ex-perience, the "wholly other" is first passively received and then actively (conceptually) "worked-up." For Schleiermacher, in contrast, religious experience always already entails some degree of conceptuality (intuition has reasons of its own). Thus, in the case of religious experience, he rejects what Otto accepts – Kant's dualistic epistemology. For my purposes, then, the distinction that Otto would draw between his and Schleiermacher's views is irrelevant.

7 This, as I recall fondly, is how my "old" professor, Malcolm Diamond,

*Contemporary Philosophy and Religious Thought* (New York: McGraw-Hill, 1974), p. 82, often described it.

8  Hayes, *Essays*, p. 95.

9  In the Glossary to Sigmund Freud's *Moses and Monotheism* (New York: Vintage books, 1939), cathexis is defined as "the process whereby ideas and mental attitudes are invested with a 'charge' of emotion."

10  Hayes, *Essays*, p. 96.

11  Ibid., pp. 96–100.

12  Ibid., pp. 100–104.

13  Quentin Skinner, *The Foundations of Modern Political Thought, Volume Two: The Age Of Reformation* (London: Cambridge University Press, 1978), pp. 347–352.

14  Hagen Schulze, *States, Nations and Nationalism*, trans. William E. Yuill (Oxford: Blackwell, 1996), pp. 91, 99, 100–103, 114.

15  Ibid., pp. 91.

16  Here I agree with Anthony Appiah's anti-Herderian view of state and nation: "Nations never preexist states. Loosely and unphilosophically defined, a nation is an 'imagined community' of culture or ancestry running beyond the scale of the face-to-face and seeking political expression. But all the nations I can think of that are not coterminous with states are the legacy of older state arrangements – as Asante is what has become Ghana, and as the Serbian and Croatian nations are in what used to be Yugoslavia.

I want, in fact, to distinguish the nation and the state to make a point entirely opposite to Herder's: if anything is morally arbitrary, it is not the state but the nation. Since human beings live in political orders narrower than the species, and since it is within those political orders that questions of public right and wrong are largely argued out and decided, the fact of being a fellow-citizen – someone who is a member of the same order – is not morally arbitrary at all." See *For Love of Country* (ed.) Martha Nussbaum and Joshua Cohen (Boston: Beacon Press, 1996), pp. 27– 28.

17  I realize that the idea of nation is older than the idea of the state. One cannot be reduced to the other. But it is also true that many, perhaps most, nationalisms want statehood – that is, they want their sense of peoplehood to be augmented and ratified by the institutions of political power. Skinner's account helps to address an important aspect of nationalist desire.

18  Hayes, *Essays*, pp. 105, 107–109.

19  Ibid., pp. 105–106.

20  See Hans Blumenberg, *The Legitimacy of the Modern Age*, trans. Robert M. Wallace (Cambridge, MA: MIT Press, 1983).

21  Obviously, Hayes' notion of the religious sense preceded Robert Bellah's notion of "civil religion" by several decades. See Robert Bellah, *The Broken Covenant* (New York: Seabury Press, 1975).

22  Hayes, *Essays*, pp. 107–108.

23  Ibid., p. 109.

24  Ibid., p. 110.

25 Frantz Fanon, *The Wretched of the Earth* (New York; New Grove Press, 1963), p. 156.

26 Wilfred Cantwell Smith, *The Meaning and End of Religion* (Minneapolis: Fortress Press, 1991), pp. 67–68. For similar comments see Max Weber, *The Sociology of Religion* (Boston: Beacon Press, 1991), p. 62.

27 According to Roger J. Corless, *The Vision of Buddhism* (New York: Paragon House, 1989), p. 115, "Tolerance does not mean vagueness. Except in a few cases, Buddhism has allowed rival cults to flourish, even when it was politically able to defeat them, but it has never had any doubt about their inferiority."

28 Garth Fowden, *Empire to Commonwealth* (Princeton University Press, 1993). For an appreciative but critical review of Fowden's book, see Andrew Louth in *Journal of Theological Studies* 46:2 (1995), 737–740. Louis H. Feldman's review, in *The Journal of the American Oriental Society* 114:4 (1994), 671–672, questions Fowden's claim that Judaism was a nonproselytizing monotheism. J. F. Drinkwater's review in *History Today* 44:9 (1994), 57–58, challenges Fowden's parallel between Constantine and Muhammad: Muhammad's status as the prophet of Allah's revelation is "literal," while Constantine's claim to be the "thirteenth apostle" of the Christian Church is metaphorical.

29 Fowden, *Empire*, pp. 3, 9, 87–88, 139, 143.

30 Ibid., p. 170.

31 Said appears to hold out hope for a form of religiosity that avoids the Dionysian spirit and sectarian madness that he describes. This would be a rather dry and sane Protestantism, which he associates with the boyhood Anglicanism of his grandmother. But the prospect of this sort of religiosity has currently, perhaps forever, been overrun by the monotheistic madness of overbearing priests, imams, and rabbis and their various entanglements with nationalism (*ALS* 154–156).

32 Smith makes several points. Hindu as a religious designation was foisted on the people of the Indian subcontinent by Muslim conquerors in the second millennium AD. This term was applied to those whom we now call Hindu and to Buddhists, Jains, and others. Most important, perhaps, was the distinctiveness of the Muslim invasion from prior invasions. The Muslims brought with them a set of organized, systematic and exclusive ideas, and were intolerant of different ideas. After several centuries, the Muslim/non-Muslim distinction has succeeded in producing a distinct Hindu consciousness. (Smith, *Meaning and End*, pp. 64–65). In contemporary language, it has succeeded in producing Hindu subjects.

33 Perhaps the most sophisticated argument for "religious nationalism" is Peter Van der Veer's *Religious Nationalism* (Berkeley, CA: University of California Press, 1994). I am sympathetic to Van Der Veer's position, but I have doubts about how much work the adjective "religious" in religious nationalism actually does.

34 Of course nationhood, "peoplehood," is a complex idea. I make no abso-

lute distinctions between nationhood and religion. Sometimes they are roughly identical but they need not be. The recent controversy in Israel over "Who is a Jew?" is instructive in this regard. The complexities of nationalism are evident in the recent "narrativist turn," where nationalism as a racialized, sexualized, and gendered discourse is a central topic of analysis.

35 Hayes, *Essays*, p. 125.

36 Emile Durkheim, *The Elementary Forms of the Religious Life*, trans. Karen Fields (New York: The Free Press, 1995), p. 215.

37 Ibid., pp. 212–213.

38 Anthony Giddens, *Durkheim on Politics and the State* (Cambridge, UK: Polity Press, 1986), pp. 230–232.

## 3 THE RELIGIOUS EFFECTS OF CULTURE: ORIENTALISM

1 Hans Blumenberg describes this process as "reoccupation." See *The Legitimacy of the Modern Age* (Cambridge, MA: MIT Press, 1983).

2 This quotation, which is on pages 114–115 of *Orientalism*, is from M. H. Abrams, *Natural Supernaturalism: Tradition and Revolution in Romantic Literature* (New York: W. W. Norton and Company, 1971), p. 66.

3 Hayden White, *Metahistory* (Baltimore: Johns Hopkins University Press, 1973), pp. x, 9.

4 *Orientalism* is metahistorical. It is also genealogical, but more Nietzschean than Foucauldian in form. Said is as interested in Orientalism as deep structure as he is in it as a series of discrete events.

5 For an extended analysis of discursive formations, see Hubert Dreyfus and Paul Rabinow, *Michel Foucault: Beyond Structuralism and Hermeneutics* (University of Chicago Press, 1982). For a similar but differently nuanced account, see Gary Gutting, *Michel Foucault's Archaeology of Scientific Reason* (Cambridge University Press, 1989).

6 James Clifford suggests that Said's description of Orientalism is confused if not confusing. See James Clifford, "On Orientalism," in *The Predicament of Culture* (Cambridge, MA: Harvard University Press, 1988), pp. 260–261. Said might rejoin by attributing the confusion these critics see to their polemical purposes rather than to the demerits of his account. These descriptions, he might argue, are not mutually exclusive. That is certainly the argument that I would make. But I can only speculate about what Said would say, since he does not address the question of whether his complex notion of Orientalism is consistent or not.

7 See Michel Foucault, *The Archaeology of Knowledge*, trans. A. M. Sheridan (New York: Pantheon Books, 1972). Said uses Freud's distinction between the latent and manifest content of dreams, which he developed in *The Interpretation of Dreams*, to illuminate the "enunciative capacity" of Orientalism – that is, its ability to place the subject in various positions in relation to language. Manifest Orientalism refers to modern, present-day descriptions of the Orient. These descriptions are the result of "commercial, political, and

other existential encounters between East and West." But these encounters, so Said's argument goes, were always constrained by the "profoundly conservative" enunciative capacities of latent Orientalism. It is latent Orientalism that determines the manifest content. As the following passage suggests, latent Orientalism determines who can speak authoritatively about the Orient and what they can say: "Transmitted from one generation to another, it was a part of the culture, as much a language about a part of reality as geometry or physics. Orientalism staked its existence, not upon its openness, its receptivity to the Orient, but rather on its internal, repetitious consistency about its constitutive will–to–power over the Orient. In such a way Orientalism was able to survive revolutions, world wars, and the literal dismemberment of empires" (*O* 221–222).

8  Compare this to Michel Foucault, "What is an Author?" in Donald F. Bouchard (ed.), *Language, Counter-Memory, Practice* (Ithaca, NY: Cornell University Press, 1997).

9  Michel Foucault, *The Archaeology of Knowledge*, trans. A. M. Sheridan (New York: Pantheon Books, 1972), pp. 54–55.

10  In his analysis of Said's attempt to create a "hybrid perspective" on the relationship between discourse and subjectivity, Clifford writes: "What is important theoretically is not that Foucault's author counts for very little but rather that a 'discursive formation'—as opposed to ideas, citations, influences, references, conventions, and the like—is not produced by authorial subjects or even by a group of authors arranged as a 'tradition.'" This is a methodological and not an empirical point. "One cannot combine within the same analytic totality both personal statements and discursive statements, even though they may be lexically identical. Said's experiment seems to show that when the analysis of authors and traditions is intermixed with the analysis of discursive formations, the effect is a mutual weakening." Arbitrary selectivity, psychologizing, and unfair reductionism, according to Clifford, are the consequences of Said's misguided assessment of authorial intentions (Clifford, *Predicament*, pp. 269–271). On this last point, also see Victor Bromert, "Orientalism and the Scandals of Scholarship," *American Scholar* 48 (1979), 537–538, and Thomas M. Greene, "One World, Divisible," *The Yale Review* 68 (1979), 579–580.

11  Michel Foucault, *The Foucault Reader*, ed. Paul Rabinow (New York: Pantheon Books, 1984, p. 116.

12  I do not mean to suggest that Said is right because he is consistent with Foucault. Foucault may not be consistent with himself. What I do want to suggest is that Foucault and Said cannot be distinguished sharply in this respect. If Said is incoherent, it is an incoherence that he shares with Foucault.

13  The idea of governing rules is not a problem for my account. Rules, as Said understands, are made to be broken.

14  Foucault, *Archaeology*, pp. 127, 130.

15  Ibid., p. 108.

16 This is not the only place where Clifford makes claims that are confusing if not confused. On one page he chides Said along with Foucault and Derrida for positing "a Western totality" against which they inveigh. On the previous page Clifford refers to Said's captivity to "the totalizing habits of Western humanism" thus presupposing what he condemns. He cannot have it both ways. Which is it? (Clifford, *Predicament*, pp. 270–271).

17 In this regard, Nietzsche is not merely being mean when he says that Socrates is ugly. Rather he is drawing a connection between Socrates' physical decadence and what he thinks that he has already, independently established, namely, Socrates' spiritual decadence.

18 "Genealogy is perhaps the most political of historical modes; but to be effective it cannot appear too openly tendentious, and Said's genealogy suffers on this score" (Clifford, *Predicament*, p. 267). From the perspective of whose notion of genealogy does Clifford speak? Certainly not from Nietzsche's perspective. If his claim is that Said's genealogy suffers by Foucault's standards, that may be true. But he does not tell us why Foucault's standards are worthy of respect. I take Said as splitting the difference between Nietzsche and Foucault's very different genealogical practices. Thus, to criticize Said for deviating from Foucauldian orthodoxy without saying why *that* orthodoxy is good is rather odd. To criticize Said's genealogical practice because it is different from Foucault's is like criticizing Foucault's genealogies because they are different from Nietzsche's genealogies. This form of criticism is legitimate, but it is also limited. It does not subject Foucauldian "scripture" to "higher criticism."

19 Michel Foucault, *Discipline and Punish*, trans. A. Sheridan (New York: Vintage Books, 1979), p. 137.

20 Ibid., pp. 27–28.

21 Albert Hourani, "The Road to Morocco," *The New York Times Review*, 8 March 1979, 27–29. See "Orientalism, an Afterword," *Raritan* (1995) for Said's response.

22 In a nice survey of the critical reception of *Orientalism* and its broad influence, Gyan Prakash adds support to the claim that Said is a founder of discursivity. The acceptance, revision, and rejection of *Orientalism* are all part of its vast influence. Thus, there are wide-ranging debates about the tensions between Said's Auerbachian high-cultural humanism and the anti-humanism of Foucauldian discourse analysis. The questionable selectivity of Said's account, which he was the first to acknowledge, is a continuing subject of discussion. Thus many critics persist in trying to undermine the force of Said's critique by highlighting his exclusion of those traditions, such as German and Russian Orientalism, that do not confirm the Foucauldian nexus of knowledge and power. Other critics make much of the uniformity of Orientalist discourse, which obscures its actual heterogeneity, selfconsciousness, and ambivalence. Nevertheless, because *Orientalism's* contradictions are often fertile rather than sterile, it established a discourse:

Said's transgression of disciplinary boundaries to force the recognition of Oriental-ism as a discipline of power has become a model for navigating between literature, history, philosophy, and anthropology, and has gone on to inspire studies in such new fields as cultural, feminist, and postcolonial studies. Established centers of area studies in the United States have been moved to confront the challenge made by the book, and Western scholarship on other cultures has undergone a noticeable change. Not only is the European presence in Africa, Latin America, and Asia rou-tinely interrogated to disclose the construction and constriction of other subjects, empire and colonialism are increasingly seen placed at the very center of Europe's constitution. The discipline of English studies appears with a colonial genealogy that can be traced to British rule in India, and French modernity is shown to be forged in Algeria and Morocco.

And, though his account is clearly limited and analytically thin, Said offers telling examples of the incestuous relationship between imperial politics and sexual politics, and the theme of Western domination as sexual con-quest has found ready elaboration. If, moreover, he does not recognize, as Robert Young claims, the Occident–Orient dichotomy as the externaliza-tion of the West's internal heterogeneity and ambivalence, his analysis, nev-ertheless, "operates precisely in the ambivalent fissures of the Western discourse. Said's work is unthinkable outside the corpus of knowledge he subjects to scrutiny, but his critique works as a catachresis, in Spivak's sense." See Gyan Prakash, "Orientalism Now," *History and Theory* 34:3 (1995), 199–210.

23 In one of the most subtle interpretations of *Orientalism*, Dennis Porter con-cludes that:

the reason why Said is unable in the end to suggest alternatives to the hegemonic discourse of Orientalism is not difficult to explain. First, because he overlooks the potential contradiction between discourse theory and Gramscian hegemony, he fails to historicize adequately the texts he cites and summarizes, finding always the same triumphant discourse where several are frequently in conflict. Second, because he does not distinguish the literary instance from the more transparently ideological forms he does not acknowledge the semi-autonomous and overdetermined charac-ter of aesthetic artifacts. Finally, he fails to show how literary texts may in their play establish distance from the ideologies they seem to be reproducing.

See Dennis Porter, "Orientalism and its Problems," in Peter Hulme, Margaret Iversen, and Diane Loxley (eds.), *The Politics of Theory*, Proceedings of the Essex Sociology of Literature Conference, University of Essex, Colchester, 1983, p. 193.

Said responds to this critique in "Orientalism Reconsidered." He remained unconvinced of the analytical benefits of a more "rigorous" his-toricizing: "the claims made by Dennis Porter (1983), among others, that I am ahistorical and inconsistent, would have more interest if the virtues of consistency (whatever may be intended by the term) were subjected to rig-orous analysis; as for my ahistoricity that too is a charge more weighty in assertion than it is in proof." (See Edward Said, "Orientalism Reconsidered," in Francis Barker, Peter Hulme, Margaret Iversen and Diane Loxley (eds.), *Literature, Politics and Theory*, Papers from the Essex Conference 1976–84 [London: Methuen, 1986], p. 221.) Said makes a Nietzschean move here. This is important because early in his account Porter describes *Orientalism* as "a Nietzschean genealogy which delimits a given field of inquiry in order to expose the multiple mystified relations between knowledge and power, culture and politics" (179). Ignoring the fact that this sounds more like Foucauldian genealogy than Nietzschean genealogy, it is important to note that Nietzsche resists, at crucial points, the very historicizing that Porter regards as Said's failure. This resistance is a central feature of "The Advantages and Disadvantages of History for Life." Regardless, Porter is surely right when he says that there is a contradiction in *Orientalism* between truth (Foucault's regime of truth) and ideology (Gramsci's hegemonic formations), between which Said vacillates. The important question, which Porter does not answer, is whether that contradiction is vicious or productive.

24  Clifford, *Predicament*, p. 262.

25  Said regrets the anti–Western construction that critics have placed on *Orientalism* . He says that this interpretation, which is common both to those who are hostile and to those who are sympathetic to the "West," is misleading. According to Said, he has never regarded Orientalism as a synecdoche, or miniature symbol, of the entire West. On the contrary, his argument "is explicitly anti–essentialist, radically skeptical about all categorical designations like Orient and Occident." Rather than separate and reify, according to Said, he has sought to connect. See Edward Said, "Orientalism, an Afterword," in *Raritan* (1995), 32–59. And the following passage should give pause to anyone who claims that Said fails to acknowledge the positive accomplishments of Orientalism: "Orientalism did a great many things. During its great age in the nineteenth century it produced scholars; it increased the number of languages taught in the West and the quantity of manuscripts edited, translated, and commented on; in many cases, it provided sympathetic European students, genuinely interested in such matters as Sanskrit grammar, Phoenician numismatics, and Arabic poetry" (*O* 96).

26  Bové defines humanism as essentialist–universalism. He claims that this notion legitimizes sexist and racist exploitation and repression. Bové's account, however, is one-sided. Human rights is also a humanist idea as are the notions that race and gender are bad reasons for treating people in invidious ways. The very idea that we owe all people, and not just some people, certain considerations is a humanist idea. Our very anger at the failed universality of humanist claims is a humanist sentiment. "Certainly, intolerable horrors have been carried out by scientists, writers, academics, and politicians camped under its banner." But so have forms of decency, consideration, and respect. Bové cites "scientific racism" in a list of "humanist horribles." But scientific racism has as much to do with nonuniversality and antihumanism as it does with humanism as the polygenesis

argument for human origins shows. Bové claims that a "genealogy of humanism makes it impossible to proceed as a humanistic intellectual without the certain knowledge that at some point the elements within humanism that make it ready to justify abuse would also compel us to revalue its potential, to see its 'complicity' with repression." My response is that every human action or judgment is subject to betrayal. Every judgment is potentially dangerous, including antihumanist actions or judgments. But that is hardly a reason for suspending action or judgment, for being a weak evaluator, weak poet, or decadent spirit.

Bové claims that *Orientalism* represents the best form of critical humanism and "the strongest weapon in struggles against domination." It is temporarily necessary "as a step on the path beyond humanism" whose "complicitous burdens would always betray humanism's generosity and creativity into domination and dogma – but not until after it had done considerable and important 'oppositional' work, precisely as *Orientalism* did do." See Paul Bové, "Hope and Reconciliation: A Review of Edward Said," in *Boundary 2* 20:2 (1993), 271. Bové has drunk deeply at the well of Foucault's "ontology of power." His account of humanism's inevitable betrayal is pure metaphysics, in the pejorative sense of the word. Humanism like any act of human imagination is fallible. Whether humanism's results are good or bad is a matter of historical contingency, not metaphysical necessity.

27 Twenty-five years later, Derrida has modified or at least qualified his views, as is evident in his comments on Heidegger's humanist teleology: "I do not mean to criticize this humanist teleology. It is no doubt more urgent to recall that, in spite of all the denegations or all the avoidances one could wish, it has remained *up till now* (in Heidegger's time and situation, but this has not radically changed today) the price to be paid in the ethico–political denunciation of biologism, racism, naturalism, etc. If I analyze this 'logic,' and the aporias or limits, the presuppositions or axiomatic decisions, above all the inversions and contaminations, in which we see it becoming entangled, this is rather in order to exhibit and then formalize the terrifying mechanisms of this program, all the double constraints which structure it. Is this unavoidable? Can one escape this program? No sign would suggest it, at least neither in 'Heideggerian' discourses nor in 'antiHeideggerian' discourses." See Jacques Derrida, *Of Spirit*, trans. Geoffrey Bennington and Rachel Bowlby (University of Chicago Press, 1991), p. 56.

28 Cliffon, *Predicament*, p. 270

29 Jacques Derrida, *Writing and Difference* (University of Chicago Press, 1978), p. 34

30 Catherine Gimelli Martin, "Orientalism and the Ethnographer: Said, Herodotus, and the Discourse of Alterity," *Criticism* 32:4 (1990).

31 See Edward Said, *Joseph Conrad and the Fiction of Autobiography* (Cambridge, MA: Harvard University Press, 1966).

32 See also Jacques Derrida, "To Do Justice to Freud: The History of Madness in the Age of Psychoanalysis," *Critical Inquiry*, 20:2 (1994). Despite his denial, Derrida renews his long standing dispute with Foucault in this article.

33 Aijaz Ahmad, *In Theory* (New York: Verso, 1992), pp. 167, 169–170, 179, 195, 217–219. Marjorie Levinson does not agree with this point. See her blistering critique of Ahmad in "News from Nowhere: The Discontents of Aijaz Ahmad," *Public Culture* 6 (1993), 97–131.

34 Said's argument would be more persuasive if he acknowledged the long-standing nature of the rivalries between the Abrahamic religions. All have engaged in polemical representations of the others from the very beginning. There is nothing distinctively Orientalist about that. Rabbinic Judaism represented early Christians as an aberrant cult. Christians represented Jews as having failed to live up to the Abrahamic and Sinai covenants and, therefore, of forfeiting to Christians the messianic promise. In turn, Muslims accuse Christians, who regard Jesus as God, of being something less than monotheists. Muslims represent Jesus as merely a prophet and Christians represent Muhammad as an impostor. These things are regrettable, but I question the usefulness of Orientalism as an account of why these things are done. They have little to do with the East–West distinction and much to do with human-all-too-human commonalities.

35 Foucault, *Discipline*, p. 27.

36 Foucault's influential reservations ("Truth and Power") about ideology are captured in the following passage:

> The notion of ideology appears to me to be difficult to make use of, for three reasons. The first is that, like it or not, it always stands in virtual opposition to something else which is supposed to count as truth. Now I believe that the problem does not consist in drawing the line between that in a discourse which falls under the category of scientificity or truth, and that which comes under some other category, but in seeing historically how effects of truth are produced within discourses which in themselves are neither truth nor false. The second drawback is that the concept of ideology refers, I think necessarily, to something on the order of the subject. Third, ideology stands in a secondary position relative to something which functions as its infrastructure, as its material, economic determinant, etc. For these three reasons, I think that this is a notion that cannot be used without circumspection.

See Michel Foucault, "Truth and Power," in *Power/Knowledge*, trans. Colin Gordon, Leo Marshall, John Mepham and Kate Soper, ed. Colin Gordon (New York: Pantheon Books, 1980), p. 118.

37 Rodinson is the author of several books on Islam and the Arab world, including *Islam and Capitalism*, trans. Brian Pearce (New York: Pantheon, 1973), *Muhammad*, trans. Anne Carter (New York: Pantheon Books, 1980), and *Europe and the Mystique of Islam*, trans. Roger Veinus (Seattle: University of Washington Press, 1987).

38 Solidad Garcia (ed.) *European Identity and the Search for Legitimacy* (London: Pinter Publishers, 1993), pp. 46–47.

4 THE RELIGIOUS EFFECTS OF CULTURE: IMPERIALISM

1 Jorge Larrain, *The Concept of Ideology* (Athens, Georgia: The University of Georgia Press, 1979), pp. 17–18, 27.

2 Plato, *The Republic of Plato*, trans. Allan Bloom (New York: Basic Books, 1968), p. 94.
3 Larrain, *Ideology*, p. 19.
4 Niccolò Machiavelli, *The Prince and the Discourses* (New York: Random House, 1950), pp. 64–66, 147, 150, 195.
5 Francis Bacon, *Advance of Learning and Novum Organum* (New York: Willey Book Company, 1944), pp. 319–331.
6 Moshe Halbertal and Avishai Margalit, *Idolatry*, trans. Naomi Goldblum (Cambridge, MA: Harvard University Press, 1992), p. 11.
7 Ibid., pp. 109–112. For a different way of conceptualizing the relationship between religion and ideology, see Louis Feuer, *Ideology and the Ideologists* (New York: Harper and Row, 1975), pp. 169–173.
8 Larrain, *Ideology*, pp. 21–22. Larrain concludes his account by briefly surveying ideology's encounter with two traditions of post-Enlightenment critical thought: French positivism and German idealism. The French tradition that grows out of the work of Auguste Comte (1798–1857) is an elaboration of the Baconian theme of distortion-free knowledge. This positivist tradition culminates, according to Larrain, in the Vienna Circle. German idealism, in contrast, culminates in Marx's materialist inversion of Feuerbach, and represents the most influential account of ideology (pp. 28–34).
9 Halbertal, *Idolatry*, pp. 112–114.
10 I refer to Louis Althusser's influential argument, *For Marx* (London: Verso, 1996), about the non-Marxist character of the early Marx. On this view, the author of the *Economic and Philosophic Manuscript of 1844* and *The Holy Family* was a Feuerbachian–humanist. Althusser also regards *The Jewish Question* and "Contribution to the Critique of Hegel's *Philosophy of Right*" as humanist. Althusser's claims are still controversial after nearly thirty years and continue to generate new responses. I side with those who "split the difference" between Althusser's claim that Marx underwent an "epistemological break" after 1845 with Hegelian–Feuerbachian humanism and those who argue that the "young" Marx is present in the "mature" Marx. They acknowledge a break, but insist on the persistence of Hegelian language, themes, and logic in what Althusser regards as the greatest work of Marx's maturity, namely, *Capital*. See Michael Rosen, *On Voluntary Servitude* (Cambridge, MA: Harvard University Press, 1996), pp. 207–219.
11 Charles Taylor, *Hegel* (Cambridge University Press, 1975), p. 91.
12 Ludwig Feuerbach, *The Essence of Christianity*, trans. George Eliot (New York: Harper and Row, 1957), pp. 5–6, 12–13.
13 Robert C. Tucker (ed.) *The Marx–Engels Reader*, 2nd edn. (New York: W. W. Norton and company, 1978), pp. 53–54.
14 Ibid., pp. 72–76.
15 There is no evidence that Marx ever used this term. The only reference to false consciousness in the Marx–Engels corpus is in a letter from Engels to Franz Mehring, where he writes the following: "Ideology is a process accomplished by the so-called thinker consciously, it is true, but with a false consciousness. The real motive forces impelling him remain unknown to

him; otherwise it simply would not be an ideological process. Hence he imagines false or seeming motive forces" (Tucker, *Reader*, p. 766).

16 Ibid., pp. 72, 74.

17 Halbertal, *Idolatry*, pp. 242–243.

18 I agree with that tradition of Marxist thought that claims that false consciousness is the least important aspect Marx's notion of ideology. According to this view, Marx construes ideology as a battlefield where competing interests fight it out. Neither Marx nor the classical Marxist tradition subscribed to the notion that ideology derived from one class and mystified another. But they did hold that ideology served class interests and that people often misperceived what their interests were or acted against those interests. See Joe McCarney, *The Real World of Ideology* (Atlantic Highlands, NJ: Humanities Press, 1980). The notion that ideology serves certain class interests but for functional reasons and without necessity is a weak claim (Rosen, *Voluntary Servitude*, pp. 184–200) when compared to conventional and vulgar notions of ideology. But this weak notion of ideology is potent enough, as Raymond Williams' *Marxism and Literature* shows. Williams says in clear language what Foucault says in his more obscure style – that Marx, especially on the issue of ideology, was a founder of discursivity. His writings and that huge tradition of "reader response" called Marxism underwrite several views, some of them contradictory. This multiplicity is a tribute more than a reproach.

19 Halbertal, *Idolatry*, pp. 244, 248–250.

20 Halbertal and Margalit are wrong when they suggest that self-deification is the ultimate consequence of *only* the inversion strategy. Marx employs language from which one can infer the notion of self-deification: "The criticism of religion disillusions man so that he will think, act and fashion his reality as a man who has lost his illusions and regained his reason; so that he will revolve about himself as his own true sun. Religion is only the illusory sun about which man revolves so long as he does not revolve about himself" (Tucker, *Reader*, p. 54). This sounds like self-deification to me. The only important difference between Nietzsche and Marx on the issue of self-deification is its individualist character for the former and collectivist character for the latter.

21 Peter Berkowitz, *Nietzsche: The Ethics of an Immoralist* (Cambridge, MA: Harvard University Press, 1995)

22 Halbertal, *Idolatry*, pp. 114–115.

23 Raymond Williams, *Marxism and Literature* (Oxford University Press, 1977), pp. 59, 77.

24 Ibid., pp. 128–135.

25 See Edward W. Said, *Joseph Conrad and the Fiction of Autobiography* (Cambridge, MA: Harvard University Press, 1966).

26 Susan Fraiman, "Jane Austen and Edward Said: Gender, Culture, and Imperialism," *Critical Inquiry* 21:4 (1995), accepts Said's call for a contrapuntal approach to the reading of texts, but she rejects the specifics of his reading of Austen. She is troubled by the kind of gender politics that underlie Said's postcolonial project. She is troubled, in particular, by Said's lack

of empathy that, by contrast, is on full display in his reading of Conrad. His analysis abstracts and isolates *Mansfield Park* from the rest of Austen's corpus and obscures the patriarchal constraints under which she wrote. Further, the conventionality of his reading shows his ignorance of recent feminist scholarship on Austen. Fraiman does not dispute Said's claim that Austen's novel, where she refers unthinkingly to Antigua, "unwittingly but systematically helped to gain consent for imperialist policies." She even refers, how ironically, I am not sure, to Austen's "imperialist crimes." Nevertheless, Fraiman does contest how these references and "crimes" should be read. They should not be read as if Austen or her protagonist, Fanny Price, were "fully acculturated Englishmen." Some account should have been given of what absent-minded references to Antigua and slavery might have meant for them, given the constraint of gender, which is at least as important as Conrad's marginality as a Polish-born émigré. I think that Fraiman is persuasive on all these points.

She describes the sexual politics of *Culture and Imperialism* as "a largely subliminal strategy" that opposes imperialism by using "a gender allegory," an unreconstructed notion of the "feminine." While I find her account illuminating, I do not find Said's use of this allegory troubling for the same reasons that she does not find Austen's reference to English womanhood as slave-like troubling. In both cases, Said's and hers-and-Austen's, an unreconstructed and devalued category is used to "tar" another practice (now imperialism, now patriarchy) regarded as bad. Fraiman remarks that "From a feminist perspective, it seems all-too-obvious that in *Mansfield Park* slavery functions similarly: not as a subtext wherein Austen and Sir Thomas converge but, on the contrary, as a trope Austen introduces to argue the essential depravity of Sir Thomas's relations to other people." Undoubtedly, it can be read this way, but that is not the only way it can be read, which is Said's point. As Said argues, "interpreting Jane Austen depends on *who* does the interpreting, *when* it is done, and no less important, from *where* it is done" (*CAI* 93). Said does not contest feminist readings such as Fraiman's, only the claim that they are the only readings or the best readings – best for whom? What I find fascinating is Fraiman's blindness to the tropological character of gender in Said's account of imperialism, which is not to say that there are not aspects of that account that are troubling. Thus Fraiman replicates the very blindness of which she rightly accuses Said. Imperialism is not rape, but neither is English womanhood slavery. On this point, it seems to me, Fraiman owes Said the same hermeneutical charity that she claims for Austen.

27 Michael Steffes, "Slavery and *Mansfield Park*: The Historical and Biographical Context," *English Language Notes* 34:2 (1996), 23–41; Peter Smith, "*Mansfield Park* and the World Stage," *The Cambridge Quarterly* 23:3 (1994), 203–229.
28 Ibid., pp. 203–229.
29 Steffes, "Slavery," 23–41.

30 See John A. Hobson, *Imperialism* (London: George Allen and Unwin Ltd., 1902).

31 Geo Widengren, *Mani and Manichaeism* (New York: Holt, Rinehart and Winston, 1965), pp. 44–45, 67.

32 Thomas Hobbes, *Leviathan* (London: Oxford University Press, 1909), pp. 56–62.

33 John Locke, "An Essay Concerning Human Understanding" in *The Empiricists* (Garden City, New York: Anchor Books, 1974), pp. 126–128.

34 Miriam Kosh Starkman (ed.) *Gulliver's Travels and Other Writings by Jonathan Swift* (New York: Bantam Books, 1962), p. 425.

35 Philip Pinkus, *Swift's Vision of Evil* (Charlottesville: University of Virginia Press, 1975), p. 54.

36 Swift, *Gulliver's Travels* (ed.) Starkman, p. 385.

## 5 THE RESPONSIBILITIES OF THE SECULAR CRITIC

1 Noam Chomsky, *The Chomsky Reader* (New York: Pantheon Books, 1987), p. 60.

2 Said might be disturbed to discover how much this notion of universality sounds like the "radical monotheism" of the Protestant theologian H. Richard Niebuhr.

3 Julien Benda, *The Treason of the Intellectuals* (New York: W. W. Norton and Company, Inc., 1928), pp. 43–45, 67, 78, 103.

4 Ibid., pp. 190–191.

5 Sigrid L. Lehnberger, "Julien Benda's Characterization of the 'Clerc,' 1927–1948," Ph.D. Dissertation, Duke University (1949), p. iv.

6 David Forgacs (ed.) *An Antonio Gramsci Reader* (New York: Schocken Books, 1988), p. 304.

7 A great intellectual injustice of the late twentieth century, and there have been injustices galore, is the collapse of Sartre's reputation. This has much to do with the efforts of post-World War II French intellectuals (whom Americans call poststructuralists) to authorize and valorize their own voices. But, like all those unfairly and prematurely dismissed, there is good reason to think that Sartre's reputation will be rehabilitated and that his ideas will recover much of their prestige.

8 For a powerful critique of this idea, see Gillian Rose, *Mourning Becomes the Law* (Cambridge University Press, 1996). Also see Gayatri Chakravorty Spivak's blistering critique of this idea in "Can the Subaltern Speak?" in C. Nelson and L. Grossberg (eds.), *Marxism and the Interpretation of Culture* (Basingstoke: Macmillan Education 1988, pp. 271–313. Spivak's critique is a devastating account of how Foucault and Deleuze mystify by conflating two different notions of representation: "representation as 'speaking for' [*vertreten*], as in politics, and representation as 're-presentation' [*darstellen*], as in art or philosophy."

9 Aijaz Ahmad thinks that this is an unworkable and an unstable hybrid.

Indeed, he thinks it is a political abomination. According to Ahmad, Said is schizophrenic – divided between "Auerbachean High Humanism and Nietzschean anti-humanism." Thus Said praises Gramsci, the Leftist militant and Benda, the reactionary. Ahmad is particularly exercised by Benda's anticommunism and antisocialism. But he gets at least two things wrong. Benda was not a political reactionary, except by rather bizarre standards. He was conservative, no doubt, but he was more fearful of fascism than of communism. He cut his political teeth during the Dreyfus affair, and was on Zola's side; the side that criticized the incipient fascism of the anti-Dreyfusards. Granted, his politics were not leftwing, and there is little in his politics to warm the heart of a committed socialist, but Benda was hardly a reactionary. It is important in politics to make the right distinctions. There is a world of difference between Benda, the mild-conservative and his fascists contemporaries. Ahmad is also wrong when he says that: "It is an index of Said's self-division that he would think of Benda, the rabid anti-communist, and Gramsci, one of the more persevering communists of the century, as occupying essentially the same theoretico-political position" (Ahmad, *In Theory*, p. 170). Of course, Said does not think any such thing. It is true, however, that Said's catholic and eclectic style, and his ability to selectively appropriate ideas from thinkers whose views he otherwise despises, makes such charges easy to make, even if on reflection they are hard to sustain.

10  Fons Elders, *Reflexive Water* (London: Souvenir Press [Educational and Academic] Ltd., 1974), pp. 168–170.

11  Ibid., pp. 170–173.

12  Ibid., pp. 173–174.

13  Economism is the notion that economic causes are the only causes or, necessarily, the fundamental or most important causes of social activity. The critique of this idea is often associated with Antonio Gramsci who believed that economism had more to do with economic liberalism than with socialism proper, that is, with the philosophy of praxis. Thus he rejects the notion that "Everything is economics." See Quintin Hoare and Geoffrey Nowell Smith (eds.), *Selections from the Prison Note Books* (New York: International Publishers, 1989), pp. 158–163.

14  Nietzsche's case is complicated. The notion that might makes right is qualified by his metaphysics of sickeness and health. Some forms of might are hygienic and others are decadent. As counterintuitive as it might sound, he believed that sickly rather than healthy forms of life were more likely to survive. This is true in part because the weak, necessarily, have a higher degree of self-consciousness and therefore, are more cunning than the healthy who rely on their instincts.

15  I do not mean to suggest that there is an antinomy between right and might. For right without power is empty and power without right is blind. According to Spinoza, right is determined not by "sound reason or power." See Benedict de Spinoza, *A Theological–Political Treatise, A Political Treatise,*

trans. R. H. M. Elwes (New York: Dover Publishing Company, Inc., 1951), p. 201.

16 Ibid., pp. 178-184.

17 Ibid., pp. 184-186.

18 Elders, *Reflexive Water*, p. 185.

19 Noam Chomsky, *Language and Responsibility* (New York: Pantheon Books, 1979), pp. 75, 77.

20 Compare Foucault's view of utopia to that of his friend and ally, Gilles Deleuze, and his collaborator, Felix Guattari. Unlike Foucault, Deleuze and Guattari cannot imagine what it would mean not to imagine utopia. According to them, "Philosophy takes the relative deterritorialization [that is the decoding, disembedding, or freeing of desire from a particular object] of capital to the absolute, it makes it pass over the plane immanance [which is simular to Foucault's discourse and the regime of truth, a nontranscendental 'place' where concepts are assembled or constructed and have their truth] as movement of the infinite and suppresses it as internal limit, *turns it back against itself so as to summon forth a new earth, a new people.*" Deleuze and Guattari compare this idea of philosophy favorably to Adorno's "negative dialectic" and the Frankfurt School's notion of the utopian.

Actually, *utopia is what links* philosophy with its own epoch, with European capitalism, but also already with the Greek city. In each case it is with utopia that philosophy becomes political and takes the criticism of its own time to its highest point. Utopia does not split off from infinite movement: etymologically it stands for absolute deterritorialization but always at the critical point at which it is connected with the present relative milieu, and especially with the forces stifled by this milieu. *Erewhon,* the word used by Samuel Butler, refers not only to no-where but also to now-here. In utopia (as in philosophy) there is always the risk of a restoration, and sometimes a proud affirmation, of transcendence, so that *we need to distinguish between authoritarian utopias, or utopias of transcendence, and immanent, revolutionary, libertarian utopias.*

(Emphasis added. See Gilles Deleuze and Felix Guattari, *What is Philosophy* [New York: Columbia University Press, 1994], pp. 99-100.) Unlike Foucault, I do not take Chomsky to be saying anything more or less than what Deleuze and Guattari are saying.

21 On this point, Chomsky offers a narrative response that takes a dialectical form. Against Foucault, he argues that a reformer or revolutionary pursues power "to bring about a more just society" (Chomsky, *Language and Responsibility*, p. 80). A naked will to power "cannot stand." This is something that both Chomsky and Nietzsche understand (although they disagree about how power should be ethically differentiated and judged) but Foucault does not. In Neitzsche's inverted Kantian world, the only good thing is a "good will to power." Thus there is good will to power and bad will to power. Nietzsche takes the first to be just (a justice that he admits few will understand) and the second to be unjust. In a similar vein, Chomsky argues that power cannot be judged in ethically neutral terms (power is not "beyond good and bad"). Some power is good and some bad. Reformers

and revolutionaries do not pursue power without making judgements between what they believe are good and bad forms of power. Nor are their judgements merely cynical masks for an otherwise naked will to power. In short, power has to be ethically justified: Nietzsche's justification takes one form, which entails the rank-ordering of human types and forms of life. Chomsky's justification takes a quasi-Kantian form. Foucault, in contrast, pretends that no justification is possible at all.

22  Paul Bové, *Intellectuals in Power* (New York: Columbia University Press, 1986), p. 210.

23  Ibid., p. 221.

24  On this point, Gayatri Spivak remarks: "Edward W. Said's critique of power in Foucault as a captivating and mystifying category that allows him 'to obliterate the role of classes, the role of economics, the role of insurgency and rebellion', is pertinent here. I add to Said's analysis the notion of the surreptitious subject of power and desire marked by the transparency of the intellectual. Curiously enough, Paul Bové faults Said for emphasizing the importance of the intellectual, whereas 'Foucault's project essentially is a challenge to the leading role of both hegemonic and oppositional intellectuals'. I have suggested that this 'challenge' is deceptive precisely because it ignores what Said emphasizes – the critic's institutional responsibility." Spivak, "Can the Subaltern Speak?", p. 75.

25  Bové, *Intellectuals*, pp. 210, 224.

26  This essay appears in Michel Foucault's *Power/Knowledge*, ed. Colin Gordan (New York: Pantheon Books, 1980).

27  Ibid., pp. 226–227.

28  Ibid., 227. Gayatri Spivak is highly critical of this view. She compares Foucault and Deleuze – whose "postrepresentational vocabulary hides an essentialist agenda," that is, the notion of an undivided subject who experiences no contradiction between power or desire and interests – unfavorably to the writers associated with the "Subaltern Studies" group: "When these writers speak, in their essentializing language, of a gap between interest and action in the intermediate group, their conclusions are closer to Marx than to the self-conscious *naïveté* of Deleuze's pronouncement on the issue. Guha, like Marx, speaks of interest in terms of the social rather than the libidinal being. . . For the 'true' subaltern group, whose identity is its difference, there is no unrepresentable subaltern subject that can know and speak itself; the intellectual's solution is not to abstain from representation." Spivak, "Can the Subaltern Speak?", pp. 75, 80.

29  Bové, *Intellectuals*, p. 228.

30  Elders, *Reflexive Water*, p. 175.

31  Michael Foucault, "Truth and Power," in *Power/Knowledge*, p. 131.

32  Bové, *Intellectuals*, pp. 229–230.

33  Ibid., 245. For a different view, see Harold Weiss, "The Genealogy of Justice; Chomsky and Said vs. Foucault and Bové," *Philosophy Today*, 33:1 (1989).

34  Bové, *Intellectuals*, p. 11.

35 Ibid., pp. 13–14.
36 Friedrich Nietzsche, *On the Genealogy of Morality*, ed. Keith Ansell-Pearson and Carol Diethe (Cambridge University Press, 1994), pp. 64, 127.
37 An unfortunate consequence of Walter Kaufmann's extensive English-language translations and interpretations of Nietzsche's work, along with the peculiar Nietzsche created by Gilles Deleuze and his French contemporaries, is the mistaken notion that Nietzsche's views do not have substantial affinities with fascist thought. The work of Kaufmann and Deleuze is a response to the interpretive excesses of Nietzsche's sister and other Nazi-sympathizers who construe Nietzsche as a proto-Nazi. Nietzsche was no Nazi. Nor was he anti-Semitic by nineteenth-century standards. But one thing is clear: he was a protofascist. In this regard, I think that Derrida's reading of Nietzsche, "Otobiographies," is better than Kaufmann or Deleuze's readings.
38 *Genealogy*, pp. 178–179.
39 Ibid., p. 55.
40 Bové, *Intellectuals*, p.18.
41 Nietzsche, *Genealogy*, p. 39.
42 Ibid., pp. 39–40.
43 Ibid., pp. 63–64.
44 Ibid., pp. 57–59.
45 Ibid., pp. 41–42.
46 Ibid., p. 43.
47 Ibid., pp. 44, 46.
48 Ibid., pp. 46–47, 54, 56, 81, 89.
49 Ibid., p. 71.
50 Ibid., pp. 89–100.
51 Ibid., pp. 98–100.
52 Ibid., p. 89.
53 Ibid., p. 108.
54 Ibid., p. 108.
55 Ibid., p. 126.

## 6 MARX, SAID, AND THE JEWISH QUESTION

1 Robert C. Tucker (ed.) *The Marx–Engels Reader* (New York: W. W. Norton), pp. 48, 50.
2 Ibid., p 26.
3 Ibid., pp. 27–32.
4 Here I refer to Hegel's notion of self-recognition, which is always mediated by an "other." In his famous allegory of "Lordship and Bondage," in *Phenomenology of Spirit*, the self-consciousness of the slave is mediated by the consciousness of the master. A person's self-hood is fully realized when it is mediated or recognized by others.
5 Tucker, *Reader*, pp. 32–40.
6 "Text" refers, minimally speaking, to signs, signification, or language. On

some interpretations, it refers to the weave or networking of language and everything else; it is a contemporary analogue of the Hindu notion of "Indra's net."

7 Tucker, *Reader*, p. 53.

8 Said's use of history, as I briefly digress, is hardly vulnerable to Robert Young's critique. Young criticizes what he regards as Frank Lentricchia's naïve, objectivist invocation of history against the skepticism and relativism of poststructuralist criticism. In turn, he traces this view of history to Hegel, the Hegelian-Marxism of Georg Lukács and Sartre's existentialist-Marxism. See Robert Young, *White Mythologies* (New York: Routledge, 1990), pp. 22–25. Said's work is clearly part of this tradition, but he is no more a naïve historicist than Foucault is a naïve structuralist or Derrida a naïve phenomenologist. Said has written his own historicist work skeptically, parasitically, and critically into the language of poststructuralism. In the body of work that Young criticizes, Said is neither poststructuralist nor antipoststructuralist – although he would later become so, at least rhetorically – but a complex hybrid. As with the word "reality," Said's use of "history" must be placed in parentheses. It is a political gesture against the unmitigated skepticism that is so common on the academic left.

9 For a persuasive argument that we inevitably construct something as scripture, see Wesley A. Kort, *Take Read* (University Park, PA: Pennsylvania State University Press, 1996).

10 Derrida's criticism looks a lot like the textuality that Said describes as ahistorical, weightless, otherworldly, and religious. In contrast, Foucault is concerned with contextuality or discourse, with the historical, social, and institutional arraignments in which texts are written. Spivak charges Said with "a profound misapprehension of the notion of textuality." See Gayatri Chakravorty Spivak, "Can the Subaltern Speak?" in C. Nelson and L. Grossberg (eds.), *Marxism and the Interpretation of Culture* (Basingstoke: Macmillan Education, 1988), pp. 271–313. Perhaps this is true. True or not, Said has, apparently, found little reason to amend his comparative praise of Foucault. Spivak and Said, therefore, disagree, perhaps not as much now as then, over the long-term usefulness of Derrida and Foucault, with Spivak preferring the former, Said the latter. Thus he once described Foucault as a critic who forces texts to reveal their "affiliations with institutions, offices, agencies, classes, academies, corporations, groups, guilds, ideologically defined parties and professions . . . and forcibly to redefine and reidentify the particular interests that all texts serve." In this earlier incarnation, Said praises Foucauldian discourse analysis for avoiding the mystifications of Derridian "undecidability," what he elsewhere calls "the 'abysmal' element of textuality" (*WTC* 182–183, 212, 224).

This claim itself might lead some to charge Said with a naïve view of text and context, reiterating the Derridian claim that there is no context (in the conventional sense) only another text. But this misses the point of Said's criticism. But Said is no naïve realist. He does not believe that contexts are simply there or "given" or that our access to them is transparent and unmediated. Contexts are always constructed with specific purposes and interests in mind, never absolute, they are always subject to a supplementary account. To speak of context, therefore, is to signal the need for a different kind of politics, which may include denying the honorific of "political" to what one contests. But this is a pragmatic, political judgment, not a strict epistemological one. For Said, there is no political discourse without the construction of contexts any more than there is philosophical or critical discourse for Derrida without the construction of "quasi-transcendentals." See Geoffrey Bennington and Jacques Derrida, *Jacques Derrida*, trans. Geoffrey Bennington (University of Chicago Press, 1993).

11  Jacques Derrida, *Specters of Marx*, trans. Peggy Kamuf (New York: Routledge, 1994), p. 28.

12  Mark Lilla, "The Politics of Jacques Derrida," *The New York Review* 45:11 (1998), 36–41, suggests that this has always been the case and that American readers can be excused if they once took this notion too literally and too absolutely.

13  Derrida, *Specters of Marx*, pp. 58–59.

14  Ibid., pp. 84–85.

## CONCLUDING REMARKS: RELIGION, SECULARISM, AND PRAGMATIC NATURALISM

1  Thomas Jefferson, *Notes on the State of Virginia*, Query xvii, in A. A. Lipscomb and A. E. Bergh (eds.), *Writings of Thomas Jefferson*, (Washington, DC, 1905), vol. 2, p. 221.

2  Romain Rolland (1866–1944) was an influential French writer and activist. The winner of the Nobel prize for literature in 1915, he was a universalist and a pacifist who opposed the Great War (World War I). In *Romain Rolland and the Politics of Intellectual Engagement* (Berkeley, CA: University of California, 1988), pp. 298–299, David James Fisher describes him "as the key transitional figure in the history of engaged French intellectuals. His mature life as a writer practically spanned the time between Zola's Dreyfusard 'J'accuse' (1898) and Sartre's existential formulations about engagement in *What Is Literature?* (1947). He lived through and reflected on every major crisis of the Third Republic."

3  Stanley Cavell, *A Pitch of Philosophy* (Cambridge, MA: Harvard University Press, 1994), pp. xi–xii.

4  The account that follows is adopted from a previously published article entitled "Cornel West: Between Rorty's Rock and Hauerwas' Hard Place," which appeared in *American Journal of Philosophy and Theology* 19:2 (1998), 151–172.

5  In *The Descent of Man*, Darwin speculated about the day when the "civilized races" would exterminate the "savage races" and anthropomorphous apes. "The [evolutionary] break will then be rendered wider, for it will intervene

between man in some more civilized state . . . than the Caucasian, and some ape as low as a baboon, instead of as at present between the negro or Australian and the gorilla." See George W. Stocking, *Race, Culture, and Evolution* (University of Chicago Press, 1982), pp. 113, 116–119.

6  See Richard Rorty, "Freud and Moral Reflection," in *Essays on Heidegger and Others* (New York: Cambridge University Press, 1991).

7  This does not commit us to Rorty's radical nominalism or to his misreading of Dewey's antinominalism as metaphysical (as in panpsychic) rather than contextual. This represents a change from a view that I expressed elsewhere. See Hart, "Cornel West," 151–172.

8  See Henry Levinson, *Santayana, Pragmatism, and the Spiritual Life* (Chapel Hill, North Carolina: University of North Carolina Press, 1992).

9  Cornel West, *The American Evasion of Philosophy* (Madison, WI: The University of Wisconsin Press, 1989), pp. 232–233. My objections to West's Kierkegaardian commitments are not epistemological. Both of us commend what he calls the "American evasion of epistemologically centered philosophy." Nor are my objections ethico-political. Our political differences are small, even trivial. Nor do my objections have anything to do with an "ethics of belief." I do not question the rationality of West's views or accuse him of seeking an irrational escape from unpleasant truths. On the contrary, my objections are what might be called an "aesthetics of belief." I do not find West's Kierkegaardian views pleasing. Those views do not fit him very well, given his otherwise pragmatic garb. True, I may suspect that this ill-fit is the result of self-deception on West's part, but that is only a hunch, for which I believe no persuasive, "knockdown" arguments can be made. On epistemological, ethical, and political grounds, I think that West is entitled to his views.

10  Postliberal refers to those Christian thinkers who, following Karl Barth, react against the theological liberalism initiated by Friedrich Schleiermacher in books such as *On Religion* and *The Christian Faith*. Following Søren Kierkegaard and Barth, they emphasize the dogmatic character of Christian faith.

11  But we disagree with James as far as he takes the "fruits" of religious belief to be unrelated to the causes of those beliefs. See Wayne Proudfoot's discussion of this matter in chapter 5 of *Religious Experience* (Berkeley, CA; University of California Press, 1985).

12  This is no simple-minded hedonism: what we want is mediated by what we, free of all moralism, ought to want. Thus I cannot imagine what is good for me without thinking about what is good for us. I cannot imagine "good" without pleasure and joy or "bad" without pain and sadness.

13  Levinson, *Santayana*, p. 87.

14  Ibid., p. 99.

15  Ibid., p. 259.

16  Of course, this is a potentially dangerous space, but what space is not? But this space is not beyond all contestation.

17  A Dewey-inspired "emancipatory social experimentalism" is the center-piece of West's version of radical democracy. This thoroughly romantic view of democratic culture accents human potential and participation. West speaks frequently about "the populace deliberating" but does not show how this would take place outside the conventions of democratic liberalism and the mechanisms of electoral politics, or why we should expect the results to be different. Creative democracy does not do away with elites. There will always be elites. They will always circulate in and (hopefully) out of the corridors of power, or between the ruling class and subdominant classes. West denies none of this. Under the regime of creative democracy, however, elites would presumably be held accountable in ways that they currently are not. West does not provide us with details about how this might be done, how those institutions would be constructed, and how the virtue that he commends would be cultivated. He does not provide a credible analysis of the prospects of creative democracy. He has often argued that the globalization of market culture systemically constrains radical democratic efforts. In light of this, it seems unlikely that creative democracy could ever amount to more than a high-minded version of liberal democratic state-capitalism, a less bureaucratic version of the welfare state. Under the constraints of global markets, even the most "Promethean" of creative democrats, *as a political actor,* is hard to distinguish from Rorty's "postmodern bourgeois liberal." They occupy the same narrow, political and linguistic space. Thus there is a certain pathos in West's description of the prospects for creative democracy. See Richard Rorty's description of this kind of democrat in the essay "Postmodernist Bourgeois Liberalism," in *Objectivity, Relativism, and Truth* (New York: Cambridge University Press, 1991). West provides a critique of this perspective in *The American Evasion of Philosophy*. Rorty's rejoinder can be found in "The Professor and the Prophet," *Transitions* 52 (1991), 70–78.

18  Steven Rockefeller, *John Dewey: Religious Faith and Democratic Humanism* (New York: Columbia University Press, 1991), p. 32.

19  Benedict de Spinoza, *On the Improvement of the Understanding, The Ethics, Correspondence*, trans. R. H. M. Elwes (New York: Dover Publications, Inc., 1955), p. 232.

20  See Gilles Deleuze, *Spinoza: Practical Philosophy* (San Francisco, CA: City Light Books, 1988).

21  See Nietzsche's analysis of Socrates in *Twilight of the Idols* (London: Penguin Books, 1968).

22  See Geoff Waite's, *Nietzsche's Corps/e* (Durham: Duke University Press, 1996). It is by far the best Marxist-oriented analysis of Nietzsche and Nietzscheans, whether "left" or "right."

23  See Michael Novack, *The Spirit of Democratic Capitalism* (New York: Simon and Schuster, 1982), for what I think is a perceptive analysis of socialist angst and self-image.

24  Alexander Nehamas, "A Touch of the Poet," *Raritan: A Quarterly Review* 10

(1990), 104–125. Levinson quotes Nehamas to make his own point. However, I think the formulation "reluctant bourgeois" is an apt description of many would-be radical democrats, myself included.

### APPENDIX A: WHOSE EXODUS, WHICH INTERPRETATION?

1 Germaine Brie, *Camus and Sartre: Crisis and Commitment* (New York: Delacorte Press, 1972), p. 82.
2 See Conor Cruise O'Brien, *Albert Camus: Of Europe and Africa* (New York: Viking Press, 1970).
3 Michel-Antoine Burnier, *Choice of Action*, trans. Bernard Murchland (New York: Random House, 1968), p. 125.
4 Michael Walzer, *Exodus and Revolution* (New York: Basic Books, 1985), pp. 5–6, 9.
5 Ibid., pp. 30–40.
6 Ibid., pp. 45–54.
7 Ibid., pp. 11–16.
8 Ibid., pp. 53, 55–70.
9 Ibid., pp. 75–76.
10 Daniel Boyarin and Jonathan Boyarin, "An Exchange on Edward Said and Difference: Towards a Dialogue with Edward Said," *Critical Inquiry* (1989), 626–633. Also see Jonathan Boyarin, "Reading Exodus into History," *New Literary History* 23 (1992), 523–554.
11 Michael Walzer, *The Company of Critics* (New York: Basic Books, 1988), p. 138.
12 Ibid., pp. 148–150.
13 Michael Walzer, "Albert Camus's Algerian War," in *The Company of Critics*, p. 140.
14 Ibid., pp. 140–142.
15 Ibid., pp. 144–147.
16 Said, "Canaanite Reading," 99–102.
17 Michael Walzer and Edward Said, "An Exchange," 257–258.

### APPENDIX B: AN EXCHANGE OF LETTERS BETWEEN MICHAEL WALZER AND EDWARD SAID

1 The same method is applied to two of my books, *Just and Unjust Wars* and *Spheres of Justice*, but Said makes such gibberish out of these two that I can't believe he ever opened them. He is convinced in any case that they are both part of the same Zionist strategy. I sometimes wish I were so single-minded!
2 Said has his own reading of the text, also designed to serve a political purpose. I don't know whether to laugh or cry at his assertion that the Israelites in Egypt were a "comprador" class. In fact, of course, only Egyptians could be compradors in Egypt: the word designates the *native* agents of outside financial interests. Said probably means to identify the Israelites with the outside interests – already in control, 3500 years ago, of

international finance. That's why they were "the targets of local rage and frustration," a nice euphemism for state enslavement.

3  Walzer's *Just and Unjust Wars* as well as his *Spheres of Justice* are based on an extension of that argument into different areas of experience. He calls my view of those two books "gibberish," although in the case of the former I made exactly the point made in nearly every review of the book, in the case of the latter I quoted Ronald Dworkin, with whom Walzer tried rather ineffectively to tilt. There is, however, a symptology to be done sometime later on Walzer's recurring obsession with "justice" and how, although it acts "unjustly," Israel is "just."

4  Here is a sample. It is a description of a play put on at the American Repertory Theatre in Cambridge: ". . . in which a visiting German businessman, an American Jewess come as an immigrant, and an Arab Palestinian find themselves taking refuge in a bomb shelter in Jerusalem under Arab siege. If there is something a bit startling about the emerging empathy between the play's German and its Jew, even less have the universalist prejudices of our culture prepared us for its Arab – a crazed Arab to be sure, but crazed in the distinctive way of his culture. He is intoxicated by language, cannot distinguish between fantasy and reality, abhors compromise, always blames others for his predicament, and in the end lances the painful boil of his frustrations in a pointless, though momentarily gratifying, act of bloodlust. This is a political play and what makes it compelling is its pessimism, which is to say its truthfulness. We have seen this play's Arab in Tripoli and in Damascus, and in recent weeks hijacking a bus to Gaza and shooting up a street of innocents in Jerusalem. On the Rep. stage he is a fictional character, of course, but in the real world it is not he but his 'moderate' brother who is a figment of the imagination" [May 4, 1984].

5  Sivan's article discusses "Edward Said's Arab critics," purporting to show that secular and Left writers in the Arab world are suspicious of me. Aside from basing his argument on two rather ambiguous cases, Sivan's article has little to say about the actual influence of my work in the Arab world, the positive effects it has had, and so on. His two prime examples are, one, a discredited Syrian "philosopher" who works directly for the Syrian régime and whose analysis of *Orientalism* rests on the assumption that I work for the CIA; and two, a Lebanese writer who lives in the United States and has no known constituency or readership in the Arab world. These inflections are missing from Sivan's solemn reporting of "the Arab world"! Needless to say, Sivan does not report how either of these writers views Israel; that will furnish him with evidence of "Arab anti-Semitism" in his next article. In going after me, he does not require that evidence!

# Select bibliography

Ahmad, Aijaz, *In Theory*, New York: Verso, 1992.

Al-'Azm, S. J., "Orientalism and Orientalism in Reverse," in *al-Istishrāq wa-l-Istishrāq Ma'kusan*, Beirut, 1981 (partially translated in *Khamsin* (London) 8, pp. 5–26).

Althusser, Louis, *For Marx*, London: Verso, 1996.

Arnold, Matthew, *Culture and Anarchy*, ed. J. Dover Wilson, Cambridge University Press, 1988.

   *Literature and Dogma* (ed.) James C. Livingston, New York: Fredrick Unger Publishing Company, 1970.

Alexander, Edward, *Matthew Arnold and John Stuart Mill*, New York: Columbia University Press, 1965.

Asante, Molefi Kete, *Afrocentricity*, Trenton, NJ: African World Press, Inc., 1988.

Bacon, Francis, *Advance of Learning and Novum Organum,* New York: Willey Book Company, 1944.

Balibar, Etienne, *Spinoza and Politics*, trans. Peter Snowdon, London: Verso, 1998.

Barker, Francis, Peter Hulme, Margaret Iversen, and Diane Loxley (eds.), *Literature, Politics and Theory*, Papers from the Essex Conference 1976–84, London: Methuen, 1986.

Bellah, Robert, *The Broken Covenant*, New York: Seabury Press, 1975.

Benda, Julien, *The Treason of the Intellectuals*, New York: W. W. Norton and Company, Inc., 1928.

Bennington, Geoffrey and Jacques Derrida, *Jacques Derrida*, trans. Geoffrey Bennington, University of Chicago Press, 1993.

Berkowitz, Peter, *Nietzsche: The Ethics of an Immoralist*, Cambridge, MA: Harvard University Press, 1995.

Bernstein, J. M. (ed.), *The Culture Industry*, London: Routledge, 1991.

Blumenberg, Hans, *The Legitimacy of the Modern Age*, trans. Robert M. Wallace, Cambridge: MIT Press, 1983.

Bové, Paul, "Hope and Reconciliation: A Review of Edward Said," *Boundary 2*, 20:2 (1993).

   *Intellectuals in Power*, New York: Columbia University Press, 1986.

Boyarin, Daniel and Jonathan Boyarin, "An Exchange on Edward Said and Difference: Towards a Dialogue with Edward Said," *Critical Inquiry* (1989), 626–633.

Boyarin, Jonathan, "Reading Exodus into History," *New Literary History* 23 (1992), 523–554.

Bradley, F. H., *Ethical Studies*, Oxford: The Clarendon Press, 1927.

Brie, Germaine, *Camus and Sartre: Crisis and Commitment*, New York: Delacorte Press, 1972.

Bromert, Victor, "Orientalism and the Scandals of Scholarship," *American Scholar* 48 (1979), 537–538.

Burke, Edmund and Thomas Paine, *Reflections on the Revolution in France/The Rights of Man*, Garden City, New York: Anchor Press/Doubleday, 1973.

Burke, Kenneth, *A Grammar of Motives*, New York: Prentice-Hall, Inc., 1945.

Burnier, Michel-Antoine, *Choice of Action*, trans. Bernard Murchland, New York: Random House, 1968.

Cavell, Stanley, *A Pitch of Philosophy*, Cambridge, MA: Harvard University Press, 1994.

Chattergee, Partha, *Nationalist Thought and the Colonial World: A Derivative Discourse*, London: Zed, 1986.

Chomsky, Noam, *Language and Responsibility*, New York: Pantheon Books, 1979.

*The Chomsky Reader*, New York: Pantheon Books, 1987.

Clifford, James, *The Predicament of Culture*, Cambridge, MA: Harvard University Press, 1988.

Corless, Roger J., *The Vision of Buddhism*, New York: Paragon House, 1989.

Crossman, Richard (ed.), *The God That Failed*, New York: Harper, 1949.

Dawson, Carl and John Pfordresher (eds.), *Matthew Arnold, Prose Writings*, London: Routledge and Kegan Paul Ltd., 1979.

Deleuze, Gilles, *Spinoza: Practical Philosophy*, San Francisco, CA: City Light Books, 1988.

Deleuze, Gilles and Felix Guattari, *What is Philosophy*, New York: Columbia University Press, 1994.

Derrida, Jacques, *Of Spirit*, trans. Geoffrey Bennington and Rachel Bowlby, University of Chicago Press, 1991.

*Specters of Marx*, trans. Peggy Kamuf, New York: Routledge, 1994.

*The Ear of the Other: Otobiographies, Transference, Translation: Tests and Discussions with Jacques Derrida*, trans. Peggy Kamuf, New York: Schocken Books, 1986.

"To Do Justice to Freud: The History of Madness in the Age of Psychoanalysis," *Critical Inquiry* 20:2 (1994).

*Writing and Difference*, University of Chicago Press, 1978.

Dewey, John, *Experience and Nature*, New York: Dover Publishers, Inc., 1958.

Diamond, Malcolm, *Contemporary Philosophy and Religious Thought*, New York: McGraw-Hill, 1974.

Dreyfus, Hubert and Paul Rabinow, *Michel Foucault: Beyond Structuralism and Hermeneutics*, University of Chicago Press, 1982.

Drinkwater, J. F., "Empire to Commonwealth: Consequences of Monotheism in Late Antiquity (book reviews)," *History Today* 44:9 (1994), 57–58.

Durkheim, Emile, *The Elementary Forms of the Religious Life*, trans. Karen Fields, New York: The Free Press, 1995.

Elders, Fons, *Reflexive Water: The Basic Concerns of Mankind*, London: Souvenir Press (Educational and Academic) Ltd., 1974.

Fanon, Frantz, *The Wretched of the Earth*, New York; New Grove Press, 1963.

Feldman, Louis H., *The Journal of the American Oriental Society* 114:4 (1994), 671–672.

Feuer, Louis, *Ideology and the Ideologists*, New York: Harper and Row, 1975.

Feuerbach, Ludwig, *The Essence of Christianity*, trans. George Eliot, New York and Row, 1957.

Fisher, David James, *Romain Rolland and the Politics of Intellectual Engagement*, Berkeley, CA: University of California Press, 1988.

Forgacs, David (ed.), *An Antonio Gramsci Reader*, New York: Schocken Books, 1988.

Foucault, Michel, *Discipline and Punish*, trans. A. Sheridan, New York: Vintage Books, 1979.

> *Language, Counter-Memory, Practice*, ed. Donald F. Bouchard, Ithaca, NY: Cornell University Press, 1977

> *Power/Knowledge*, ed. Colin Gordon, New York: Pantheon Books, 1980.

> *The Archaeology of Knowledge*, trans. A. M. Sheridan, New York: Pantheon Books, 1972.

> *The Foucault Reader*, ed. Paul Rabinow, New York: Pantheon Books, 1984.

> *The Order of Things*, New York: Vintage Books, 1973.

Fowden, Garth, *Empire to Commonwealth*, Princeton University Press, 1993.

Fraiman, Susan, "Jane Austen and Edward Said: Gender, Culture, and Imperialism," *Critical Inquiry* 21:4 (1995).

Freud, Sigmund, *Future of an Illusion*, trans. James Strachey, New York: W. W. Norton and Company, 1961.

> *Moses and Monotheism*, New York: Vintage Books, 1939.

> *The Interpretation of Dreams*, New York: Avon Books, 1965.

> *Totem and Taboo*, New York: Vintage Books, 1946.

Garcia, Solidad (ed.), *European Identity and the Search for Legitimacy*, London: Pinter Publishers, 1993.

Giddens, Anthony, *Durkheim on Politics and the State*, Cambridge: Polity Press, 1986.

Girard, René, *Violence and the Sacred*, trans. Patrick Gregory, Baltimore: Johns Hopkins University Press, 1977.

Greene, Thomas M., "One World, Divisible," *The Yale Review* 68 (1979), 579–580.

Gutting, Gary, *Michel Foucault's Archaeology of Scientific Reason*, Cambridge University Press, 1989.

Halbertal, Moshe and Avishai Margalit, *Idolatry*, trans. Naomi Goldblum, Cambridge, MA: Harvard University Press, 1992.

Hart, William David, "Cornel West: Between Rorty's Rock and Hauerwas' Hard Place," *American Journal of Philosophy and Theology* 19:2 (1998), 151–172.

Hayes, Carlton J. H., *Essays on Nationalism*, New York: The MacMillan Company, 1928.

Heffner, Richard (ed.), *A Documentary History of the United States*, New York: New American Library, 1985.

Hegel, G. W. F., *Introduction to The Philosophy of History*, trans. Leo Rauch, Indianapolis, Indiana: Hackett Publishing Company, 1988.

Heidegger, Martin, "The Ontotheological Nature of Metaphysics," in *Identity and Difference*, trans. Joan Stambaugh, New York: Harper and Row, 1969.

Hoare, Quintin and Geoffrey Nowell Smith (eds.), *Selections from the Prison Note Books*, New York: International Publishers, 1989.

Hobbes, Thomas, *Leviathan*, London: Oxford University Press, 1909.

Hobson, John A., *Imperialism*, London: George Allen and Unwin Ltd., 1902.

Hourani, Albert, "The Road to Morocco," *The New York Times Review*, 8 March 1979, 27–29.

Hulme, Peter, Margaret Iversen, and Diane Loxley (eds.), *The Politics of Theory*, Proceedings of the Essex Sociology of Literature Conference, University of Essex, Colchester, 1983.

James, C. L. R., *Beyond a Boundary*, London: Hutchinson, 1963.

James, David, *Romain Rolland and the Politics of Intellectual Engagement*, Berkeley, California: University of California, 1988.

Jefferson, Thomas, *Notes on the State of Virginia*, Query XVII, in A. A. Lipscomb and A. E. Bergh (eds.) *Writings of Thomas Jefferson*, Washington, D.C., 1905, vol. 2.

Kort, Wesley A., *Take Read*, University Park, PA: Pennsylvania State University Press, 1996.

Larrain, Jorge, *The Concept of Ideology*, Athens, GA: The University of Georgia Press, 1979.

Lehnberger, Sigrid L., "Julien Benda's Characterization of the 'Clerc,' 1927–1948," Ph.D. Dissertation, Duke University (1949).

Levinson, Marjorie, "News from Nowhere: The Discontents of Aijaz Ahmad," *Public Culture* 6 (1993), 97–131.

Lilla, Mark, "The Politics of Jacques Derrida," *The New York Review* 45:11 (1998), 36–41.

Livingston, James, *Matthew Arnold and Christianity*, Columbia, SC: University of South Carolina Press, 1986.

Locke, John, "An Essay Concerning Human Understanding," in *The Empiricists*, Garden City, New York: Anchor Books, 1974.

Louth, Andrew, "Empire to Commonwealth: Consequences of Monotheism in Late Antiquity (book reviews)," *Journal of Theological Studies* 46:2 (1995), 737–740.

Machiavelli, Niccolò, *The Prince and the Discourses*, New York: Random House, 1950.

Martin, Catherine Gimelli, "Orientalism and the Ethnographer: Said, Herodotus, and the Discourse of Alterity," *Criticism* 32:4 (1990).

McCarney, Joe, *The Real World of Ideology*, Atlantic Highlands, NJ: Humanities Press, 1980.

Milbank, John, *Theology and Social Theory*, Oxford: Basil Blackwell, Ltd., 1990.

Mill, J. S., *Considerations on Representative Government*, London: Longman, Green, Longman, Roberts, and Longman, 1865.

Mufti, Aamir R., "Auerbach in Istanbul: Edward Said, Secular Criticism, and the Question of Minority Culture," *Critical Inquiry* 25:1 (1998), 95–125.

Nehamas, Alexander, "A Touch of the Poet," *Raritan: A Quarterly Review* 10 (1990), 104–125.

Nietzsche, Friedrich, *On the Genealogy of Morality and Other Writings*, ed. Keith Ansell-Pearson and Carol Diethe, Cambridge University Press, 1994.

*Twilight of the Idols*, London: Penguin Books, 1968.

Novack, Michael, *The Spirit of Democratic Capitalism*, New York: Simon and Schuster, 1982.

Nussbaum, Martha and Joshua Cohen, *For Love of Country*, Boston: Beacon Press, 1996.

O'Brien, Conor Cruise, *Albert Camus: Of Europe and Africa*, New York: Viking Press, 1970.

Palmer, Bryan D., *Descent into Discourse*, Philadelphia: Temple University Press, 1990.

Pinkus, Philip, *Swift's Vision of Evil*, Charlottesville: University of Virginia Press, 1975.

Plato, *The Republic of Plato*, trans. Allan Bloom, New York: Basic Books, 1968.

Prakash, Gyan, "Orientalism Now," *History and Theory* 34:3 (1995), 199–210.

Proudfoot Wayne, *Religious Experience*, Berkeley, CA: University of California Press, 1985.

Robbins, William, *The Ethical Idealism of Matthew Arnold*, University of Toronto Press, 1959.

Rockefeller, Steven, *John Dewey: Religious Faith and Democratic Humanism*, New York: Columbia University Press, 1991.

Rodinson, Maxime, *Europe and the Mystique of Islam*, trans. Roger Veinus, Seattle: University of Washington Press, 1987.

*Islam and Capitalism*, trans. Brian Pearce, New York: Pantheon Books, 1973.

*Muhammad*, trans. Anne Carter, New York: Pantheon Books, 1980.

Rorty, Richard, *Essays on Heidegger and Others*, New York: Cambridge University Press, 1991.

*Objectivity, Relativism, and Truth*, New York: Cambridge University Press, 1991.

"The Professor and the Prophet," *Transitions* 52 (1991), 70–78.

Rose, Gillian, *Mourning Becomes the Law*, Cambridge University Press, 1996.

Rosen, Michael, *On Voluntary Servitude*, Cambridge, MA: Harvard University Press, 1996.

Said, Edward, *After the Last Sky*, photographs by Jean Möhr, New York: Pantheon Books, 1986.

*Beginnings: Intention and Method*, New York: Columbia University Press, 1985.

*Covering Islam*, New York: Pantheon Books, 1981.

*Culture and Imperialism*, New York: Alfred A. Knopf, 1993.

*Joseph Conrad and the Fiction of Autobiography*, Cambridge, MA: Harvard University Press, 1966.

"Michael Walzer's *Exodus and Revolution*: A Canaanite Reading," *Grand Street* 5 (1985–6), 86–106.

*Musical Elaborations*, New York: Columbia University Press, 1991.

"Nationalism, Human Rights, and Interpretation," *Raritan* 12:3 (1993), 26–51.

"Orientalism, an Afterword," *Raritan* (1995), 45–46.

*Orientalism*, New York: Vintage Books, 1979.

*Peace and Its Discontents*, New York: Vintage Books, 1996.

*Representations of Intellectuals*, New York: Pantheon Books, 1994.

*The Politics of Dispossession*, New York: Pantheon Books, 1994.

*The Question of Palestine*, New York: Vintage Books, 1980.

*The World, the Text, and the Critic*, Cambridge, MA: Harvard University Press, 1983.

Schleiermacher, Friedrich, *On Religion*, Cambridge University Press, 1988.

*The Christian Faith*, Edinburgh: T. and T. Clark, 1928.

Schulze, Hagen, *States, Nations and Nationalism*, trans. William E. Yuill, Oxford: Blackwell, 1996.

Skinner, Quentin, *The Foundations of Modern Political Thought, Volume Two: The Age Of Reformation*, London: Cambridge University Press, 1978.

Smith, Peter, "*Mansfield Park* and the World Stage," *The Cambridge Quarterly* 23:3 (1994), 203–229.

Smith, Wilfred Cantwell, *The Meaning and End of Religion*, Minneapolis: Fortress Press, 1991.

Spinoza, Benedict de, *A Theological–Political Treatise, A Political Treatise*, trans. R. H. M. Elwes, New York: Dover Publishing Company, Inc., 1951.

*On the Improvement of the Understanding, The Ethics, Correspondence*, trans. R. H. M. Elwes, New York: Dover Publications, Inc., 1955.

Spivak, Gayatri Chakravorty, "Can the Subaltern Speak?" in C. Nelson and L. Grossberg (eds.), *Marxism and the Interpretation of Culture*, Macmillan Education: Basingstoke, 1988, pp. 271–313.

Starkman, Miriam Kosh (ed.), *Gulliver's Travels and Other Writings by Jonathan Swift*, New York: Bantam Books, 1962.

Steffes, Michael, "Slavery and *Mansfield Park*: The Historical and Biographical Context," *English Language Notes* 34:2 (1996), 23–41.

Stocking, George W., *Race, Culture, and Evolution*, University of Chicago Press, 1982.

Taylor, Charles, *Hegel*, Cambridge University Press, 1975.

Tocqueville, Alexis de, *Democracy in America*, trans. George Lawrence, ed. J. P. Mayer, New York: HarperPerennial, 1988.

Trilling, Lionel, *Matthew Arnold*, New York: Harcourt Brace Jovanovich, 1939.

Tucker, Robert C. (ed.), *The Marx–Engels Reader*, 2nd edn., New York: W. W. Norton and Company, 1978.

Van der Veer, Peter, *Religious Nationalism*, Berkeley, CA: University of California Press, 1994.

Viswanathan, Gauri, *Outside The Fold: Conversion, Modernity and Belief*, Princeton University Press, 1998.

Waite, Geoff, *Nietzsche's Corps/e*, Durham, NC: Duke University Press, 1996.

Walcott, Fred, *The Origins of Culture and Anarchy*, University of Toronto Press, 1970.

Walzer, Michael, *Exodus and Revolution*, New York: Basic Books, 1985.

*Just and Unjust Wars,* New York: Basic Books, 1977.

*Spheres of Justice,* New York: Basic Books, 1983.

*The Company of Critics,* New York: Basic Books, 1988.

Walzer, Michael and Edward Said, "An Exchange: Michael Walzer and Edward Said," *Grand Street* 5 (1985–6), 246–259.

Weber, Max, *The Sociology of Religion,* Boston: Beacon Press, 1991.

Weiss, Harold, "The Genealogy of Justice; Chomsky and Said vs. Foucault and Bové," *Philosophy Today* 33:1 (1989).

West, Cornel, *The American Evasion of Philosophy,* Madison, WI: The University of Wisconsin Press, 1989.

White, Hayden, *Metahistory,* Baltimore: Johns Hopkins University Press, 1983.

Widengren, Geo, *Mani and Manichaeism,* New York: Holt, Rinehart and Winston, 1965.

Williams, Raymond, *Culture and Society,* New York: Columbia University Press, 1983.

*Marxism and Literature,* Oxford University Press, 1977.

Wittgenstein, Ludwig, *Philosophical Investigations,* trans. G. E. M. Anscombe, New York: Macmillan Publishing Co., Inc., 1953.

Young, Robert, *White Mythologies,* New York: Routledge, 1990.

# Index of names